The Inner Architect

The Inner Architect

Designing a Mindset That Rebuilds Itself

Kiran Saito

Mindful Pages

Published in 2025

ISBN: 9789371340946 (PB)
ISBN: 9789371770453 (eBook)

Published by

Mindful Pages
Imprint of Alpha Editions LLC
312 W. 2nd St #1834
Casper, WY 82601, USA

This book was developed using advanced writing tools to support the drafting and ideation process. All content has been thoughtfully curated, refined, and reviewed to ensure quality and relevance.

Content

Introduction
Welcome to the Reconstruction Site

Resilience has become something of a modern fetish. It's splashed across corporate HR manuals, echoed in TED Talks, hashtagged to death on social media. Wherever there's burnout, break-up, redundancy or just the slow erosion of meaning, we're told to bounce back. Chin up. Push through. Stay strong. The prevailing wisdom is uncomplicated and relentlessly upbeat: resilience is just a question of resolve—of clenching your jaw and soldiering on.

But what if that's the wrong metaphor entirely?

What if the goal isn't to bounce back at all, but to build forward? After all, who really wants to return to the same structure that cracked under pressure?

This book, then, is not another volume of platitudes. It's not a motivational script. Nor is it a tidy handbook of life hacks or feel-good mantras. *The Inner Architect* offers a radical reframe: what if the mind isn't a battlefield or a garden or some mythical "machine"? What if it's a structure—a physical, buildable thing? Something you can dismantle, reinforce, refine, and redesign with deliberation rather than desperation.

The problem with much of today's personal development is that it assumes the framework is sound. It tells you to hang prettier curtains on crumbling walls. Paint over the cracks. Smile through the aftershocks. This book suggests a different path: stop trying to salvage what collapsed, and begin the architectural work of rebuilding. From scratch if you must.

You are not broken. You may simply be inhabiting a structure no longer fit for the weather of your life. And unlike your genetic traits or childhood memories, structures can be reimagined.

This isn't metaphor for metaphor's sake. It's quite literal. Like any architectural body, the mind requires design integrity. It needs its load-bearing beams, its thermal insulation, its intelligent flow between rooms. When people fold under stress, it's often not about weakness of character. It's about inadequate design—mental routines that can't bear the weight of uncertainty, habits that trap rather than support, identities so tightly bound to status or schedule they fracture the moment either is lost.

So, what if the way you think, act, and adapt is not fixed by nature, but shaped by architecture?

Before anything can be built, rubble must be cleared. The first chapters dismantle some well-worn myths. You'll see burnout for what it truly is—not moral failure, but collapse of infrastructure. You'll examine what lies in the debris: the leftover emotions, the lost scripts, the confusion that clouds action. You'll question the cultural overreliance on motivation, and why it so often betrays us when we need it most. Before we start building, we must know what cannot be relied on.

Then, we start the work.

We shift from reaction to design. From fumbling through self-improvement trends to crafting something solid and durable. This is blueprint thinking. You'll learn to distinguish between cosmetic habits and structural ones—those that merely look good from those that truly hold under pressure. Together, we'll map your cognitive architecture: what you believe, how you respond, where you leak energy, and what scaffolding you actually need to thrive.

And then, subtraction.

In a culture addicted to accumulation—of tasks, inputs, data, ambition—we forget that clarity is usually a matter of less, not more. This is not about aesthetic minimalism. It's not about inbox zero. It's a mental discipline: the removal of clutter that clouds thought and confuses purpose. You'll explore how to create mental space through intentional neglect. How simplicity becomes strength. How subtracting noise makes room for signal.

Next comes habit architecture—not the flashy kind sold by influencers, but the quiet, structural kind. Habits not as ends, but as beams. You'll explore how to design behaviours that reinforce identity and reduce daily decision fatigue. The key isn't willpower—it's load management. The more your mind is freed from trivial choices, the more resilient it becomes in the face of real ones.

From habit, we move to wiring.

Behavioural engineering sounds technical—and it is. It's also deeply human. This is where you rewire your autopilot, interrupt unhelpful patterns, and install new, durable scripts. Most of us live reflexively, shaped by echoes of past experience and ambient cultural pressure. This section shows you how to override those loops—not with brute force, but with strategic redesign. This isn't about being "better." It's about being structurally sound.

But even the best structure collapses under overload. That's where cognitive load comes in. Your attention is not limitless. Your emotional bandwidth has a ceiling. This book treats overwhelm not as weakness, but as signal. You'll learn how to design your day—and your mental ecosystem—to offload what doesn't require active attention, leaving space for the things that do. Information, after all, is not the same as understanding. Emotion is not the same as wisdom.

At some point, we must also reckon with meaning.

Structure without meaning is lifeless. And so we turn, unavoidably, to values—not as marketing slogans, but as foundational beams. What do you stand on when the world around you shifts? What holds steady when your plans fall apart? These aren't lofty ideas. They're practical, load-bearing realities. Get them wrong, and your mental architecture cracks in the next storm. Get them right, and everything else aligns.

No design is complete until it's tested by weather.

Emotional weather. Disruption. Loss. Change. Good architecture doesn't promise protection from storms. It offers preparation. Here, you'll learn not to suppress emotion but to build for it—to design space for grief, frustration, fear. This isn't weakness; it's reinforcement. True resilience isn't stoicism. It's adaptive flexibility.

By the later chapters, the architectural metaphor reveals itself not just as useful but necessary. Mindset is not about feeling good. It's about inhabiting a well-built space. Those who emerge from life's inevitable collapses intact tend to be those who had real foundations—not decorative inspiration, but structural intention.

And finally, identity.

Perhaps the most overlooked—and essential—structure of all. Too often, we define ourselves by the things that can be lost: job titles, relationships, aesthetics. But when the scaffolding falls away, what remains? In these final pages, you'll explore identity not as inheritance but as deliberate construction. You are not your past, nor your résumé. You are the one who builds. And rebuilds.

That's the promise here. Not a mindset to wear like a T-shirt on bad days. Not a dose of encouragement for another Monday morning. But a full architectural shift—from foundation to wiring to purpose. From inherited scripts to chosen structures. From short-term fixes to long-term coherence.

This is not about being optimistic. It's about being precise.

Not about performing inspiration.

About inhabiting integrity.

It isn't self-help.

It is self-architecture.

Welcome to the reconstruction. Let's get to work.

Chapter 1
Clearing the Rubble – What Burnout Leaves Behind

Burnout is not a fleeting emotion or a rough patch in an otherwise manageable week. It isn't something you can sweat out with sleep, fix with a meditation app, or dissolve with a few sun-drenched motivational quotes. No, burnout is something more severe—structural collapse. A failure in the unseen frameworks of your thinking, your daily systems, and even the identity you've spent years performing. What follows isn't mere tiredness; it's wreckage. Broken bits of belief, shattered rituals, a destabilised self now stripped of the familiar scaffolding that once held it upright.

This chapter is about what comes *after*. Not the dramatic implosion—though that gets most of the attention—but the disquieting silence that follows. That strange mental stillness littered with psychic debris. Tangled thought patterns, emotional residue, fragments of frameworks that, even in their dysfunction, once offered a kind of coherence. This aftermath isn't just inconvenient—it demands confrontation. And that confrontation must be approached not with guilt, nor forced optimism, but with a kind of mental engineering. With sober-eyed clarity.

We live in a world expertly designed to optimise for output. A person's sense of self is so often entangled not in *who* they are, but in *what* they accomplish. The job title. The caretaking. The polished image. The inbox that never dares reach double digits. These aren't just daily tasks. They're the invisible beams holding up our identities. So, when these structures fall—whether via professional collapse, personal loss, illness, or quiet detachment—it's not just the routine that breaks. It's the compass. Meaning, once fixed to external rhythms, now swings unmoored.

And in that disarray, people don't merely feel tired—they feel foreign to themselves.

The instinct, naturally, is to rebuild. To chase the old cadence, revive the former roles, wear again the costume of "who I was before." But this rush is a kind of denial. Burnout, like a failed building, lays bare the faults embedded in the original blueprint. It exposes how ill-suited the design was to the pressures placed upon it. And this post-collapse period—though jarring—is fertile ground, *if* we resist the urge to reconstruct too quickly.

The first order of business isn't rebuilding at all. It's dismantling.

Emotional debris doesn't advertise itself. It hangs about like smoke—impossible to see but corrosive all the same. You'll find it in inexplicable anger, persistent exhaustion, the numbness that trails even minor successes. This is not fragility. It's the psychological echo of overload—evidence that circuits, pushed beyond their limits, have twisted out of alignment.

Your mind doesn't default to blankness after breakdown. It retains. Thought patterns once formed in survival mode fossilise into "the way things are." Emotional short-cuts like numbness, urgency, or detachment linger long after the fires are out. And so, what's left is not clarity, but noise—mental clutter that gums up decision-making and fosters confusion.

You might appear functional. You may even feel better. But the structure within remains unsound.

Which means motivation isn't the solution—at least not yet. The urgent task is subtraction. To tear down routines, beliefs, and aspirations inherited under duress. "I must be needed to matter." "If I stop, I'll be overtaken." "Rest is indulgent." These are not wisdoms; they are architectural hazards. Load-bearing lies that once held up a collapsing identity. They must go, if anything stable is to take their place.

But this clearing is no simple matter of will. It requires discernment. Emotional remnants rarely come with name tags. Fatigue gets mislabelled as laziness. Numbness parades as composure. Excessive busyness wears the mask of commitment. It's easy to double down on effort and call the problem a lack of character. But what's really happening? A misdiagnosis of design.

There's another layer—quieter, subtler, more existential. When structure collapses, so too does identity.

If your self-worth has been forged in the fires of competence, dependability, or constant achievement, then losing the mechanisms that propped up those traits doesn't just interrupt your day. It unsettles your sense of self. People often feel unrecognisable without their function—be it their career, their role in a family, their position in a social group. That absence feels less like freedom, and more like erasure.

This isn't weakness. It's the human mind confronting an identity unmoored. Not a loss of *who* you are, but of the reference points used to navigate that question. What remains, once the familiar is gone? Often, the answer is dissonance: grief, relief, fear, numbness. But nestled within that fog is something potent—possibility.

Because identity, like a structure, can be redesigned. And disorientation? That's the clearing. The prelude to construction. Those raw materials—old assumptions, inherited values, worn-out ambitions—are yours to sort through. You are not confined to the self you built under stress. You are now standing in the open ground where something more stable might rise.

But it requires rejecting the clichés.

Pop psychology loves to start with motivation. "You just need to want it." "Visualise your best self." "Find your why." These mantras are catchy. They sell. And they collapse under the slightest strain.

Real change does not begin with willpower. It begins with design.

Motivation is not the match that lights the fire. It is the warmth that follows once the hearth has been built. Asking someone in collapse to summon motivation is like asking a person caught in a downpour to lay bricks. The psychological ground is too soaked to hold anything stable. The inner systems—values, patterns, routines—must first be rebuilt.

In this sense, motivation isn't a catalyst. It's a symptom of integrity.

And that realisation is liberating. It removes the shame that so often shadows exhaustion. It clarifies why productivity tricks so often backfire. Why you can follow someone's ten-step morning routine and still end the day drained. Because surface tweaks don't resolve structural flaws. You can't paint over rotted beams and expect the house to stand.

So then, what does it mean—truly—to clear the rubble?

It means recognising emotional residue as evidence, not failure. It means disentangling the survival tactics that once served you from the constraints they've become. It means asking hard questions about the beliefs you inherited—about work, about rest, about worth—and deciding which still deserve space.

It also means honouring your previous self. Not with nostalgia, but with realism. That person—the one who coped, who powered through, who made it this far—wasn't a mistake. They were a draft. And drafts exist so we can revise.

In the pages ahead, you won't find a programme. You'll find questions. You won't be told to push harder—you'll be asked to pause. You'll be invited to pay attention: to thought patterns that loop, to the voices that echo authority long gone, to the decisions you make when no one's watching.

Because this is not motivational labour. It's architectural.

And every thoughtful rebuild begins with demolition.

We clear not to abandon, but to prepare. We unlearn not to regress, but to lay honest foundations. We sit, often uncomfortably, with the mess—the unstructured days, the disassembled identity, the quiet ache of not knowing what's next. Not because it's easy, but because this pause is necessary. Only from here can something genuinely new take shape. Not a replica. Not a performance. A design.

So before you rush to recover, linger. Survey what remains. Sort through the wreckage with patience, with care. Look at the beams that broke, the supports that cracked under pressure. Learn from them. Because within that rubble lies not just failure—but insight.

This chapter is your invitation to examine it. To stop asking when you'll get back to how things were. And to start asking what might be possible, now that the old design is gone.

The Myth of Bouncing Back

Resilience, once a quietly revered trait, has been recast as a social imperative—an expectation worn like a badge, invoked in boardrooms, classrooms, TED talks, and therapy sessions alike. Its popular interpretation, however, has drifted from psychological substance into cultural caricature. Today, resilience is too often defined not by depth but by *speed*—how fast one recovers, how efficiently one returns to baseline, how quickly the visible signs of distress are erased. To "bounce back" is now held up as a moral and mental ideal, the implied measure of strength.

But strength, real strength, is not elastic. It is structural.

This chapter sets fire to the myth of bouncing back—not because recovery is undesirable, but because its popular framing is conceptually unsound, psychologically misleading, and ultimately counterproductive. The glorification of swift recovery reduces resilience to performance: the re-establishment of outward functionality, rather than the honest reconstruction of inner integrity. In doing so, it suppresses complexity, punishes slowness, and rewards denial.

Consider what it means, semantically, to bounce back. The metaphor is mechanical: a rubber ball dropped from a height, returning to form with no visible distortion. But human beings are not rubber balls. We are not objects that passively absorb impact. We are systems of memory, emotion, values, physiology, and experience. To experience a significant disruption—burnout, trauma, dislocation, loss—and then return unchanged is not resilience. It is stasis. Or worse, it is self-erasure in the service of maintaining appearances.

The idea that we should "get back to normal" after destabilising events betrays a deeper cultural discomfort with psychological messiness. It suggests that restoration to previous levels of productivity, emotional tone, or identity is always the goal—that what was must be preserved at all costs. But sometimes, what was is exactly what needs to be dismantled. A toxic routine, a distorted value system, an identity built entirely around external validation. In such cases, bouncing back is not courageous. It is maladaptive.

This is where the architectural metaphor becomes essential. A building that collapses under stress does not benefit from being rebuilt identically. Structural engineers study failure not to replicate the past, but to *learn from it.* They ask: what load points were miscalculated? What materials buckled? What design assumptions proved false under pressure? Only through such interrogation can a safer, more resilient structure be created. The same applies to psychological design. The mind, like architecture, benefits more from conscious reconstruction than from emotional elasticity.

Yet much of contemporary self-help discourse skips this stage entirely. It champions recovery, but discourages the deep auditing of what led to collapse in the first place. One reason for this is cultural: Western societies in particular prize momentum. There is prestige in endurance, in demonstrating speed of return. Delay, introspection, emotional fatigue—these are framed as indulgent or inefficient. Even mental health initiatives, however well-intentioned, can become co-opted by the productivity ethic: mindfulness as a tool for workplace performance, therapy as a means to "optimise" output.

But real psychological resilience resists quantification. It is not a metric of speed or a return-to-baseline timeline. It is a process of adaptive reorganisation—of rethinking, reframing, and rebuilding the internal systems that govern meaning, emotion, decision-making, and identity. It does not always look impressive. It does not always produce short-term gains. And it often requires tolerating ambiguity far longer than most institutions or social norms will comfortably allow.

Let us look briefly to the science. Studies in post-traumatic growth, notably those emerging from the work of psychologists Richard Tedeschi and Lawrence Calhoun, suggest that significant psychological disruption can serve as a catalyst for growth—not despite the disruption, but *because* of it. However, this growth is neither automatic nor immediate. It requires reflection, support, and deliberate reorientation. It involves asking hard questions: What assumptions were shattered? What values feel hollow now? What roles no longer fit? There is nothing speedy about this. It is not bouncing. It is building.

Equally important are the insights from neurobiology. The human stress response is not a switch to flip off but a wave to regulate. After prolonged exposure to stress—chronic work pressure, caregiving overload, prolonged uncertainty—the nervous system recalibrates to interpret the world as threatening by default. This recalibration doesn't dissipate just because a deadline is met or a crisis abates. The nervous system needs time, safety, and new signals to *downshift.* Pushing for rapid return, whether through internal pressure or external expectation, can leave individuals trapped in a reactive, dysregulated state—functional, perhaps, but far from well.

From an ethical standpoint, the glorification of fast recovery can also be a form of gaslighting. It suggests that if one is still struggling weeks or months later, the problem is insufficient will or faulty mindset. It erases context: structural inequality, systemic overwork, invisible caregiving burdens, racialised trauma, economic precarity. It reduces suffering to a solvable riddle of personal resilience, rather than recognising the broader architectural failures that may have contributed to collapse in the first place.

The alternative is not learned helplessness or eternal victimhood. It is *conscious reconstruction*—the deliberate, effortful act of examining what broke, deciding what matters, and rebuilding with intention. This reconstruction respects time, context, and complexity. It recognises that returning to work is not the same as returning to self. That functional behaviour is not evidence of psychological integration. And that the goal is not to bounce back, but to emerge with better design.

This shift in perspective also reframes our understanding of support. When we expect people to recover quickly, we offer them short-term encouragement: "You've got this." "You're stronger than you think." "Just take a break and come back swinging." These phrases, while well-meaning, often bypass the deeper work. Conscious reconstruction requires a different kind of holding space—less about cheerleading and more about listening, witnessing, scaffolding. It asks communities, workplaces, and institutions to invest not just in recovery plans, but in *rebuilding processes*—those that honour change, not merely restore normalcy.

Practically, this reframe has implications for how we design systems around us. In workplaces, for instance, resilience training often focuses on helping individuals adapt to unsustainable conditions, rather than questioning the conditions themselves. A conscious reconstruction mindset would ask: why are employees burning out in the first place? What values are being enacted through policy? What rhythms are people being asked to live within, and are those rhythms humanly sustainable? The answers to these questions are inconvenient, but necessary. You cannot build adaptive minds in maladaptive systems.

Even in education, we see the consequences of the bounce-back myth. Students are rewarded for fast recovery from failure, high test performance, and visible composure under stress. What's rarely taught is how to sit with uncertainty, how to unlearn unhealthy ambition, or how to reconstruct identity when one's original path collapses. Resilience, as currently taught, becomes another performance metric. What is needed is architectural literacy: the ability to map, question, and rebuild one's internal frameworks with humility and skill.

This doesn't mean reconstruction is linear or permanent. There will be regressions. Rebuilding is iterative. What matters is that each iteration is conscious, not compulsive. That each redesign reflects what has been learned, not what is socially demanded. True resilience is slow, sometimes invisible, and often lonely. But it is also the only kind that sustains.

In psychological terms, we might call this *adaptive integration*: the process by which disruption becomes growth through meaningful reconstruction. It demands courage—not the courage to "bounce," but to stay with the ruins long enough to understand them. To see what parts of the former self were ornamental, which were essential, and which were never yours to begin with.

In closing—not as a summary, but as a distillation—the myth of bouncing back is not just a linguistic problem. It is a design flaw in our collective thinking. It reduces complex human experiences into timelines, metrics, and narratives of triumphant return. It silences those still in the rubble. It privileges the visible over the real. And it distracts us from the deeper work of reconstructing internal systems that can endure—not by springing back, but by holding firm, bending wisely, and redesigning when necessary.

This chapter is not about denying the human capacity for recovery. It is about redefining what recovery should mean. Not a return to what was, but an emergence into what is newly possible.

Not bouncing.

Building better.

Emotional Debris and Cognitive Clutter

Mental fatigue doesn't simply fade with rest—it lingers, quietly rearranging the architecture of our thinking. After periods of prolonged stress, overwhelm, or emotional strain, what remains is not just exhaustion. It is residue. Invisible to others, often unnoticed by ourselves, this residue accrues in the form of thought patterns, emotional habits, and reactive mental loops that compromise our clarity long after the source of fatigue is gone. Most people assume that when the pressure lifts, the mind resets. But human cognition is not designed like a machine. It is more like a sponge—porous, impressionable, and slow to dry.

This chapter confronts what is left behind. Not the dramatic fallout of crisis, but the low-grade psychological sediment that accumulates in the aftermath of prolonged intensity. Whether it's months of overwork, caregiving fatigue, chronic anxiety, or living under emotionally unsafe conditions, these experiences leave behind a cognitive and emotional clutter that subtly distorts how we think, feel, and respond. And unless consciously addressed, this clutter becomes the scaffolding for future behaviour—flawed inputs generating flawed outputs.

To understand this phenomenon clearly, we must first reject the popular notion that stress is a switch—on during difficulty, off during recovery. Neuroscience tells a different story. Chronic stress changes brain function, particularly in regions governing executive control and emotional regulation. The prefrontal cortex—the site of planning, decision-making, and impulse regulation—shows reduced connectivity, while the amygdala—the brain's threat detector—becomes hypersensitised. The result? Even after the acute stressor has passed, the brain continues to over-prioritise threat cues and underperform in strategic thinking. *This is the cognitive architecture of clutter: a mind that defaults to reactivity, repetition, and hypervigilance.*

From a psychological perspective, this translates into a series of inherited distortions. You might become indecisive, not because you're inherently uncertain, but because your cognitive bandwidth has been eroded by months of mental triage. You might start catastrophising small setbacks, not due to pessimism, but because your neural filters have been rewired to expect disruption. These are not abstract tendencies. They are neuropsychological adaptations that persist unless consciously reset.

But the issue goes deeper. Emotional debris often accumulates in unprocessed feelings that are set aside during crisis but never revisited. When navigating high-stakes environments—whether corporate burnout, caregiving crises, or life transitions—emotions are frequently triaged: "Now's not the time," we tell ourselves. We defer anger, repress fear, sideline grief. This strategy can be functional in the short term, but it comes at a cost. Deferred emotions don't disappear. They sediment into the emotional infrastructure of the mind, emerging later as irritability, apathy, cynicism, or disproportionate emotional responses. What looks like mood volatility is often the delayed discharge of unmanaged experience.

The workplace offers a particularly vivid context for this pattern. Consider the manager who, after surviving an intense product launch, continues to exhibit hyper-controlling tendencies long after the deadline has passed. Or the healthcare worker who, months after a staffing crisis, remains emotionally numb in the face of patient distress. These are not flaws of character. They are evidence of *residual emotional load*—emotions that were never metabolised and have now altered behavioural norms. Without intentional clearing, they become default settings.

There's also a cognitive analogue to this emotional debris: mental clutter in the form of unfinished thoughts, open loops, and low-level background anxiety. The modern brain, especially in high-performing individuals, is flooded with stimuli. Email threads left unresolved. Tasks half-completed. Conversations replayed. Plans imagined but never executed. This backlog creates what psychologists term the "Zeigarnik effect": the tendency of the mind to fixate on incomplete tasks. Left unmanaged, this mental residue creates a kind of cognitive noise that reduces working memory, impairs decision quality, and fragments attention.

What makes this particularly insidious is that we often interpret the effects of cognitive clutter as moral failings. A distracted mind becomes labelled as "lazy." A cluttered memory as "disorganised." A lack of emotional range as "burned out," full stop—as if that were the end of the story. But these symptoms are not character indictments. They are signals of architectural overload. Just as too many files slow a hard drive, too many open loops—emotional, mental, or behavioural—compromise mental fluidity. *Clarity is not a mindset—it is the result of internal space.*

There is also a philosophical dimension here. Cognitive and emotional clutter subtly constrains freedom—not just in attention, but in agency. When our internal world is shaped by unresolved impressions, we act not from intention but from momentum. Habits of urgency, defensiveness, or avoidance become scripts we follow unconsciously. In the absence of mental space, we stop choosing and start repeating. Over time, this repetition ossifies into identity: "I'm just someone who…" becomes the rationalisation for inherited thought loops. What we experience as personality is often merely the residue of untreated experience.

Conscious clearing, then, is not therapeutic indulgence. It is *a discipline of sovereignty*. It is the process by which we reclaim authorship over our thoughts and behaviours—not by effort alone, but by *subtraction*. By pausing to identify what we've unconsciously internalised. By distinguishing what is ours from what was merely adaptive. And by recognising that clutter, emotional or cognitive, is not benign. It shapes the architecture of our mind—what it holds, how it holds, and how long it can hold before cracking.

Practically, the work of clearing involves three layers: identification, validation, and release. Identification is the ability to name what lingers. This could be a recurring thought ("I always mess up the important things"), an emotional loop (irritation masking unacknowledged fear), or a behaviour that once made sense but now sabotages growth. Validation is the recognition that these patterns were, at one point, *functional*. Emotional clutter is not inherently irrational. It is the residue of previously adaptive logic. Finally, release is the practice of creating new systems: habits of reflection, environments of stillness, and thought structures that are architecturally intentional, not inherited.

One powerful example can be found in the transition from crisis caregiving to ordinary life. Many caregivers report that after the crisis ends—whether due to a loved one's recovery, death, or institutionalisation—they remain trapped in hypervigilant patterns. They scan for signs of danger, feel unable to relax, and often struggle with guilt when they do. The crisis is over, but the architecture remains. These individuals aren't "failing" to move on—they are *still living inside the psychological structure that crisis built.* The same principle applies to professionals exiting burnout-inducing jobs, soldiers returning from deployment, or people leaving high-conflict relationships. Emotional debris is not a dysfunction. It is a *footprint.*

So why don't we clear it more often? Partly because clutter has become culturally normalised. In high-demand environments, busyness is valorised, and emotional processing is stigmatised. We're expected to "move on," "let it go," "focus on what's next." But these imperatives encourage suppression, not clarity. They prioritise forward motion over foundational integrity. The problem is that when the mind becomes a hoarder of unprocessed impressions, it loses its responsiveness. Like a cluttered workspace, everything becomes harder—finding what matters, seeing what's possible, and acting with precision.

What's needed is a shift from performance-oriented recovery to architecture-based restoration. This means recognising that healing is not something we *feel our way into*, but something we *design our way through*. It is a process of creating internal conditions—mental stillness, reflective routines, structural thinking—that allow for true cognitive and emotional recalibration. This may involve journaling not as catharsis, but as cognitive offloading. Meditation not as spiritual aspiration, but as neural defragmentation. Conversations not as venting, but as pattern exposure.

Ultimately, emotional debris and cognitive clutter are not signs that we are broken. They are evidence that we've been overloaded. The mind leaves traces. What matters is whether we choose to see them. In the architecture of inner life, clearing is not a luxury. It is the prerequisite for rebuilding. For resilience that is more than a slogan. For clarity that is more than a moment. And for strength that does not collapse under the weight of what it refuses to release.

This is not a call to purge emotion or eliminate thought. It is a call to *curate the contents of your inner world with the same intentionality you would bring to a physical space you must live in every day*. Because that's what the mind is—not a battlefield, not a black box, but a living space. And clutter, when ignored, becomes structure. The work is not just to feel better. It is to *build better.*

When Identity Collapses with Structure

When your routines disintegrate and your roles are stripped away, who remains?

This is not a rhetorical exercise. It is a psychological crucible faced by people across all stages of life—often abruptly, and always disruptively. The collapse of structure—whether triggered by burnout, redundancy, divorce, illness, caregiving, retirement, or relocation—frequently brings with it a collapse of identity. That collapse is disorienting. But it is not pathological. *It is the honest exposure of how tightly many of us have welded our sense of self to external scaffolding.*

The deeper challenge is that we rarely notice the merger until the structure vanishes. People don't typically walk around declaring, "I am my morning routine," or "I am the meetings I run." But beneath the surface, identity is quietly coded into patterns of action, external validation, and recurring feedback loops. Roles become personality. Productivity becomes self-worth. Social function becomes private truth. And when the rhythms stop—the work ends, the relationship dissolves, the caregiving ceases, the calendar empties—there is often no emotional floor beneath them. What felt like personal stability reveals itself as contingent structure.

We should begin by acknowledging the uncomfortable reality: this merger between identity and structure is often *efficient.* It produces socially coherent individuals—predictable, self-regulating, productive. It facilitates coordination within institutions, relationships, and economies. It simplifies psychological navigation. You don't need to ask who you are when the world consistently tells you: you're the dependable parent, the high-performing analyst, the supportive spouse, the competent leader. These labels, reinforced through routines, slowly harden into identity. And over time, that identity becomes an unconscious constraint on what we believe we are allowed to feel, think, or want.

The problem arises not when these identities function well, but when the structures that sustain them disappear—and with them, the signals that confirm we are who we thought we were. Without the scaffolding of action and role, we begin to feel blank. This blankness is often misread as depression or failure, but it is neither. *It is the cognitive dissonance of a person whose self-concept was built atop transient routines.*

Take the example of a professional who steps down from a senior leadership role after a long period of burnout. They may describe feeling untethered—not simply because their calendar is empty, but because their value, confidence, and emotional regulation were encoded into a schedule, a team, and an organisational hierarchy. Or consider a parent whose identity has revolved entirely around their caregiving function. When children leave home, or the demands shift, the absence of need is experienced not as relief but as erosion. These are not unusual reactions. They are the expected psychological consequences of identity rooted in external design.

In psychology, this is closely related to the concept of *role engulfment*—a term used to describe when an individual's self-concept becomes dominated by a single role or identity, often to the exclusion of other dimensions of the self. Role engulfment may initially offer clarity and purpose, but over time it becomes a liability. When the role is altered or removed, there is no internal architecture to compensate. The result is an identity vacuum—marked by emotional confusion, decision paralysis, and in some cases, existential fatigue.

The field of identity theory, particularly in sociology and developmental psychology, provides further nuance. Scholars such as Sheldon Stryker and Peter Burke have long argued that identity is not a monolith, but a system of internalised role expectations shaped by interactional contexts. The more salient and reinforced a role becomes, the more central it is to our self-definition. Yet what the literature also shows is that adaptive identity systems are *plural and flexible.* In other words, resilience lies not in strengthening a single role-based identity, but in developing a diversified internal identity ecosystem—one capable of weathering structural change without total collapse.

Unfortunately, this pluralism is often undermined by cultural messaging that prizes specialisation and clarity. From an early age, individuals are taught to aspire towards *coherence*—to find a calling, pursue a path, define a brand, be consistent. While these goals have utility in certain domains (career progression, professional networking, strategic planning), they come at the cost of adaptability. When coherence is prioritised over multidimensionality, individuals lose the muscle required to hold ambiguity, reconfigure identity, and construct meaning outside pre-existing roles.

This is where the architectural metaphor regains its potency. If we imagine identity not as essence, but as *a designed structure*, we can begin to ask generative questions: What are the load-bearing beams of my self-concept? Which parts are decorative? What's built for durability, and what's built for display? And crucially—what is left when the scaffolding is removed?

These are not abstract philosophical musings. They are essential to recovery from burnout, trauma, or any major life transition. The work is not to *rebuild the same identity with different tools*, but to *interrogate the assumptions baked into the previous structure*. Who were you trying to prove something to? What rhythms were inherited, not chosen? Which parts of your former self served others but silenced you?

Philosophically, this inquiry touches the work of thinkers like Simone de Beauvoir and Erich Fromm, who challenged essentialist views of selfhood. Fromm, in particular, warned against *having* an identity rather than *being* in a state of continuous creation. To have an identity—as possession—is to risk losing it through structural change. To be in identity, as a verb, is to accept its malleability and engage in active authorship. The collapse of external structure thus becomes an *invitation to return to authorship.*

This re-authorship is not instantaneous. The blank space that follows structural collapse is often psychologically taxing. Ambiguity is metabolically expensive. The brain prefers prediction and routine. Yet it is in this ambiguity—this destabilised in-between—that real design becomes possible. Not reactive reconstruction, but conscious architecture. Not a return to past roles, but the emergence of deeper foundations based on values, curiosity, and agency.

Practical strategies here matter. Individuals navigating identity collapse often benefit from narrative reframing—using reflective writing or dialogue to map past roles without equating them with essence. This is not about rewriting history, but about seeing structure *as structure*, not as self. Language becomes a powerful tool. "I was someone who led large teams" is different from "I am a leader." The former acknowledges temporality; the latter risks rigidity.

There is also immense value in intentional experimentation. Without former routines to anchor us, the temptation is to remain inert—waiting for clarity before taking action. But clarity often follows movement. Low-stakes engagement in diverse activities—creative, relational, physical—can serve as probes into new identity possibilities. Not because they *define* the self, but because they *test its edges*. This kind of architectural sketching allows for new designs to emerge organically, informed by direct experience rather than inherited expectation.

Social context must also be addressed. Identity reconstruction is rarely a solitary act. It occurs within relational fields. Unfortunately, others often struggle to accept new designs. People who benefitted from your previous roles may resist your redefinition. Colleagues may question your shift in ambition. Family members may grieve the reliable version of you they once leaned on. This friction is not a sign you're on the wrong path. It is proof that your prior identity was entangled in systems that now require renegotiation.

None of this makes identity collapse easy. But it does make it *meaningful.* To be confronted with the question "Who am I without that?" is not a crisis to be medicated, but a design brief to be engaged. It is the blueprint stage—the raw material from which something more honest, more flexible, and more sustainable can be built.

The danger is not the loss of identity. The danger is mistaking the former structure for the only possible self. What matters now is not how quickly you fill the gap, but how consciously you redraw the frame. Identity is not found. It is constructed. And the collapse, however painful, is an opening—a structural clearing that, if approached with care and creativity, allows for the emergence of an architecture better aligned with who you are becoming.

The mind can rebuild. But only when it remembers that it is the architect, not just the occupant.

Why Motivation Doesn't Matter Yet

Motivation is frequently positioned as the holy grail of personal change—a spark to be captured, a mindset to be summoned, the precondition for meaningful action. Popular psychology, self-help literature, and performance coaching routinely treat motivation as the necessary starting point. "You just need to want it more." "Find your why." "Harness your inner drive." These are the refrains of a culture obsessed with emotional propulsion. But they misrepresent how sustainable change actually occurs.

Motivation is not the cause of durable behaviour; it is the consequence of sound psychological design.

This is not merely a semantic reversal. It is a reframing with deep implications. If motivation is a byproduct, not a catalyst, then waiting for it—searching for it, willing it into existence—becomes a form of stalling. And the advice that insists we must feel driven before we act becomes not only unhelpful but intellectually dishonest.

Let us begin with the fundamental problem: *motivation is state-dependent.* It fluctuates in response to mood, sleep, blood sugar, social context, hormonal rhythms, and a wide spectrum of environmental variables. Even the most disciplined individuals—athletes, writers, surgeons—report that their drive oscillates. What distinguishes their consistency is not greater access to motivation, but a system of internal scaffolding that renders motivation unnecessary in the moment of action. They have designed habits, roles, and routines that *do not require them to feel like it* in order to begin.

This insight is not new. Behavioural psychology has long emphasised the role of *contextual cues and environmental shaping* in behaviour maintenance. B.F. Skinner's operant conditioning, later refined by scholars such as James Clear and Charles Duhigg, made it clear that habit formation is more about cue-routine-reward loops than inner desire. But the modern fixation on motivation has obscured this evidence. We still idealise the person who rises early to train, not because of a sleep-conditioned routine and a pre-laid outfit, but because they are somehow intrinsically driven. We romanticise effort when it looks emotional, even when it's unreliable.

What this means for those in recovery from burnout, disorientation, or identity collapse is essential: *the absence of motivation is not a sign that something is wrong with you—it is a signal that your current architecture cannot yet support action.* This is especially true during transitional periods. When mental structure is compromised—when routines have evaporated, emotional clutter abounds, and the self feels fragmented—waiting for motivation is a deeply flawed strategy. You are attempting to ignite fuel in a system that lacks the wiring to carry the spark.

Consider a person emerging from prolonged professional burnout. Their energy is low, their sleep erratic, and their former identity as a productive contributor feels either fragile or fraudulent. They want to "get back to it," but the emotional residue of collapse is unresolved. In this state, exhortations to "just start small" or "find your passion again" are at best premature and at worst harmful. *What's needed is not motivation, but new mental scaffolding*: micro-structures of stability, cognitive anchors, behavioural guardrails. From these, momentum—and later, motivation—can emerge.

This logic aligns with self-determination theory (SDT), one of the most empirically robust models of human motivation, developed by psychologists Edward Deci and Richard Ryan. According to SDT, intrinsic motivation—genuine, self-sustaining drive—arises not from sheer effort, but from the presence of three psychological nutrients: autonomy, competence, and relatedness. Each of these requires *infrastructure* to support it.

Autonomy doesn't mean being untethered. It means acting from integrated values within a designed structure. Competence doesn't arrive magically. It develops through repeated engagement in appropriately scaffolded challenges. Relatedness requires connection, but connection is rarely possible when the self is architecturally incoherent. In short, if the mind is in ruins, motivation cannot grow. You do not will your way into self-determination. You *build the conditions that make it possible.*

This raises a critical ethical point. The cultural insistence on motivational readiness can easily become a moral judgment. Those who struggle to initiate are seen as lacking willpower, grit, or "mindset." But a person without a house does not lack the desire for shelter. They lack walls. Likewise, a person whose internal architecture has collapsed under stress is not weak. They are *temporarily without the structural affordances that support agency.*

We must also acknowledge that motivation is not a neutral tool. It is shaped by ideological assumptions. Much of what we call motivation is, in fact, internalised pressure—residual performance scripts inherited from capitalism, patriarchy, or familial expectation. The desire to "get back to work," to "prove oneself," or to "reclaim lost time" may feel motivational, but it often conceals unexamined obligations. In such cases, chasing motivation is not a path to authenticity—it is a shortcut back to misalignment.

So what, then, replaces motivation at the start of a rebuild?

Scaffolding. The intelligent construction of minimal viable structures that reduce friction, preserve decision energy, and gradually reintroduce agency. These include environmental design (e.g., changing physical spaces to reduce resistance), temporal design (e.g., attaching new behaviours to existing rhythms), and relational design (e.g., shared commitments or identity-aligned accountability). These are not tactics for productivity. They are *tools of reconstruction*—ways to create the conditions under which the nervous system can begin to trust action again.

One of the most effective forms of scaffolding is *identity-based design.* Rather than setting outcome goals ("I want to write a book"), the individual builds identity-aligned routines ("I am the kind of person who writes for 20 minutes after coffee"). This approach is supported by cognitive-behavioural research showing that repeated behaviour not only changes habits, but shifts self-perception—*and it is self-*

perception, not emotional enthusiasm, that sustains long-term change. Identity is stabilised not by intention but by enacted patterns.

This is especially vital during times when the emotional system is untrustworthy. Following emotional exhaustion, the body often sends inconsistent signals: fatigue, resistance, bursts of overcommitment followed by crash. These are not reliable motivators. They are evidence of a system still recalibrating. To expect stable motivation from this system is to misread its function. The better question is: *What scaffolding can I build so that I do not need to feel ready in order to begin?*

We can draw a useful parallel from architecture itself. When constructing a bridge, engineers do not begin by spanning the full distance. They begin with supports. Temporary structures that allow for weight distribution before the permanent form can hold. The same principle applies to psychological reconstruction. Until the new mindset is load-bearing, it requires *externalised support*—structured repetition, reduced choice architecture, environmental cues. These are not crutches. They are intelligent preconditions.

This reframing also guards against the trap of motivational fetishism—the idea that we must constantly feel inspired in order to be authentic. In reality, many of the most important actions in life are preceded not by excitement, but by neutrality or even resistance. Caregivers show up not because they're motivated, but because they've designed their days to accommodate care. Writers write not because they're inspired, but because they've structured their mornings to include writing. The presence of motivation becomes, in time, a *pleasant side effect*, not a necessary fuel source.

Finally, there is a moral freedom in this understanding. If motivation doesn't matter *yet*, then your lack of drive is not a disqualifier. It is a context. And context can be designed. Rather than interrogating yourself—"Why don't I feel like doing this?"—you can begin to ask, "What would make this feel less heavy, less complicated, more frictionless?" This is the architectural lens: shifting from inner scrutiny to external design.

To rebuild well, you do not need to feel energised. You need to *design around the assumption that energy will be inconsistent.* To stop waiting for motivation is not to lower your standards. It is to respect the complexity of human behaviour and to approach change with structural intelligence rather than emotional pressure.

When you build scaffolding first, motivation arrives later—*as the mind realises it can trust itself again.* And that is when real change begins to hold.

Chapter 2
Blueprint Thinking – Designing Your Inner Infrastructure

Every human mind possesses an architecture. The question is not whether it exists, but whether it's intentional or haphazard.

Most people inhabit a mental framework that was never consciously constructed. It's inherited—pieced together from cultural scripts, childhood impressions, societal cues, and the imperatives of survival rather than meaning. Over time, this patchwork scaffolding becomes so familiar it passes for self. And then—often suddenly—it doesn't hold.

When individuals crumble beneath psychological strain—burnout, emotional collapse, prolonged overwhelm—it is too often construed as a failure of will: not enough grit, not enough stamina. But these are not root causes. They are the visible signs of something deeper giving way. What's failing isn't character, but construction—the inner framework that was never engineered to withstand the cumulative pressures of modern existence. What's needed isn't more motivation, but a better blueprint.

This chapter offers an alternative to reactive self-help: what might be called blueprint thinking. It's the practice of designing a mind with intention—one that prioritises strength, coherence, and adaptability over surface optimisation. Blueprint thinking doesn't ask what you want to achieve—it asks what sort of internal system can reliably sustain purpose and clarity, especially when circumstances deteriorate.

It's tempting to reach for performance upgrades—tweaked schedules, fine-tuned habits, morning routines borrowed from digital prophets—but these are surface solutions. They often obscure the real question: what, structurally, is your mind built to carry? And more critically: where does it begin to fracture?

This requires drawing a sharp distinction between structural integrity and aesthetic design. Much of the self-improvement industry trades on appearances—planners, trackers, affirmations arranged like furniture in a tastefully staged home. But structure lies behind the walls. It's what keeps the roof on when the winds rise. A person may function seamlessly in optimal conditions, yet disintegrate when stress mounts. That disintegration reveals not a personal flaw, but an architectural oversight.

Consider the distinction between a routine and a ritual. Routines are often scheduled performances—meditate, hydrate, stretch, repeat. They look admirable on paper but are easily abandoned when life gets messy. Rituals, by contrast, are embedded in one's identity and environment. They're sustained not by discipline alone, but by alignment. They bend without breaking. They are the psychological equivalents of reinforced beams.

To build at that level, one must first map the internal terrain. This is not self-reflection for its own sake. It's architectural surveying. Think of it as drafting a cognitive floorplan. You're identifying where your attention naturally flows and where it clogs. Which beliefs carry weight, and which sag under contradiction. What thoughts precede your best decisions—and what triggers your worst. You are not simply cataloguing quirks. You are uncovering your mind's load paths.

Take, for example, the person who reflexively perfects under pressure. They may appear committed to excellence, but a closer look often reveals something else entirely: a central beam of belief—perhaps, "If I err, I lose worth"—bearing far more than it should. Around that beam grows a structure warped by avoidance, overextension, and control. The solution here isn't encouragement. It's redesign. That belief isn't noble. It's unstable. And if it's to remain, it needs either reinforcement or replacement.

Which brings us to a key principle: design for stress, not for ideal conditions. Too many lives are built like holiday homes—functional when the weather's fine, uninhabitable when storms come. Blueprint thinking asks: what happens to your mental routines when sleep is compromised, when ambiguity reigns, when grief descends? A resilient structure doesn't prevent such things; it endures them. Through redundancies. Through simplification. Through wise load distribution across fewer, more reliable pillars.

Decision fatigue offers a perfect case study. We know—both from research and experience—that decision-making is a depletable resource. Without scaffolding—clearly defined values, defaults, and constraints—the cumulative weight of tiny choices becomes overwhelming. Those who function at high levels don't necessarily think harder. They've just built better decision structures. It's not about pushing harder—it's about holding smarter.

There is, as ever, a deeper philosophical layer. We are culturally conditioned to treat identity as something inherent: a buried self waiting to be uncovered. But blueprint thinking disrupts that romanticism. It suggests the self is not a fixed core, but an ongoing construction project. Change, then, is not betrayal. It is redesign. It is, in fact, the mark of thoughtful construction.

This reframe also exposes the limitations of willpower, long mythologised as the engine of change. But neuroscience—and daily life—tell us otherwise. Willpower flickers. It fades. It is reactive, not renewable. Systems, however, endure. Defaults informed by identity, routines aligned with context, and structures built to anticipate resistance—these conserve effort and yield consistency. That's not laziness. That's engineering.

Blueprint thinking, then, is a shift in posture. A refusal to outsource one's inner life to culture or chance. It's the decision to approach the mind with the same intentionality a skilled builder brings to their craft. You would not construct a house on inherited blueprints without checking the load distribution. Why build a life that way?

This chapter begins the reversal of that pattern. It invites you to identify which of your habits are decorative and which are structural. It offers a method to audit your cognitive layout—to notice where clarity accumulates and where tension builds. It asks you to think not about doing more, but about building better.

Perfection is not the target. Structural coherence is. A mind with integrity doesn't need constant stimulation or heroic levels of discipline. It holds its shape under ambiguity. It remains aligned under pressure. It doesn't shatter; it adjusts.

This is the blueprint stage. Not the final build. But the moment to stop guessing at your design and start shaping it with deliberation. You're not just the resident here. You're the architect. Let's begin.

From Reaction to Construction

Most people live in a state of low-grade reactivity, mistaking it for normalcy. They wake up to alarms they didn't set with intention, open phones filled with obligations they didn't choose, and enter routines they've never consciously designed. Their day unfolds as a sequence of responses—to emails, expectations, interruptions, moods, minor crises. This is not a life built. It is a life absorbed.

Reactive living, by its nature, is externally anchored. It is governed by inputs. The input could be a deadline, a disapproving glance, a social comparison, or a bad night's sleep. But whatever the source, the self that responds is rarely the self that designs. It is the self in autopilot mode—pattern-driven, emotionally entangled, strategically shallow. And the cost of this state is subtle but profound: a loss of authorship.

This subchapter proposes a structural correction. *To live well, one must shift from reaction to construction.* Not occasionally, when life is calm, but systemically—through the deliberate development of inner infrastructure that governs action from intention rather than stimulus. This transition is not motivational. It is architectural. It involves understanding how the reactive mind is formed, and how a constructed mind can be designed.

To understand the appeal of reactivity, we must first recognise its neurological efficiency. From an evolutionary standpoint, the reactive brain is adaptive. It ensures survival by prioritising threat detection, rapid decision-making, and energy conservation. The limbic system—especially the amygdala—is tasked with flagging urgency. It doesn't wait for reflection. It scans and responds. This worked well when threats were immediate and physical. But in modern life, where psychological complexity outpaces physical danger, the same circuitry misfires. *A difficult email can trigger the same stress response as a predator.* And over time, this creates a baseline of anxious vigilance.

Reactivity is not just a personal habit. It's a systemic condition. Modern environments—particularly digital ones—are designed to maximise engagement through interruption. Notifications, performance metrics, gamified interfaces, and infinite scrolling do not merely compete for attention; they *train the brain to expect intrusion.* And when the brain expects interruption, it abandons construction. It waits to be directed.

This is where the concept of intentional inner architecture becomes critical. A constructed mind is not merely more focused. It is *structured to generate direction internally.* It does not rely on moods to act, nor on external prompts to choose. It contains internal scaffolding—mental routines, metacognitive practices, values-driven priorities—that organise behaviour without the need for constant motivation or friction.

Construction begins with *awareness of reactivity as a default.* This awareness is not theoretical. It is behavioural. For example, consider a moment when your attention shifts involuntarily—toward an email notification, a reactive thought, a flash of irritation. These shifts are not failures of discipline. They are expressions of an unprotected cognitive architecture—one without boundaries, buffers, or filters. The reactive mind lets everything in and must deal with everything as if it matters equally. This is untenable.

A constructed mind, by contrast, begins with *selectivity.* It establishes cognitive architecture by prioritising what gets processed and when. This does not mean becoming indifferent or detached. It means designing *thought gates*—structured times for reflection, protected spaces for deep work, routines that make priorities visible, and habits that reduce decision fatigue. These are not productivity tools. They are *design principles* that reduce noise and reinforce clarity.

Take, for instance, the use of structured reflection. Research in cognitive behavioural therapy and mindfulness-based cognitive science demonstrates that the ability to *observe* a thought without immediately reacting to it correlates with lower emotional volatility and higher executive function. This capacity—sometimes called "metacognitive awareness"—is foundational to construction. When a person can pause, label, and assess their thoughts before acting, they reclaim design authority. The brain stops being a reactor. It becomes an architect.

This shift is not about becoming hyper-controlled or emotionally muted. It is about becoming *responsive on purpose*. Responsiveness and reactivity are not synonyms. Responsive action arises from internal alignment—what matters most, what's contextually relevant, what honours a broader design. Reactive action, in contrast, is governed by immediacy and internal noise. The difference lies in who sets the agenda: the world or the self.

Philosophically, this returns us to ancient principles that modern science is only now empirically confirming. The Stoics, for example, were early practitioners of construction. Marcus Aurelius wrote extensively on the discipline of thought selection—not as self-denial, but as sovereignty. The freedom to choose one's focus, and thereby one's emotional state, was not merely a coping tool. It was the essence of agency. Similarly, in Buddhist psychology, particularly in the Abhidhamma tradition, the mind is described as a field to be cultivated—a place where intentional design fosters clarity and liberation.

But modern psychology offers another powerful layer: the understanding that the brain is plastic. Neural pathways are not fixed; they are *sculpted by repetition*. When a person reacts compulsively, they are not failing—they are reinforcing well-worn pathways. When a person pauses, reflects, and chooses intentionally, even once, they begin to form new scaffolding. Over time, the reactive loop loses strength. This is not mysticism. It is neuroarchitecture. What fires together, wires together. Construction is both a metaphor and a material fact.

Practically, transitioning from reaction to construction begins with a shift in design questions. Instead of asking, "How do I stop reacting?" the individual begins to ask, *"What needs to be built so I don't need to react?"* The answer is rarely a single tactic. It is often an ecosystem. For example: a clear decision protocol reduces emotional hijacking; a defined morning structure limits the chaos of low-energy choices; a values hierarchy simplifies prioritisation. These components form a mental operating system—*not to control life, but to navigate it without constant improvisation.*

The benefits of this architecture extend beyond personal wellbeing. Leaders who construct their mental frameworks are far less susceptible to reputational reactivity—rash emails, impulsive reversals, misaligned initiatives. Creatives who build boundaries around their attention produce more consistent work, even when uninspired. Parents who install pause mechanisms in their communication respond with intentionality rather than projection. These outcomes are not personality traits. They are the result of design.

Still, it's important to acknowledge the cultural tension embedded in this model. Many people are praised precisely for their reactivity: their speed, their availability, their capacity to "pivot." Construction, by contrast, often requires *slowness at the front end*: time to think, space to design, deliberate withholding of response. In fast-paced cultures, this can look like inefficiency. But the paradox is clear—*slowness in design leads to speed in execution.* You do not want to make faster decisions. You want to design environments where fewer decisions are needed.

There is also a deeper philosophical payoff. When one begins to live from construction, a different kind of peace emerges—not the absence of conflict, but the absence of compulsion. You do not need to say yes out of guilt, or respond out of fear, or act out of inherited expectation. Your actions, even under pressure, align with structures you've chosen. This is not about becoming inflexible. It is about becoming *internally coherent.*

Ultimately, the shift from reaction to construction is not just a mental upgrade. It is an ethical stance. It says: I will not be dictated to by noise, pressure, or performance cues. I will build a mind that can hold what matters, discard what doesn't, and act with clarity even when the world is chaotic. This is not perfectionism. It is psychological craftsmanship. You are not here to react well. You are here to *build something worth inhabiting.*

And that work starts now. Not with another productivity tool. But with the decision to stop living by reaction—and start constructing from within.

Structural Integrity vs. Surface Design

In architecture, a building that looks impressive but collapses under stress is not a marvel—it is a liability. The same holds true for the mind. Mental habits that appear effective on the surface but lack structural integrity are often mistaken for strength. Yet when pressure mounts—during burnout, conflict, disruption, or failure—these surface designs falter, exposing the absence of foundational support beneath the display. This subchapter draws a clear line between psychological facades and functional infrastructure. It argues that personal development must not prioritise how habits *look*, but how they *hold.*

There is a significant distinction between building for performance and building for durability. Performance-driven habits are calibrated for visibility, efficiency, or aesthetic appeal. They are often mimetic—borrowed from productivity trends, influencers, or organisational norms. They generate temporary results and external validation but fail to deliver long-term stability. Foundational habits, by contrast, are those that regulate internal coherence. They are less visible, slower to develop, but essential to withstanding real psychological load.

Consider the example of two individuals with a structured morning routine. One wakes at 5:00 a.m., journals, runs, meditates, and posts an inspiring quote before breakfast. The other wakes at 6:30, makes tea, sits in silence for ten minutes, and reviews one value-aligned intention for the day. The first routine is dense, impressive, and may indeed be effective. But if it is not internally grounded—if each component is performed without connection to a broader inner architecture—it is vulnerable to collapse. A single disruption (a sick child, a travel delay, a poor night's sleep) can derail the entire sequence. The second routine, while minimal, is built on *fewer but deeper load-bearing elements*—deliberate stillness, grounding, and alignment. It is resilient, not because it is minimal, but because it is integrated.

This is the difference between *surface design* and *structural integrity*. Surface design is reactive and decorative. It often seeks optimisation without asking what is being optimised *for*. It adds complexity under the assumption that more equals better. Structural integrity, by contrast, starts with subtraction: *What needs to hold when everything else fails?* What mental habits reinforce clarity, values, and action when motivation disappears?

Cognitive behavioural science supports this distinction. Surface-level habits are often driven by external reinforcement—rewards, feedback loops, gamified metrics. These can work, but only when the environment supports them. When reinforcement disappears—when feedback is delayed, results are unclear, or the task becomes emotionally difficult—these habits decay. Foundational habits are internally regulated. They rely on intrinsic drivers—meaning, identity, coherence. They are *anchored in how a person thinks about themselves and their life*, not just what they do on a good day.

Structural habits also interact differently with stress. Surface-level routines often collapse under pressure because they are additive—they require energy, attention, or ideal conditions. Foundational habits absorb pressure because they are designed to function *within* it. For example, a foundational habit might be a daily evening reflection practice that helps recalibrate attention and identify distortion in thought patterns. This isn't glamorous, but it acts as a *structural anchor*—a way to release accumulated cognitive noise and restore internal alignment. It does not depend on emotional readiness; it *restores* emotional readiness.

Another example lies in how people manage time. Surface design focuses on calendaring, apps, productivity frameworks. These tools have their place, but when people feel overwhelmed, they often default to doing more faster. Structural integrity in time design might mean clearly defined *non-negotiable boundaries* around energy—knowing that two hours of deep work is more valuable than ten hours of interrupted effort, and having a repeatable system for protecting those hours. This isn't time management. It's *cognitive load engineering.*

The danger of surface design is that it can produce the illusion of progress. In the language of systems thinking, it creates *shallow feedback loops.* You complete a checklist. You feel productive. You receive praise. But if the tasks are misaligned with deeper priorities, the structure they reinforce is brittle. Many professionals, particularly high-achieving ones, live in structures that reward appearance over integrity. They perform composure while privately spinning. They deliver outcomes while accumulating internal dissonance. The long-term result is not success, but silent erosion.

This phenomenon has cultural roots. Western cultures especially emphasise *outward indicators of success*—busyness, output, polish. Organisational life often elevates those who can *signal competence under pressure,* even if that pressure is unsustainable. Over time, this incentivises surface design: performance rituals, image management, shallow adaptability. Rarely is the question asked: *Does this person's psychological infrastructure support sustainability?* We reward deliverables, not design.

But when real disruption hits—grief, illness, organisational upheaval, relational rupture—it becomes painfully clear who has built structural integrity. These individuals may wobble, but they do not fall apart. Why? Because their internal systems are not held together by public image or external validation. They are built around slow, deliberate, low-maintenance habits—*ones that serve not their output, but their orientation.* They know what they value, how to reset under stress, where their attention defaults, and what practices restore function.

There is also a philosophical dimension to this work. At its core, structural integrity requires a kind of *introspective honesty*—a willingness to ask: *What am I building? Who am I building it for? And will it hold when no one is watching?* Surface design tends to avoid these questions. It prefers quick wins, visible improvement, measurable outputs. But deep design requires confronting complexity. It involves tolerating slowness, ambiguity, even temporary inefficiency. The goal is not to *look* stable. It is to *be* stable.

Consider the contrast between two forms of self-reflection. One person journals each morning, tracking gratitude and wins—a practice that reinforces positivity. Another person engages in weekly internal audits, asking: *What did I avoid this week? Where did I act out of fear rather than principle? Which behaviours reflect my values, and which reflect my conditioning?* Both are reflective, but only the latter develops structural insight. One is maintenance. The other is design work.

To develop structural integrity, a person must engage in what organisational theorist Chris Argyris called *double-loop learning*—not just adjusting behaviours within existing frameworks, but re-examining and redesigning the frameworks themselves. Surface habits operate in a single loop: if a result isn't achieved, tweak the input. Foundational habits step back: *Why is this result even meaningful? What assumptions underlie this input-output logic?* This kind of reflection is not always efficient. But it is *necessary for durability.*

In practical terms, the development of foundational habits involves identifying and reinforcing a few key domains:

Cognitive alignment – Habits that improve clarity of thought, reduce distortion, and centre decisions around internal logic rather than emotional volatility. This includes reflection, metacognition, and structured pause.

Emotional containment – Habits that allow emotions to be processed without suppression or impulsivity. Not distraction, but containment. This includes expressive writing, containment rituals, and safe interpersonal processing.

Attention design – Habits that regulate what gets your attention, when, and why. This includes environment shaping, intentional information diets, and conscious disengagement from attention economy traps.

Identity anchoring – Habits that regularly reconnect behaviour to chosen values and long-term design, not to inherited scripts or transient ambition. This might include slow, analogue rituals, deliberate solitude, or consistent engagement with source material (texts, mentors, principles).

None of these habits appear on a glossy productivity tracker. But they are what hold a person up when the conditions for peak performance no longer exist. They are what make a person internally navigable—*a mind that does not collapse simply because the world does.*

The temptation to optimise surface-level routines is understandable. It offers speed, visibility, and reinforcement. But the deeper work—building structural integrity—offers something rarer: a psychological system that does not need to be constantly rescued. One that sustains clarity under ambiguity, traction under turbulence, and alignment without performance. This is not an aesthetic project. It is *a structural one.*

And it is worth building well. Because what holds you under pressure will not be how polished your habits look. It will be how deeply they are wired into who you are—and how intelligently they were designed to bear weight.

The Cognitive Floorplan

Most people understand that physical spaces influence behaviour—architecture, layout, lighting, and acoustics all affect how we move, think, and feel. Yet few realise that the same is true for the internal spaces of the mind. Just as buildings are designed (or not) with load distribution, flow, and functionality in mind, so too is the psyche shaped by an internal structure: a cognitive floorplan. This floorplan consists of the habitual pathways our thoughts take, the assumptions that shape our perception, the emotional loops we fall into under stress, and the unseen stress points where that system begins to distort. But unlike a building, most people never pause to map the layout of their minds. They live inside a structure they've never examined—and pay the price in disorientation, inefficiency, and preventable collapse.

This chapter introduces the practice of cognitive floorplan mapping—not as a metaphor, but as a disciplined process for understanding and redesigning the architecture of one's inner world. Done well, this mapping allows us to see where clarity flows, where meaning gets trapped, where stress accumulates, and where our cognitive scaffolding no longer supports the psychological load it's forced to carry. Mapping your internal layout is not introspection for its own sake. It's structural analysis: a foundation for building intentional, resilient mental design.

To begin, we must acknowledge that every person operates within a network of automatic mental patterns. These patterns were not chosen consciously; they are the byproducts of experience, social conditioning, emotional reinforcement, and repeated decisions. Over time, these patterns become *default routes.* Just as people navigate their homes without thinking—turning left out of habit, avoiding a squeaky stair—they navigate thought in familiar, often unconscious ways. A stressful situation triggers the same defensive posture. A compliment activates self-doubt rather than confidence. A free afternoon generates guilt, not ease. These routes are not personality traits. They are architectural features, and like any structure, they can be examined and altered.

The field of cognitive psychology gives us tools for doing just that. Aaron Beck's early work on cognitive distortions—such as catastrophising, personalisation, or black-and-white thinking—was never just about correcting irrational thoughts. It was about mapping how thought patterns *organise our perception of reality.* More recent work in schema theory builds on this, showing how early life experiences create mental frameworks that shape interpretation long into adulthood. These schemas are not beliefs we hold consciously. They are structural elements in the mind—walls, hallways, bottlenecks—that filter what gets noticed and what gets ignored.

So what does it mean to map your cognitive floorplan? It begins with observation: *Where does your mind go when it's under stress? What thoughts repeat themselves most often—regardless of context? Which emotional reactions arrive faster than they should, and which ones never seem to find expression at all?* These are not idle curiosities. They are coordinates on a psychological map. Over time, patterns emerge: perhaps you always frame uncertainty as danger. Or you consistently undervalue rest, treating downtime as debt. Or you become performative in the presence of authority. Each of these patterns reflects a structural logic—some form of psychological layout that, at one point, served a purpose but may now be distorting your perception of the present.

The goal is not to eliminate complexity. A rich cognitive structure is meant to be multidimensional. The problem arises when certain parts of the mental floorplan become *overused* while others atrophy. For example, the analytical corridors of the mind may be overdeveloped, leading to overthinking and paralysis, while the reflective or intuitive spaces remain under-accessed, resulting in shallow decision-making. Or the emotional processing wing is perpetually bypassed in favour of immediate action, leading to unresolved tension that leaks into unrelated areas of life. These are design flaws—not character flaws. And like any design, they can be corrected through deliberate restructuring.

One of the most common structural imbalances in modern minds is the *overconcentration of attention in reactive zones*. That is, a disproportionate amount of mental energy is allocated to anticipating outcomes, scanning for threat, or managing appearances. These mental rooms are not illegitimate; they have their uses. But when the entire floorplan is arranged around reactivity, the self becomes fragmented—always scanning, rarely settling. There's no space for ideation, depth, or integration because the architecture doesn't include a room for it.

In such cases, redesign becomes imperative. And redesign begins with *inventory*: what mental spaces exist, and how are they used? Where is energy consistently lost? Where are thoughts recursive, not productive? Where is the floorplan bottlenecking—forcing every idea, emotion, or intention through the same narrow channel until everything jams? These questions move the work from reflection to strategy. They require not just psychological insight but design thinking.

Design thinking, originally formulated for innovation and product development, is increasingly relevant in the psychology of self-construction. It teaches us to iterate, to prototype, to test new layouts without needing immediate perfection. A redesigned mental floorplan might involve something as small as inserting a 90-second pause between stimulus and response. Or as large as reconfiguring core assumptions—such as shifting from "My worth is determined by output" to "My output is only as good as the system that supports it." These are not affirmations. They are *load-bearing redesigns.*

Another key insight from architectural thinking is the importance of *flow*. In physical spaces, poor flow creates inefficiency, congestion, and even danger. In the mind, the equivalent is *cognitive fragmentation*—a state in which thoughts compete for limited attention, emotional states bleed into unrelated tasks, and meaningful goals are obscured by logistical noise. A well-mapped floorplan identifies these blockages and designs pathways around them. This might involve external tools (like structured decision journals or habit triggers), or internal ones (such as values hierarchies or emotional check-ins). What matters is not the tool, but the alignment: each mental hallway must lead somewhere intentional.

Mapping your cognitive floorplan also reveals where structural support is missing entirely. Many people lack a clear conceptual space for rest, for example—not just time off, but *permissioned mental stillness*. Or they lack a mental room for grief, and so every loss gets boxed into denial and placed in the attic of the mind, where it silently undermines structural stability. Others have no architectural space for uncertainty, which means ambiguity triggers frantic control mechanisms rather than curiosity. When these absences are identified, they can be designed for. New rooms can be built—through ritual, language, practice, and environment.

The ethical implications of floorplan mapping are also worth considering. The way we mentally structure the world affects not just how we live, but how we see others. A floorplan dominated by scarcity or threat produces a worldview that is suspicious, zero-sum, and reactive. One shaped by unexamined privilege may lack rooms for empathy or perspective-taking. These are not just private architectural choices—they are moral frameworks. Designing a mind with structural space for nuance, complexity, and responsibility is not just wise. It is *civic*.

It's also important to note that floorplans evolve. Life events—crises, transitions, relationships—can and should prompt renovations. A person who becomes a parent must redesign their attention flow. Someone recovering from burnout must reconfigure energy thresholds. Someone moving into a leadership role must redesign how they house complexity and ambiguity. The danger lies in trying to navigate a new life phase with an outdated cognitive layout.

In closing—not as summary, but as pivot—the work of cognitive floorplan mapping is foundational to everything that follows in this book. Without a clear sense of your mental layout—your thought corridors, your stress points, your architectural blind spots—any attempt at change risks being misdirected. You cannot build what you cannot see. You cannot reinforce what you do not know is load-bearing. You cannot declutter what you do not believe you're carrying.

Mapping is not passive introspection. It is *the first act of intentional self-design.* Done well, it changes not just how you think, but how you *inhabit your own mind.* Not reactively. Not performatively. But architecturally. With clarity, precision, and structure that holds.

Designing for Load – Handling Psychological Weight

Psychological collapse doesn't usually begin with a dramatic event. It begins with accumulation. A missed lunch. An unresolved tension. A poorly slept night. A dozen open loops competing for attention. Most people don't burn out because of one catastrophic failure—they burn out because their inner systems were not designed to carry the weight they routinely bear. Just as buildings must be engineered to hold predictable and variable loads—weather, occupancy, use over time—so too must the human mind be *deliberately constructed* to support emotional, cognitive, and relational pressure. This subchapter explores what it means to *design for load*: to intentionally reinforce the internal structures that allow a person to remain functional, composed, and value-driven, even under stress.

It is not a question of *if* stress will appear. It is a question of *whether the structure you've built can absorb it.* Most people treat stress as an intrusion—an aberration from normal functioning. But this framing is both inaccurate and dangerous. Stress is not an anomaly; it is a structural constant. Daily life in the modern world—particularly for professionals navigating complexity, ambiguity, and relational responsibility—*guarantees* a certain baseline of pressure. The problem is not that people experience psychological load; it's that they've never been taught to distribute, reinforce, or release it. They endure it reactively until the structure buckles.

Let's begin with a clear distinction: there is a profound difference between *managing stress* and *designing for load.* Stress management tends to focus on relief—rest, relaxation, emotional regulation, mindfulness. These are important. But they are palliative measures—responses once stress has already taken hold. Designing for load, by contrast, is *preventative architecture.* It asks: How can the mind be constructed in such a way that it resists overload to begin with? What are the psychological equivalents of load-bearing walls, redundancy systems, and reinforcement points?

To answer these questions, we must first understand the anatomy of psychological weight. In engineering terms, "load" includes *dead load* (static, predictable weight), *live load* (variable or moving weight), and *environmental load* (external forces like wind or seismic stress). Translating this to the mind:

Dead load is the baseline structure of life—your core responsibilities, identity commitments, habitual thought patterns, and self-expectations.

Live load includes unpredictable demands: new projects, interpersonal conflict, urgent decisions, illness, or temporary crises.

Environmental load encompasses societal, cultural, or systemic stressors—economic uncertainty, political instability, social inequity.

A structurally sound mind doesn't remove these loads; it is *designed to distribute and absorb them without deformation.* This involves conscious construction of internal features that anticipate stress rather than merely respond to it.

The first of these features is *cognitive bandwidth allocation.* Human attention is a limited resource. Decision fatigue, as demonstrated by the work of Roy Baumeister and others, depletes mental function long before emotional resilience gives out. Yet people often organise their cognitive effort based on urgency rather than load—investing equal effort into trivial decisions (what to wear, which email to answer first) and meaningful ones (how to handle a conflict, whether to take a job). Structurally designed minds *reserve bandwidth* for high-impact decisions by automating or externalising the rest. This is not laziness. It's engineering. Every decision not made in the moment preserves psychological load capacity for where it actually matters.

Second, the mind needs *emotional containment systems*. Emotions are not inefficiencies. They are signals. But uncontained emotional responses become disruptive—either by bleeding into unrelated domains or by mutating into distorted narratives. A designed mind does not suppress emotion. It *houses* it. This may involve dedicated processing time (journaling, conversation, structured solitude), but more critically, it involves architectural features that *hold emotion in place* until it can be metabolised. The alternative is emotional leakage: the meeting where irritation surfaces as sarcasm, the deadline panic that becomes hypercontrol, the family dinner ruined by displaced anxiety. Psychological design requires allocating *emotional holding spaces*—rituals, environments, or inner scripts that allow for pause before release.

Another foundational element is *value-aligned priority structure*. When under pressure, reactive minds default to urgency. But urgency is a poor proxy for importance. Structurally designed minds return to *principled design*—prioritising action based on internal alignment, not emotional tempo. This is what allows people to make clear decisions during conflict, remain calm under scrutiny, and persist without burnout. The clarity comes not from grit, but from load-aware scaffolding. The mind has a pre-established template for what matters, and this template absorbs noise.

One compelling application of this principle can be found in military decision-making models, such as the OODA loop (Observe–Orient–Decide–Act), developed by strategist John Boyd. In high-stress environments, decision-makers are taught not to rely on instinct alone, but to move through structured layers of orientation before taking action. The model creates *mental buffer zones*—space for thought before reaction. Similarly, load-designed minds embed these buffers into everyday cognition. They don't just react. They *process through a known architecture*, which dramatically reduces stress-induced error and emotional volatility.

There's also a neurological argument to be made. The autonomic nervous system—particularly the balance between the sympathetic (fight-or-flight) and parasympathetic (rest-and-digest) responses—can be trained, but only when internal systems are stable. Polyvagal theory, proposed by Stephen Porges, suggests that safety perception is not just emotional but *physiological.* The brain constantly scans for cues of safety or threat. A designed mind introduces *predictable internal rhythms*—habits, rituals, and mental models—that signal safety even in unstable environments. These rhythms are structural reinforcements. Without them, the brain interprets variability as danger, and stress becomes chronic.

Another form of reinforcement is *redundancy*. Good buildings have fail-safes—backup systems that absorb excess when the primary system is overwhelmed. Most people lack psychological redundancy. They rely on a single coping strategy (working harder, venting, withdrawing), and when it fails, collapse feels total. Structurally designed minds cultivate *multiple stabilisers*: restorative practices, values-based communities, alternative frames for meaning-making. These are not backups in the traditional sense; they are *distributed supports*, reducing the load any one system has to bear alone.

Equally important is *psychological load auditing*. Engineers routinely inspect buildings under strain to identify structural fatigue. Minds require the same rigour. This means developing habits of review—not only after crisis, but *during functioning*. A designed mind doesn't wait for collapse to recalibrate. It checks for load signals: emotional reactivity, decision lag, cognitive clutter, withdrawal, or uncharacteristic aggression. These are not mood swings; they are structural warnings. In a well-designed system, they prompt inspection, not shame.

There is also a cultural critique embedded here. Much of modern life is designed around *maximising capacity*—fitting more into a finite system. But architecture teaches a different lesson: systems that are always operating at full capacity are *vulnerable by definition*. Sustainable design requires *load buffering*—unused capacity held in reserve, not because it's inefficient, but because it protects integrity. In psychological terms, this means creating margins: white space on the calendar, hours unscheduled, tasks left undone, not as a luxury but as a *load-bearing feature.* The culture of optimisation sees margin as waste. The discipline of design sees it as wisdom.

Finally, there's the moral dimension. A structurally designed mind is not just personally resilient—it is *relationally ethical.* When a person has built the internal capacity to handle stress without externalising it, others are spared the secondary trauma of their reactivity. Colleagues aren't walking on eggshells. Partners aren't absorbing displaced frustration. Children aren't navigating adult volatility. Psychological load is inevitable, but *where it lands is a design decision.* If it's not absorbed by internal systems, it will be displaced outward.

Designing for load, then, is not simply a matter of personal development. It is a form of *psychological architecture with systemic consequences.* It requires conscious construction, honest auditing, and rigorous maintenance. But it offers extraordinary returns: a mind that holds under pressure, a self that acts with integrity even in duress, and a life that does not fracture when the world does what it inevitably will—press, stretch, and weigh down.

If the mind is to be a space worth living in, it must be engineered to hold. Not with optimism, but with structure. Not with willpower, but with design. That is the promise—and the responsibility—of building for psychological weight.

Chapter 3
The Minimalist Mindset – Subtract to Strengthen

Modern life leans heavily towards accumulation. More goals. More apps. More hacks. More content. Always more. The dominant narrative suggests that to grow is to add: expand your skillset, grow your network, develop your personal brand. In this paradigm, success is not merely earned—it's tallied. And self-worth, subtly but insistently, becomes a running total of what one has achieved, acquired, or consumed. But—here's the tension—what if our deepest leverage lies not in what we add, but in what we choose to remove?

This chapter offers a different architecture: the minimalist mindset. Not a lifestyle trend. Not a Pinterest aesthetic. But a deliberate, and often uncomfortable, design principle for the mind. Subtraction here isn't about reduction for its own sake. It's about pruning down to structural integrity—doing only what reinforces the whole. It's psychological scaffolding, not spiritual whim. Think of minimalism not as less, but as precision: an act of engineering rather than taste. In this context, it becomes a method of managing mental load—not just managing time.

At the heart of it is a simple truth, often neglected: the mind cannot hold everything and remain lucid. When it's flooded—with ambitions, ideas, obligations, inputs—it fragments. Decision-making slows. Focus thins. Emotional resilience wanes. What begins as a chase for productivity morphs into incoherence. The structure still appears intact, but inside, it's buckling. Enter the minimalist mindset: a necessary intervention, a call to audit not just what's being built, but how it's expected to hold.

To see this more clearly, we must first address the broader cultural scaffolding—the architecture of excess. Today's models of success are glutted. Certifications piled on. Outputs tracked religiously. Colour-coded calendars that map out every breath. We treat productivity as moral currency. "Busy" is synonymous with value.

Yet most of what floods our lives is not essential. It's aspiration dressed up as necessity. The minimalist approach rejects that equation entirely. It pivots success away from pace and towards alignment. Not: What more can I do? But: What am I ready to not pursue?

This introduces one of the chapter's keystone practices: strategic neglect. In a world obsessed with prioritisation, very few are taught its counterpart—the skill of deliberate disregard. This isn't laziness. Nor is it detachment. It's triage. It's the recognition that your time, attention, and emotional bandwidth are finite—so not every door deserves to be knocked on. Not every expectation warrants fulfilment. Not every curiosity must be capitalised. Every goal taken on without structural purpose is a weight borne by your foundation. Spread yourself too thin, and the beams bend.

Professionals, especially those driven by potential, often fall into this trap. To keep options open. To remain "available." To prove capability across domains. It looks admirable—on paper. But ambition without boundaries is not ambition. It's architectural foolishness. Think of the designer who builds without load limits: the structure may be grand, but it collapses under its own sprawl. The minimalist mindset insists on constraints—not as sacrifices, but as preconditions for longevity.

Among these constraints, few are as pivotal as clarity around what "success" means. In overloaded cultures, success tends to blur—defined not by internal markers, but by shifting comparisons and glittering outcomes. It becomes vague. And that vagueness is a trap. Undefined success leads to perpetual motion without fulfilment. The minimalist reframing is sharp: strip away excess and ask instead—What does success look like if no one's watching? What if success meant not forward movement, but lasting coherence? What if it left you energised, not spent?

These aren't rhetorical musings. They're design criteria. Provocations. Instead of chasing visibility, ask: Does this decision reinforce my internal structure? Instead of optimising every moment, consider: Does this invite clarity, or clutter? Minimalist logic defines success as fewer things done better, with deeper presence. Fewer tasks. Better fit. Deeper roots. It's a slower metric—but a sturdier one. Not what can be sustained in a sprint, but what can be borne steadily without fraying.

This ethos isn't new. It's echoed across disciplines. In design, minimalism holds because every element must justify its inclusion. Stoic philosophy prizes not accumulation but restraint—freedom through containment. Zen finds clarity not by adding understanding, but by clearing obscuration. Neuroscience tells us: quality thinking emerges when cognitive load is reduced. No matter the domain, the same principle recurs: intelligently designed subtraction yields strength.

So to live minimally is not to scale back your ambitions. It's to sharpen them. It's to build a narrower channel through which your energy flows—not to limit, but to concentrate. Minimalists don't think smaller. They filter harder. They don't simply do less—they do what matters, cleaner. It's not asceticism. It's engineering. Every act of removal is not absence, but an assertion: this is what I'm choosing to carry, and nothing more.

Nowhere is this more crucial than in how we meet silence. A cluttered mind cannot sit still—it treats quiet as an emergency. But a minimalist mind recognises silence as architecture: an intentional space carved out for reorganisation, recovery, and return. These are not wasted areas. They are the cognitive equivalent of an atrium—rooms designed to reduce pressure and redistribute flow. Without them, the corridors of the mind jam. Decisions bottleneck. Burnout creeps in unnoticed.

In this framework, quiet isn't simply a break from input. It is curated stillness. Intentional withdrawal. Mental habits such as deliberate non-doing, analogue routines, purposeless reflection, and planned disengagement from the information feed are not indulgences. They are infrastructural. They lower ambient noise. They reclaim attention. They create the conditions in which intention can resurface.

There's a moral dimension to this, too. Excess isn't merely wasteful. It externalises harm. Overburdened individuals offload stress—onto colleagues, families, institutions. Systems built on perpetual reach leave others picking up the slack. The minimalist stance resists this. It promises less, but honours what it offers. It doesn't commit on impulse and cancel later. It resists the dopamine rush of visibility, choosing instead the quieter discipline of reliability. Volume is traded for integrity.

To adopt such a stance requires a shift in inquiry. Not: How can I fit more in? But: What can be taken away to make the essential more stable? Not: What new pursuit awaits? But: What has outlived its usefulness? These aren't stylistic preferences. They're decisions about what kind of internal structure one is willing to live within. Minimalism rejects the glossy façade of a life that looks impressive but cannot endure its own demands. It builds inward. It prizes coherence over decoration, and subtraction not as loss—but as construction.

In the pages that follow, this chapter will explore three key dimensions of this inner architecture: how to strip success of its unnecessary layers, how to say no without guilt, and how to cultivate spaces within the mind that are not voids, but designed rooms for clarity to echo in. This is not a prescription for renunciation. It's an invitation to craft less—so that more of what matters can stay intact.

In this light, subtraction is not absence. It is presence—sharpened, unburdened, deliberate. It is the act of removing what cannot hold, so that what remains can—solidly, gracefully, and for the long haul. Let's begin.

Cognitive Clutter is Emotional Noise

Resilience is often misrepresented as sheer tenacity—the ability to endure, to push through, to persist no matter what. But a more precise definition frames resilience not as brute force, but as *clarity under pressure*. The resilient mind does not simply absorb impact; it *processes with fidelity*. It knows what to respond to, what to delay, and what to discard entirely. What undermines this capacity is not the presence of hardship, but the internal disorganisation that precedes it. And in this disorganisation, *cognitive clutter is the silent saboteur*.

The term "cognitive clutter" is often associated with distraction: too many tabs open, too many apps pinging, too many things on the to-do list. But its more insidious form is internal—accumulated, unresolved thought fragments and emotional residue that hijack mental bandwidth. These are not simply inefficiencies. They are structural flaws in mental design that distort perception, interrupt focus, and drain adaptive capacity. *Cognitive clutter is not a harmless side effect of a busy life; it is a primary driver of emotional noise*—a continuous low-frequency hum that makes clear thinking and stable feeling difficult, if not impossible.

To understand how this happens, consider the architecture of working memory. The brain's capacity to hold and manipulate information in real-time is finite. George A. Miller famously estimated the number to be seven (plus or minus two) items at once. More recent cognitive science places that number even lower. When that limited space is filled with half-formed worries, unresolved conversations, phantom tasks, and media fragments, *what's left for intentional thought or emotional regulation is marginal.* The brain, overloaded with fragments, becomes reactive. And reactivity is the enemy of resilience.

But the effects are not merely cognitive. Cluttered thoughts do not remain isolated in abstract logic. They bleed into affect. When information comes faster than it can be meaningfully processed, the nervous system responds with *irritability, anxiety, numbness, or impulsivity*—not because the person is weak or undisciplined, but because their inner system is saturated. The brain does not distinguish cleanly between cognitive data and emotional weight. Unprocessed mental inputs become *emotional noise*—a persistent sense of overwhelm that has no clear source, and therefore no direct solution.

This dynamic is visible across professional and personal contexts. A manager who spends the day oscillating between email, team dynamics, strategy, and personal worries will find their thinking increasingly blunt. Not because they lack intelligence, but because their *executive function is occluded by excess*. Likewise, a parent attempting to be present with their child while mentally toggling through financial concerns, social media notifications, and unresolved work issues is not emotionally disengaged—they are neurologically *diminished by bandwidth overload.* The resulting behaviours—snappiness, withdrawal, inability to focus—are not moral failings. They are *load responses.*

It is important to distinguish here between complexity and clutter. Complexity is not inherently harmful. Humans are capable of managing complexity when systems are well-structured. Clutter, by contrast, is unmanaged accumulation—*information and emotion without order, hierarchy, or containment.* This is where resilience begins to fray. Not at the moment of external pressure, but much earlier, when internal space has already been compromised.

This principle is well-supported in psychological research. Studies on *decision fatigue*—the cognitive depletion that follows too many decisions—show that even minor choices (what to eat, what to wear) consume executive bandwidth. Over time, cluttered minds become more risk-averse, emotionally volatile, and susceptible to biased thinking. Similarly, research in affective neuroscience shows that *emotional regulation depends on prefrontal-limbic coherence.* When the cognitive system is over-engaged, that coherence breaks down, and emotions are either suppressed or over-amplified.

What, then, is the antidote? It is not productivity hacking. It is not multitasking. It is not motivational mantras. The antidote is *deliberate cognitive minimalism*—the practice of removing, reducing, and reordering internal inputs so that the mind can function as a coherent structure rather than a noisy corridor of distractions.

This involves several disciplines. First, it requires the *curation of inputs.* Not all information is worth absorbing. Not every notification needs checking. Not every thought warrants follow-through. The minimalist mind does not passively consume; it *filters with intent.* In practice, this means reducing exposure to high-frequency, low-value stimuli—news cycles, superficial content, unnecessary meetings—because each input, however trivial, claims a piece of working memory. Over time, these fragments accumulate into a noisy baseline that makes reflective thinking difficult.

Second, cognitive minimalism involves the *externalisation of memory*. Rather than rely on the mind to hold lists, reminders, obligations, and uncertainties, minimalist thinkers use *external systems*: notebooks, whiteboards, trusted task managers. This is not mere organisation—it is *load redistribution*. It frees the mind from the burden of recall and allows it to focus on judgment, synthesis, and presence.

Third, and most critically, the minimalist mindset involves *emotional decluttering*. Emotional clutter is subtler than mental clutter, but no less disruptive. It consists of unresolved feelings, lingering interpersonal tensions, moral ambiguities, and unexpressed needs. Left unprocessed, these emotional fragments distort cognitive function. The brain becomes preoccupied with unconscious scanning—searching for resolution, avoiding pain, rehearsing hypothetical scenarios. The result is reduced clarity, impaired decision-making, and chronic background stress.

This is where the disciplines of reflective writing, therapy, mindfulness, and structured solitude become architectural tools. Not because they are trendy or therapeutic, but because they serve a functional purpose: *they clear emotional residues so that the cognitive system can operate with fidelity*. When you metabolise a difficult feeling, you reduce noise. When you resolve an inner conflict, you reclaim bandwidth. When you say what needs to be said, you end a loop that otherwise spins indefinitely in the background.

There is an analogy worth considering here. Just as poor acoustics can make even a well-designed concert hall unusable, *emotional noise degrades the performance of otherwise capable minds*. The music of thought—the rhythm, the clarity, the harmony—can only be appreciated when the environment is not distorted by echo and interference. Cognitive clutter is not just an obstacle; it is a design flaw that needs correcting at the foundational level.

One might ask: isn't some degree of mess inevitable? Life, after all, is complex. People have multiple roles, unpredictable emotions, and competing demands. Yes. But the issue is not mess. The issue is *accumulated, unprocessed mess*. The difference is critical. Just as a professional kitchen can be chaotic during dinner service but remains functional due to tight systems, the mind can withstand temporary chaos if it is supported by *regular routines of clearing, organising, and filtering.*

Minimalist thinkers do not chase permanent clarity. They cultivate *resilient clarity*—the kind that can be quickly restored. They do not fear complexity. They fear unmanaged complexity. They do not obsess over perfection. They value *reduction with purpose.* They understand that inner silence is not a luxury but a precondition for meaningful thought.

This mindset is not about becoming monastic or emotionally detached. It is about becoming *intellectually and emotionally available to what matters most.* It is about preserving enough internal space to respond with discernment rather than compulsion. It is about building a mental structure that does not collapse under the weight of its own disorganisation.

When cognitive clutter is removed, emotional noise fades. What remains is not emptiness, but *precision.* Not sterility, but *alignment.* This is not productivity. It is architecture. It is resilience made visible in design.

And in this architecture, every removed distraction, every resolved feeling, every simplified input becomes not a sacrifice, but a *support beam*—holding the mind with less, so it can do more of what truly counts.

Redefining Success Without Excess

The dominant definition of success in modern culture is not only dated—it is *damaging.* For decades, we've been told, directly and indirectly, that to be successful is to accumulate: titles, wealth, achievements, followers, square footage, accolades, experiences, and now even metrics of wellness. Under this model, success becomes a quantitative pursuit, with progress measured in external symbols and upward movement. But what if the ladder leads nowhere meaningful? What if the structure itself is faulty? *At what point does pursuit become pathology?*

The modern professional—especially in high-performing, knowledge-based economies—can often feel as though they're building a cathedral out of moving parts: constantly redesigning, constantly upgrading, never pausing. There's always another milestone to reach, another KPI to optimise, another aspect of life to enhance. Yet behind the polish of curated timelines and professional bios, there is often a persistent hum of disquiet. The quiet unease that whispers: *You have everything they said you needed. Why doesn't it feel like enough?*

The issue is not with ambition per se. Ambition, when grounded in values and clarity, can be a force for integrity and contribution. But ambition that is unexamined—anchored to borrowed metrics—becomes a source of distortion. This distortion shows up as burnout disguised as dedication, consumption disguised as self-care, and perpetual motion mistaken for meaning. At the heart of this misalignment is an outdated success architecture: *one that confuses scale with substance, and expansion with depth.*

Minimalism, when applied to mindset and not just aesthetics, offers a radical alternative. It suggests that success isn't defined by what we acquire, but by *what we deliberately choose not to pursue.* This is not a philosophy of deprivation. It is a discipline of discernment. And in a world flooded with possibilities, *discernment is the new success metric.*

Consider this contrast: a person earns a high income, maintains an enviable lifestyle, and is considered impressive by their peers—but they wake with anxiety, end each week exhausted, and secretly dread the pace they must maintain. Another individual may earn less, live with intentional constraints, and be invisible to most—but they feel anchored, energised, and mentally unburdened. Who is more successful? The answer depends on which blueprint you're using. The minimalist reframing of success asks us to scrutinise the blueprint itself—not just how well we're executing it.

Philosophically, this is not a new idea. The Stoics, the Taoists, and even certain strands of Christian and Buddhist ethics have long warned against the tyranny of external validation and material accumulation. What's changed is the *urgency.* The cognitive and emotional costs of excess—be it in data, goals, relationships, or expectations—are no longer just moral concerns; they are neurological and structural.

Cognitive science supports this. The human brain is not built to sustain infinite streams of ambition. We are wired for focus, for purpose, for coherence. When success is defined as "more," coherence breaks. We chase conflicting objectives, enter environments misaligned with our values, and tolerate systems that reward output at the expense of wellbeing. The result is not just stress, but identity fragmentation—people living lives they don't fully endorse, because the metrics they use to guide decisions were never truly their own.

The minimalist approach to success begins with *subtraction as strategy*. This does not mean settling or opting out. It means asking a more demanding question: *What is essential, and what is noise?* And then having the courage to design around the answer.

Practically, this means interrogating inherited success metrics. Do you truly need to scale your business—or have you assumed growth is always better than sustainability? Do you need to run faster—or would deeper mastery at a slower pace create more value? Do you actually want visibility—or have you mistaken exposure for relevance? These are not questions to answer once. They are design questions—ongoing prompts that must be built into your internal architecture.

Minimalist success reframes productivity as *alignment with purpose*, not speed. It reframes wealth as *sufficiency for autonomy*, not accumulation for status. It reframes time as *space for depth*, not as a container to be filled with efficiency. And it reframes legacy not as what is remembered, but as *what is transferred—principles, not profile.*

This approach has profound implications for goal-setting. Traditional goal structures often compound excess by stacking milestones without examining motive. Minimalist design asks: *What are you willing to not pursue?* It demands the kind of clarity that turns down promotions, declines high-paying but low-alignment projects, and walks away from attention in favour of privacy. Not because these things are bad, but because *they may not be true to your architecture.*

Take the example of high-performing professionals who reach the top of their industries and begin to experience a phenomenon known as "success depression"—the disillusionment that comes after achieving externally validated milestones, only to find that the internal sense of meaning remains absent. This is not due to psychological fragility. It is a design failure. The structure of their success was misaligned with their actual values. The minimalist mindset acts as a correction mechanism—one that prioritises *alignment over applause*.

It also resists the growing trend of quantifying every dimension of life. The quantification of self—tracking sleep, steps, screen time, income, productivity, even mood—can lead to metric fatigue. We begin to live not as embodied humans, but as dashboard managers. Minimalist success reclaims *qualitative metrics*: depth of attention, consistency of integrity, quality of relationships, richness of solitude. These are harder to measure but far more reliable as indicators of a life well-built.

There is also a social and ethical dimension to minimalist success. When people abandon the endless race for more, they reduce not only personal stress but collective pressure. They stop modelling scarcity. They stop feeding systems that reward burnout. They create cultures—organisational, familial, relational—where people are valued for who they are, not just what they achieve. In this way, minimalist success is not just personal—it is *culturally subversive.* It is an act of resistance against hyper-capitalist ideals that equate human worth with market value.

But this path is not easy. It requires unlearning. It requires saying no to things that look impressive but feel empty. It requires enduring the discomfort of silence, space, and slow growth—while watching others sprint. It demands *inner conviction over outer conformity*. Most of all, it requires a new metric: *does this support the life I am willing to live with full presence and responsibility?*

Minimalist success is not a downgrade. It is an *upgrade in consciousness*. It shifts the question from "How much can I achieve?" to "What am I building that can actually hold my values under pressure?" The former leads to expansion. The latter leads to *integration.* The former chases visibility. The latter cultivates *stability.*

Ultimately, success is not a title to earn, but a *structure to inhabit.* It should not require performance, pretence, or perpetual acceleration. It should feel like a home—one that fits, functions, and fortifies. Minimalist success does not ask us to lower the bar. It asks us to *move the bar to where it actually belongs.*

And in that relocation, we do not lose ambition—we regain authorship.

The Power of Strategic Neglect

There is a quiet discipline more powerful than focus, more liberating than motivation, and more essential than productivity hacks: the discipline of *strategic neglect.* In a world engineered to fragment attention and stretch ambition across infinite pursuits, the ability to *consciously ignore* becomes a mark of cognitive maturity, not carelessness. Neglect, when wielded with intention, is not laziness—it is architecture. It is the deliberate refusal to scatter energy toward what does not structurally support your core design.

Modern life relentlessly promotes accumulation: of goals, of projects, of aspirations, of skills to acquire and benchmarks to reach. Every day brings invitations to expand—to optimise one's morning, network more effectively, develop a new side hustle, launch another initiative, or "10x" yet another aspect of life. While each ambition may seem worthwhile on its own, the *aggregate effect is erosion*: mental bandwidth collapses under the weight of constant engagement. Strategic neglect is the counterforce—*not a withdrawal from effort, but a redesign of investment.*

The term "neglect" carries a pejorative charge. It conjures images of irresponsibility or decay. But when prefixed with strategy, it becomes a sophisticated act of selection: the conscious decision to *not pursue, not respond, not prioritise.* This is not failure to act—it is mastery over *what not to act on.* It requires clarity, discipline, and, above all, a personal philosophy that ranks coherence above appearance.

Strategic neglect is distinct from avoidance. Avoidance is reactive; it is a fear response, an escape from discomfort. Strategic neglect is proactive. It emerges from alignment. You ignore what does not belong—not because it is hard, but because it is *misaligned.* This distinction matters. Where avoidance fragments integrity, strategic neglect reinforces it. You are not shrinking from challenge; you are *editing your architecture.*

One of the most significant benefits of strategic neglect is cognitive clarity. Neuroscience has long affirmed that the brain has limited executive bandwidth. This is not merely a metaphorical constraint—it is a *biological fact.* The prefrontal cortex, which governs planning, prioritisation, and impulse control, can only manage a finite set of active goals. Overloading it leads to what psychologists term "goal competition," where multiple, incompatible aims dilute focus and produce decision fatigue. Put simply: *you can't build coherence when your attention is being siphoned by everything you could be doing.*

A case study illustrates this clearly. Consider a mid-career professional who excels in her field but feels chronically unfulfilled. Her calendar is packed, her reputation stellar, yet her work feels hollow. Upon examination, it becomes evident that she has accumulated a dozen parallel ambitions: she mentors junior colleagues, leads multiple committees, writes a newsletter, takes night courses, volunteers weekly, and is considering launching a podcast. Each endeavour is noble, but none are rooted in a central value structure. Her schedule is optimised—but her life is not *designed.* Once she begins practising strategic neglect—intentionally pausing or exiting commitments that don't reinforce her core architecture—clarity returns. Focus sharpens. Energy regenerates. Fulfilment, once elusive, re-emerges. Not through *addition*, but through *elimination.*

There is a cultural resistance to this idea. We are conditioned to measure worth by activity. To be busy is to be needed. To be involved is to be relevant. To opt out is often perceived as weakness or disinterest. But this is a false binary. *Involvement is not the same as impact.* When the mind is stretched across a dozen loosely connected pursuits, depth vanishes. Strategic neglect reclaims depth. It allows you to go *further* by going *fewer.*

There is also an ethical dimension. When people pursue goals out of obligation, image maintenance, or borrowed ambition, they often deliver mediocre engagement. Strategic neglect is an act of integrity. It says: "I will not commit to what I cannot sustain with care." In doing so, it honours both the self and others. It prevents the slow erosion of credibility that comes from overpromising and under-delivering. It protects the quality of one's attention—the most generous and undervalued currency in human relationships.

In the psychological literature, this discipline finds echoes in *goal disengagement theory*. Researchers such as Carsten Wrosch and Gregory Miller have shown that people who are able to *let go of unattainable or misaligned goals* enjoy better physical health, less emotional distress, and more adaptive coping mechanisms. Letting go, counterintuitively, is a sign of resilience—not failure. Strategic neglect, in this context, is not merely a productivity strategy; it is a *wellbeing imperative.*

Critically, strategic neglect must be anchored in a design philosophy. You cannot subtract meaningfully if you have not first defined what you *are* building. This is why it cannot be reduced to generic "saying no" advice. It requires a rigorous internal audit: What are the load-bearing values in your architecture? Which goals reinforce them, and which distract from them? Which ambitions are authentic, and which are performative? Neglect is only strategic when it is *principled.*

A helpful heuristic is to ask: *What am I unwilling to neglect?* The answers that emerge—health, relationships, solitude, mastery, contribution—become design anchors. From there, you subtract not arbitrarily, but architecturally. You redesign your commitments around what truly matters. And you accept that neglecting the nonessential is not only permissible—it is necessary.

Strategic neglect also guards against *ego inflation.* Many pursuits are fuelled not by purpose but by prestige. We say yes because we like how it sounds when we tell others. We add responsibilities because they signal status. But these ego-driven yeses often become architectural liabilities—flimsy extensions that destabilise the whole structure. Minimalist design requires ego deconstruction. It demands that we trade the approval of many for the coherence of self.

There's a parallel here with the minimalist design movement in architecture. Great architecture is not about ornamentation—it is about utility, proportion, and flow. Similarly, a well-structured inner life is not filled to the edges. It has white space. It breathes. Strategic neglect carves that space—not through indifference, but through intention.

One might ask: how does this apply in high-demand environments—startups, academia, caregiving, medicine—where the margin for refusal seems thin? The answer lies in *micro-neglect*: the disciplined avoidance of unessential tasks within even the most demanding roles. It might mean not replying to every non-urgent email, not engaging in habitual rumination, not chasing prestige projects that divert attention from core objectives. Even within constraint, neglect can be applied as an act of precision.

It is also important to differentiate strategic neglect from chronic under-functioning. Neglect becomes destructive when it is a coping mechanism for fear or apathy. The point is not to do less for the sake of comfort, but to do *less of what weakens structure*. The key litmus test: does neglecting this improve the integrity of my inner architecture? If yes, proceed. If not, reconsider.

Perhaps the most transformative benefit of strategic neglect is the emergence of *mental stillness*. When the mind is not compulsively managing a thousand micro-ambitions, it regains its most powerful capacity: *awareness*. In that stillness, insight emerges. Patterns become visible. Priorities realign. And from that clarity, a mindset is built—not based on perpetual striving, but on deliberate construction.

To ignore wisely is to think architecturally. It is to know that every yes must be supported by a hundred nos. It is to understand that cognitive clarity is not found in more, but in *selective design*. The world will continue to offer infinite invitations. But those with an inner blueprint will not accept them all. They will decline strategically—not to withdraw from life, but to build one that can actually *hold them*.

Quiet Spaces in the Mind

The most radical act in a chronically overstimulated world is not protest or productivity—it is *stillness*. Not the passive kind confused with laziness or surrender, but the deliberate creation of internal space in which the mind can *hear itself think*. Quiet spaces in the mind are not a luxury or a reward—they are an architectural necessity. Without them, the mind becomes reactive, brittle, and confused, trapped in an echo chamber of urgency. With them, thought becomes design: structured, deliberate, capable of supporting depth and resilience.

Contemporary life is a continuous transaction of attention. Everything competes for it—emails, deadlines, notifications, conversations, inner scripts, self-surveillance. The modern mind is rarely *with itself*. It is either broadcasting or buffering, scanning or solving. And when it does pause, the silence is so unfamiliar that it feels awkward, even threatening. Stillness, long neglected, has been recast as unproductive. But the brain does not thrive on relentless output; it thrives on rhythm. And rhythm includes *rest*—mental rest, emotional quiet, and cognitive spaciousness. Without these, the mind is not thinking. It is merely processing.

The cognitive cost of constant stimulation is significant. Research in neuroscience and psychology has repeatedly shown that the brain's default mode network—the network active when we are not focused on external tasks—is essential for *self-reflection*, *emotional integration*, and *creative insight*. This is the system that gets activated during mind-wandering, daydreaming, or contemplative pauses. When we eliminate quiet time, we impair these functions. Thought becomes linear, shallow, and anxious. It cannot consolidate complexity. It cannot reorient. In effect, the absence of internal silence leads to *structural weakening* of the mind's architecture.

Consider the metaphor of architectural load: a building must have not just material strength, but intelligent distribution of space—gaps, corridors, atriums. These negative spaces are not wasted—they're functional. They support light, movement, and integrity. Similarly, the mind's negative spaces—its quiet zones—are essential for psychological coherence. Without them, thoughts collide and accumulate, like clutter in an overfilled hallway. Quiet, then, is not an escape. It is a *framework*.

Cultivating quiet spaces requires more than turning off devices. True mental quiet is not simply the absence of noise; it is the *presence of conscious, undistracted awareness*. Silence without awareness is idleness. Awareness without silence is chaos. The practice is to bring both together. And to do so reliably, we must design for it—not wait for it to arrive.

One of the most effective practices for this is *structured stillness*: allocating time each day where nothing is consumed, produced, or responded to. This is not meditation in the traditional sense, though it may take meditative form. It is a designed pause—a clearing in the day's structure where the mind can *breathe without being steered*. The goal is not relaxation, though that may occur. The goal is *presence*. It is in this presence that the mind self-corrects, self-organises, and sometimes, unexpectedly, solves.

Another practice is the cultivation of *deliberate non-engagement*. This means stepping back not only from technology, but from the compulsion to resolve, to fix, to optimise. It involves letting a question remain unanswered, letting a feeling unfold without immediate analysis. This is deeply countercultural. We are trained to interpret silence as a problem and uncertainty as failure. But much of the mind's deeper work happens *beneath* verbal thought. When we rush to label or intervene, we interrupt this process. In quiet, insight often comes—not as a lightning bolt, but as a gradual unfurling. This is the mind rearranging itself from the inside.

Historical traditions have long recognised this principle. Stoicism valued inner tranquillity (*ataraxia*) not as a passive detachment, but as an *active state of internal order*. Zen practice speaks of *shoshin*—beginner's mind—a quiet openness that precedes understanding. In Christian monasticism, the concept of *hesychia* referred to a stillness so deep it became a form of prayer. And in the writings of thinkers like Blaise Pascal or Soren Kierkegaard, solitude was not a retreat from responsibility, but the precondition for meaningful thought. Across these traditions, quiet is not ornamental. It is foundational.

In more recent psychological frameworks, quiet is increasingly seen not as mere absence of stimuli, but as an *enabler of executive function.* Studies show that short periods of silence enhance memory consolidation, strengthen cognitive control, and reduce stress hormone levels. Not coincidentally, some of the most effective thinkers—scientists, designers, writers—protect time for what they call "white space." These are unscheduled windows where mental drift is permitted and even encouraged. It is in such spaces that innovation tends to appear—not as forced insight, but as something found when the noise dies down.

Practising mental stillness does not mean eliminating thought. It means creating *room* between thoughts. That room allows for perspective. It allows us to distinguish between signal and noise, between what demands attention and what only impersonates urgency. In that space, emotional residue can settle. Cognitive clutter can dissipate. The mind can move from reactivity to reflection.

Yet quiet is not always comfortable. Often, when we stop moving mentally, we encounter what we've been outrunning: unresolved questions, buried emotions, unmet needs. For this reason, many people avoid quiet not because they dislike silence, but because they fear *what silence might surface.* But this surfacing is essential. It is the only way to move from suppression to integration. *What we do not process in quiet, we project in noise.*

To support this practice, we can borrow from architectural minimalism: remove what distracts, prioritise what supports structure, and introduce symmetry and flow. For the mind, this may mean:

– Creating consistent daily "quiet blocks" where no input is allowed
– Designating spaces in the home or office as stimulus-free zones
– Practising transitions between tasks that include a minute of breath or silence
– Journaling not to analyse, but to *empty* mental residue without judgment

These are not rituals of self-indulgence. They are *infrastructure upgrades*. They clear the cognitive floorplan and reinforce structural integrity. They teach the mind that stillness is safe, valuable, and productive in its own right.

The deeper aim is this: to transform quiet from an interruption into a design element. Not a break from life, but part of its structure. When quiet becomes habitual, it changes the default mental setting. You no longer seek stimulation reflexively. You no longer fear your own thoughts. You become more selective about what enters, and more capable of processing what remains. The mind begins to resemble a well-designed interior: spacious, coherent, intentional.

Ultimately, quiet spaces in the mind are not found. They are *built.* They are the result of subtractive design, of choosing clarity over consumption, stillness over stimulation. And as with all architecture, what we build reflects what we value. If we value resilience, depth, and coherence, then silence is not a retreat—it is a structural pillar. To create space is to create capacity. And it is in that capacity—not in noise, not in speed—that clarity lives.

Chapter 4
Habit Architecture – Building Routines That Hold Under Pressure

There's a curious contradiction in how we approach habits in the modern age. On the one hand, we lionise them—early wake-ups, cold plunges, gratitude journaling—treating them as personal revolutions. Yet, when real pressure intrudes, these very rituals often evaporate. What looked like commitment turns out to have been performance. The truth? Many habits we adopt are built not to withstand reality, but to gesture at it. This chapter, then, isn't concerned with collecting shinier routines. Its concern lies elsewhere: in designing habits as internal architecture—structures built to hold under strain, not collapse at its onset.

To begin, we must reconsider the very nature of a habit. It's not a lifestyle accessory, nor a symbol of aspiration. A solid habit is akin to a load-bearing beam in a house: unglamorous, essential, and utterly non-negotiable. Their job is not to dazzle or inspire, but to stabilise. Still, we often mistake the visible for the vital. A colour-coded planner, a finely curated morning sequence—these are too frequently confused for structures that can actually carry weight. But the proof of their strength lies in this: Do they hold when life begins to tilt? When energy wanes, when time thins—do they still stand?

To answer that, we need to distinguish between two classes of habit: anchors and ornaments. Anchor habits sink deep. They are those quiet, recurring actions—rising at a consistent hour, journaling without audience, taking unhurried walks, reading before bed—that shape the rhythm of a mind. They don't seek applause. Their power lies in how little they require and how much they return. Ornaments, by contrast, are often complex, overly engineered, and tied to circumstance. They look impressive. Until, of course, they don't. Under stress, they fall away, revealing they were never integrated into the framework of a lived day.

This chapter invites a shift—from seeing habits as spectacles to recognising them as reinforcements. Just as buildings are engineered with seismic joints or wind buffers, our mental routines must be designed with psychological stressors in mind: cognitive overload, emotional fatigue, digital noise, and chronic ambiguity. Sustainable habits aren't those that boost performance on your best day. They're the ones that soften the fall on your worst.

Building such habits requires intention and, more to the point, design. Any structure that endures does so because it adheres to certain principles: it suits its environment, it avoids unnecessary complexity, and it can absorb impact. Translated to habit-formation, the formula is similar—alignment, simplicity, and repeatability. Alignment grounds the habit in your sense of self. Simplicity ensures it's frictionless, even amid chaos. Repeatability means it survives the rough days because it doesn't demand optimal conditions.

Think of something as simple as five minutes of reflection at day's end. No gadgets. No prompts. Just you, sifting through thoughts, recalibrating. This routine asks little, yet offers profound grounding. It steadies the psyche, prevents emotional spirals, and supports adaptive clarity. That's habit as architecture—not flash, but framework.

Contrast that with the elaborate digital productivity setup that depends on perfect alignment: the right mood, the right tech, the right window of time. Miss one element, and the whole mechanism sputters. Such systems give the appearance of control, but add their own weight to an already burdened mind.

Another overlooked factor? Environment. No architect designs without considering landscape and weather. Likewise, no habit should be formed without accounting for its surrounding cues. Even the most promising routine will erode if housed in a disruptive environment. A focused work habit falters in a cluttered room. A sleep habit can't root itself in glare and noise. Subtle adjustments—tidying, quieting, repositioning—are not superficial. They are structural. The aim is to let your surroundings whisper you into action, rather than demand effort at every turn.

Take the mundane example of object placement. A meditation cushion that's already in place quietly increases the chance you'll sit.

A book at your bedside nudges you towards reading without fanfare. These are not minor details; they're load-bearing supports. The smallest moments of resistance—digging for headphones, fumbling with app folders—can become deciding factors in whether a habit survives. Especially under duress, small frictions snowball.

Furthermore, sustainable habits rarely stand alone. Just as bridges use overlapping components to absorb shock, habits form stronger systems when interwoven. A routine that begins with hydration, transitions to light movement, and ends with brief reflection is far more likely to endure than isolated attempts at self-discipline. This isn't habit-chaining for aesthetic effect. It's resilience through interdependence. If one piece slips, others remain to hold the structure.

There is, too, a philosophical underpinning here. Habits are not mere utilities. They are manifestations of how you've chosen to live. What you do, over and over, is what you believe—not in the abstract, but in practice. To construct enduring routines is to articulate an inner ethic: *this is the sort of mind I want to preserve, regardless of turbulence.* Not an aspiration, but a design decision. When chaos strikes, your shelter is the habit that asks for nothing more than what you already gave it yesterday.

So, what follows in this chapter is not a roundup of productivity hacks or motivational affirmations. It is, instead, a set of principles—guidelines to help you identify which habits deserve reinforcement, which need redesign, and which must be let go entirely. You will learn to view your environment not as a neutral backdrop but as a co-conspirator in your routines. And you'll come to understand habits not as accomplishments, but as the quiet scaffolding that holds you upright in a world that constantly shifts its ground.

The goal isn't to craft a sleeker version of yourself. It's to root a sturdier one. A self that doesn't need to reinvent itself after every crisis, because its daily rhythms—modest, consistent, deeply integrated—don't depend on circumstance. That is the subtle difference between a habit and a hinge. One is a checklist. The other bears weight. And that's what this chapter is here to help you build.

The Architecture of Micro-Habits – Presents habit stacking as mental reinforcement

If habits are the structural framework of the mind, then micro-habits are the rivets, fasteners, and interlocking joints that determine whether the whole structure endures or collapses under load. We have been conditioned to overvalue dramatic overhaul—30-day transformations, wholesale lifestyle redesigns, grand New Year's resolutions—while undervaluing the architecture of the microscopic. The irony, however, is that *the durability of our behavioural systems hinges far less on the ambition of our intentions than on the architecture of our smallest actions.* Micro-habits, when designed and connected strategically, serve not just as behavioural hacks, but as cognitive reinforcement mechanisms. They stabilise identity, restore continuity under pressure, and build a form of mental infrastructure that scales naturally with time and capacity.

In behavioural science, micro-habits are defined as actions so small they seem trivial in isolation: one push-up, two lines in a journal, thirty seconds of mindful breathing. But this apparent triviality is precisely where their psychological power lies. They sidestep the brain's resistance to effort, lower the activation energy required to start, and—most importantly—*create patterns.* And it is these patterns, rather than any single act of willpower, that form the basis of sustained change. As researchers like BJ Fogg and James Clear have outlined, change that lasts does not begin with motivation but with structure—specifically, with actions embedded in *reliable cues and reinforced through consistency.*

Yet much of the modern discourse around micro-habits remains trapped in tactical superficiality. Popular articles treat them as gimmicks: floss one tooth, drink one glass of water, and so on. While the intention is to overcome inertia, what's often missing is *architecture.* Micro-habits are not meaningful because they are small; they are powerful because they are *structured in relation to one another.* This is the principle of habit stacking—not a productivity trend, but a foundational concept in behavioural architecture. It is not just about linking one action to another. It is about *creating chains of mental reinforcement*, where each habit supports the next, not just temporally, but cognitively.

Consider the following example: you wake up, drink a glass of water, sit on your cushion for three minutes of stillness, write a sentence of intention, and then begin your first focused task. Each micro-habit in that sequence may take less than a minute. But together, they *prime the nervous system*, reinforce identity ("I am someone who starts the day with intention"), and reduce cognitive friction for the harder tasks that follow. If any one element falters, the chain still holds. But when all are active, they *amplify each other's strength*. This is not efficiency for its own sake—it is *resilience by design*.

It is worth stepping back to explore why micro-habits matter more than ever in today's context. We live in an era of overstimulation, cognitive overload, and accelerated decision fatigue. In such an environment, large habits—no matter how noble—are often the first to break. They require time, energy, and favourable conditions. Micro-habits, by contrast, *survive adversity* because they are frictionless, flexible, and inherently modular. They are not aspirational. They are architectural.

Psychologically, micro-habits also offer a form of *self-signalling*. Every time you perform even a small action aligned with your values, you reinforce an internal narrative: "I am consistent. I follow through. I take care of my mental environment." These signals compound into identity. And identity, once formed, *drives behaviour with far less friction*. This is what makes micro-habits disproportionately powerful. They do not demand belief or motivation upfront. They *build belief through behaviour*. And once identity becomes stable, behaviour begins to follow with far less effort.

From a neurological perspective, micro-habits offer something subtler: they engage and stabilise neural circuits through repetition rather than strain. The basal ganglia, where habit loops are encoded, does not differentiate between grand or trivial acts. What matters is *cue, routine, and reward*. If that loop is consistent, the habit embeds. If that habit is stacked—triggered by a preceding one and preparing for the next—the system becomes more than the sum of its parts. This is what psychologists call *chunking*: the process of grouping actions into a singular behavioural unit. Once formed, such sequences become almost automatic—*which is exactly the point*. In pressure scenarios, we do not rise to the level of our intentions. We fall to the strength of our systems. Micro-habits are the bricks that allow those systems to hold.

Critically, micro-habits also avoid the trap of false confidence that comes from temporary intensity. This is an under-discussed psychological danger in habit formation. When individuals experience a spike in motivation, they often commit to high-effort routines—daily workouts, strict diets, long meditation sessions—that are sustainable only under perfect conditions. When motivation drops, these routines shatter. And with them, self-trust erodes. Micro-habits, on the other hand, are not built on intensity. They are *calibrated for the average day*, not the ideal one. Their sustainability is what allows them to function as scaffolding during emotional turbulence, fatigue, or chaos.

There is also a philosophical aspect to this discussion. Micro-habits are exercises in humility. They ask us to *value the imperceptible*, to trade performative ambition for private discipline. In a culture that glorifies scale and spectacle, it takes intentional design to prioritise what does not broadcast status. And yet, it is precisely these invisible rituals—done without external validation—that reinforce the deepest forms of internal coherence. To brush your teeth mindfully, to stretch for ninety seconds before sleep, to repeat one grounding phrase when entering a meeting—these are not tasks. They are *architectural anchors* in a disorienting world.

To design micro-habits well, however, certain conditions must be met. First, the cue must be obvious and contextually stable. Vague intentions ("meditate more") do not become micro-habits. Specific, situational links ("After I put my coffee mug down, I will sit for one minute") do. Second, the action must be scalable. That is, it should be achievable on your worst day, and expandable on your best. Finally, the habit must connect to identity, not outcome. When a micro-habit is reduced to its outcome ("one glass of water for health"), it may fade when the result is not immediate. When it is linked to identity ("I am someone who honours small commitments"), it becomes more durable.

This subchapter has intentionally avoided the superficial language of lifehacks or behavioural trends. Micro-habits are not a novelty. They are *a foundational principle of resilient self-design.* They allow us to create structural continuity even when everything external becomes volatile. They reduce the cognitive load of willpower by embedding stability into the very fabric of our daily flow. And perhaps most importantly, they remind us that transformation is not a matter of dramatic overhaul. It is the product of *thoughtfully designed sequences*—quiet, repeatable, anchored in values, and executed without spectacle.

The architecture of micro-habits is not about doing more. It is about *doing smarter, smaller, and better connected.* It is about building internal systems that can withstand not only ambition, but fatigue, stress, and distraction. When we habit stack with intention—when each small act reinforces the next, when cues are clean and routines interlock—we are no longer living reactively. We are engineering the mind to sustain itself. And in a world where mental erosion often comes from small cracks, the smallest reinforcements often make the greatest difference.

Anchor Habits vs. Vanity Habits – Identifies habits that offer deep stability versus superficial results

Modern culture is enamoured with habits. Bookshelves overflow with titles promising effortless routines for weight loss, productivity, wealth creation, mindfulness, and happiness. Social feeds are saturated with morning routines, performance hacks, and self-optimisation blueprints, often presented as if any well-assembled sequence of behaviours could unlock a frictionless life. But beneath this surge of habit-related enthusiasm lies a critical problem: not all habits are built equally. Some stabilise us when life becomes volatile; others crumble under the slightest pressure. Some habits reinforce identity, mental resilience, and long-term coherence. Others are performative, fragile, and context-dependent. To navigate this complexity with clarity, we must draw a hard line between *anchor habits* and *vanity habits.*

Anchor habits are those rare routines that provide disproportionate psychological return. They serve as internal ballast—offering structure, predictability, and continuity, especially under emotional or cognitive strain. These are the habits that continue even when motivation falters, when the external environment becomes chaotic, or when other routines fall away. Vanity habits, by contrast, are typically designed around performance or image. They look impressive, but they do not hold up under pressure. They are often aspirational, driven more by external metrics than intrinsic alignment. And when the conditions that supported them change, they tend to collapse.

To understand the distinction, consider a common example: the elaborate morning routine. A person might wake at 5:30 a.m., journal for twenty minutes, follow a prescribed workout, prepare a macro-counted breakfast, read for fifteen minutes, and visualise their goals before work. On paper, it's admirable—disciplined, comprehensive, well-orchestrated. But strip away just one support—sleep quality, a calm household, a stable schedule—and the entire sequence may unravel. This is not resilience; it is conditional performance. It is *stacked fragility*. Unless a habit can be sustained through stress, its value remains aesthetic, not architectural.

Anchor habits are usually smaller, quieter, and less dependent on optimal circumstances. They may include stretching for five minutes before bed, checking in with a mentor weekly, writing down three clear intentions before starting a workday, or preparing meals in silence without screens. They rarely show up on social media. They don't broadcast performance. But they do something more important: they *stabilise the mental environment.* When established well, they form the structural beams that hold identity steady even when mood, energy, or confidence fluctuate.

Psychological research supports this differentiation. Habits that are anchored to *identity* tend to be more enduring than those based on *outcomes*. When a person sees themselves as "someone who cares for their physical wellbeing," the act of walking daily—even without measuring steps or weight loss—becomes self-reinforcing. But when the habit is tied to visible results ("I go to the gym to look toned"), it is more vulnerable to interruption, criticism, or external judgement. Motivation rooted in identity behaves like gravity: subtle, invisible, and constant. Motivation rooted in performance behaves like weather: shifting, variable, and sometimes violent.

Moreover, anchor habits tend to be designed with emotional architecture in mind. They soothe rather than stimulate. They reduce complexity rather than add layers of behavioural debt. The writer who reviews their three core values before each drafting session is building coherence, not just discipline. The leader who spends five minutes decompressing between meetings—without opening a screen or checking Slack—is reinforcing emotional bandwidth, not just managing time. These rituals do not shout. They *anchor*.

By contrast, vanity habits are often vulnerable to trend cycles and peer comparison. They may include productivity rituals copied from high-performing executives, meditation apps used only to check streaks, or elaborate nutrition protocols that collapse during travel. While they may offer short-term benefits, their sustainability is often inversely proportional to their visibility. When behaviour is driven by image, deviation can feel like identity failure. This is not sustainable. It is *psychological liability disguised as optimisation.*

One of the most overlooked dimensions in habit design is *load-bearing capacity.* Just as architects design buildings not for sunny days but for storms, mental architects must assess whether a habit can hold emotional, cognitive, or existential weight. Can this practice continue when your schedule breaks, your mood dips, or your sense of purpose falters? If the answer is no, the habit is decorative, not foundational. Designing a habit that only functions under optimal emotional weather is like building a bridge that holds only when no one is walking across it.

This brings us to the role of *contextual resilience.* Anchor habits are often less sensitive to environmental volatility. For example, an anchor habit may involve pausing before responding to emotionally triggering emails. It requires no equipment, no perfect setting, no time block. It simply asks for presence. That habit, repeated consistently, can reshape the tone of a work culture, reduce reactivity, and improve self-regulation. In contrast, a vanity habit—say, reviewing twelve productivity metrics before breakfast—may offer the illusion of control but rarely withstands the entropy of a demanding week.

Historically, many great thinkers and leaders were known more for their anchor habits than their performance habits. Marcus Aurelius wrote meditations not to project wisdom but to *ground himself.* Gandhi's evening spinning of thread was a ritual of simplicity and self-reliance. Maya Angelou wrote in anonymous hotel rooms because it removed distractions and anchored her in creative solitude. These routines were not grandiose. They were humble, durable, and internally anchored.

In practical terms, distinguishing between anchor and vanity habits requires rigorous self-inquiry. Ask: *Does this habit feed my ego, or my nervous system? Can I sustain this when I'm under pressure, or does it depend on mood, environment, or appearance? Is this a ritual of return—to myself, my values, my clarity—or a ritual of projection?* The answers reveal more than time-tracking ever will.

The path forward is not to abandon challenging or impressive routines, but to build a foundation underneath them. Anchor habits first. Then stack complexity. This sequencing matters. Without stable anchors, ambitious habits become fragile. With them, even complexity can be navigated without cognitive depletion. And when life inevitably disrupts your routines—as it always does—it will be the anchor habits that survive. They are what allow you to return to yourself, not because you were perfect, but because *you designed for disruption.*

The cultural shift required here is subtle but significant. We must stop treating behaviour as branding. We must shift our focus from how impressive a habit looks to how stabilising it feels. Performance is transient. Stillness is structural. And the habits that hold under pressure are the ones that offer not visibility, but *continuity.*

Anchor habits, then, are not just behavioural tools. They are the psychological infrastructure of the self. They are where discipline meets compassion, where repetition becomes resilience, and where small actions do the silent work of holding everything else in place. Without them, even the most impressive routines are exposed to collapse. With them, even modest routines can grow into cathedrals of personal integrity.

Design Principles of Enduring Routines – Habits Aligned with Identity and Longevity

There is a subtle tyranny in how habits are often portrayed: a shallow optimism that assumes if something is easy, it will last. "Make it automatic," say the guides. "Stack it with something else. Reward yourself after." And while these strategies may work at the behavioural surface, they do little to answer a more enduring question—*what makes a habit last not just through ease, but through adversity?* What distinguishes the routines that collapse under life's pressure from those that evolve and fortify across decades?

To answer that, we must step back from hacks and shortcuts, and ask instead: *What does it mean to design a routine that is truly structural?* That is not merely efficient but essential? The routines that endure—those that hold across job changes, relocations, pandemics, grief, joy, and aging—share a quality that few habit manuals address directly: they are embedded in identity, not discipline. And they are built with design principles that echo architecture, not engineering alone.

First, enduring routines are constructed around *who we believe we are*, not what we wish to accomplish. This is a critical distinction. A routine tied to an outcome—say, meditating to reduce anxiety—may falter once the outcome is reached or disrupted. But a routine grounded in identity—"I am someone who engages with stillness daily"—is self-reinforcing. It doesn't wait for anxiety to return. It doesn't require a countdown app. It becomes a natural expression of self-maintenance.

This insight is supported by a growing body of psychological research. Studies in self-determination theory and behavioural identity show that habits tied to intrinsic values and self-concept are not only more likely to be adopted, but also more likely to survive interruptions. As James Clear rightly observes, "Every action you take is a vote for the type of person you wish to become." But identity-based routines go a step further: they *are* the vote. They don't just reflect identity; they actively *sculpt* it.

Second, routines that endure tend to be built with *elasticity*. They are not rigid protocols that collapse under change. Instead, they contain the seeds of adaptation. Consider a habit like daily reading. A brittle version of this routine might demand thirty minutes of uninterrupted literary focus, logged into a tracker. But what happens when your child is ill, or work spills into your evening? The habit fails, and with it, the fragile sense of "being a reader." But an elastic version—*ten pages wherever possible, one paragraph if needed, one audiobook chapter while walking*—preserves continuity. It allows for life to intervene without identity breaking.

Elasticity is not a concession to laziness. It is a recognition of reality. Lives are complex, nonlinear, and emotionally dynamic. Routines that do not account for this fact are destined to fail the moment perfection becomes inaccessible. Enduring routines, then, are less about precision and more about preservation. Their genius lies in their flexibility.

Third, enduring routines are *anchored to context*. The environment in which a habit is practiced matters as much as the habit itself. As research by Wendy Wood and others in habit formation confirms, context cues—time of day, location, social presence—are key to behavioural persistence. But context must be *intentional*. If a routine depends on the gym being open, or the weather being fair, or your office being quiet, then it is not structurally sound. To be enduring, the routine must be portable or context-agnostic.

For example, the habit of daily reflection can be shaped into a question asked over coffee, a mental scan during a commute, or a short entry in a notebook before bed. It survives by not being married to a place. Similarly, the habit of gratitude may live in a nightly family ritual, a private journaling practice, or a silent moment before sleep. Its strength lies not in its method but in its *reliability*. Context-aware routines endure not by being perfect, but by being repeatable across imperfect contexts.

Fourth, enduring routines are *psychologically rewarding* in a non-performative way. This means they create an immediate, intrinsic sense of stability, clarity, or connection. They don't require external validation. You don't need to post your cold plunge. You don't need a smartwatch to validate your breathwork. The reward is inherent. You feel better after, not because someone else knows you did it, but because your system *needed* it.

This is where so many contemporary habits fail. They are built to be seen. They are aesthetic rituals rather than stabilising ones. The performance orientation—"Did I do it well? Did it track? Did I win today?"—can quickly erode the internal reward loop. Enduring routines, by contrast, often involve subtle but meaningful shifts in state: a sense of coherence, a restored rhythm, a moment of agency reclaimed. These sensations are the *structural glue* of long-term habits. They bind the behaviour to your emotional centre, not your social identity.

Fifth, and perhaps most critically, enduring routines are designed *with decay in mind.* That is, they are intentionally built to resist entropy. Just as buildings require maintenance to stay intact, so do routines. They degrade over time without intentional restoration. This is not failure—it is entropy at work. Enduring routines include within them *recovery loops*: reassessment rituals, moments of reflection, or check-ins that refresh motivation and design.

For example, someone with a writing habit might schedule a monthly review not to judge productivity, but to notice emotional resistance, pattern drift, or creative depletion. They might ask: "Is this still the right time of day? Has the purpose of this routine shifted? Am I writing from alignment or obligation?" These are not efficiency questions. They are architectural. They test for stress points, alignment, and integrity. And just like engineers monitor bridges for microfractures, thoughtful individuals monitor habits for subtle misalignments.

Sixth, longevity is supported by *emotional friction reduction.* The best routines are not just repeatable—they are *welcome.* They feel like a return, not a burden. This requires wise design. Consider someone who wants to adopt a reading habit. If their routine begins with a race to finish a book per week, the activity may become another arena for self-judgement. But if the routine begins with an atmosphere—a lit candle, a quiet space, no goal but presence—then the emotional context is restorative. The cue itself becomes soothing. The friction is low not because the task is easy, but because the affective state is *welcoming.*

Finally, routines with endurance are not pursued in isolation. They are *integrated with other systems of meaning.* Whether they tie into spiritual beliefs, creative missions, relational commitments, or professional ethics, they are not siloed behaviours. They *belong to a larger architecture.* This is perhaps the ultimate marker of an enduring routine: it makes *sense* in your life. It is not borrowed. It is not fashionable. It is not a "should." It is an expression of *values-in-motion.*

When we understand routine-building in this way—as a process of structural design rather than behavioural coercion—we stop asking shallow questions like "How long does it take to build a habit?" and start asking better ones: *Is this habit built on identity or performance? Will it hold when everything else changes? Is it portable? Is it elastic? Is it restorative? Does it belong here?*

These questions do not lend themselves to quick fixes. But they do lead us to better architecture. And in the long arc of a complex life, it is not the glamorous routines that hold us up. It is the ones that were built with wisdom, for our actual lives, over time.

Enduring routines, then, are not found in productivity books or morning routine reels. They are forged in quiet acts of alignment. They are the architecture of the self when it has matured beyond performance. They are not merely efficient—they are *anchored.* Not merely visible—they are *vital.* And their design is not just a behavioural challenge. It is a philosophical one.

Environmental Cues as Structural Supports – How Surroundings Sustain What Willpower Can't

To speak of habits without speaking of environment is to study architecture without ever mentioning gravity. Yet this omission is frequent. In the public discourse on behaviour change, the spotlight so often falls on internal motivation, discipline, or neurochemical loops, while the quiet, ambient power of physical and social context is relegated to an afterthought. This is a conceptual error, and a costly one. If we are to understand why some routines decay while others embed, or why even the most disciplined intentions collapse under stress, we must examine not just the *actor*, but the *stage.*

At its core, an environmental cue is any element in one's surroundings that triggers, reinforces, or sustains a behaviour. It can be as obvious as a gym bag by the door or as subtle as the scent of coffee triggering morning journaling. It can be architectural—open floor plans encouraging social interaction—or temporal, such as daylight influencing wake times. But regardless of form, the role of the environment is *structural.* It provides the scaffolding within which routines either hold or falter.

This idea is not speculative. Across behavioural science, the evidence for environmental influence is overwhelming. B.F. Skinner's early work on operant conditioning highlighted the power of surroundings in shaping repeated action. Later, Wendy Wood's empirical studies showed that up to 45% of daily behaviours are automatic responses to environmental context—not the result of deliberate decision-making. James Clear echoes this with a blunt truth: "You do not rise to the level of your goals. You fall to the level of your systems. And systems are shaped by your environment."

So why does this matter? Because even well-designed habits, aligned with identity and intention, will *not persist* if they are perpetually undermined by ambient friction. A reader's routine will wither in a room dominated by noise, screens, or visual clutter. A meditation practice cannot reliably survive a schedule that offers no uninterrupted stillness. A writing habit will not thrive in a chair that hurts or a desktop littered with chaos. These examples aren't personal failures; they're failures of environmental design.

The key insight is this: *environment is not neutral.* It either supports or obstructs. This means that sustainable habits are rarely the result of brute willpower; more often, they are the product of frictionless design—spaces and cues so well-aligned that the behaviour becomes the path of least resistance.

Consider the office worker trying to reduce digital distractions. Blocking websites or installing focus apps may help temporarily, but unless the workspace itself is redesigned—notifications off, phone out of sight, browser stripped of temptation—the behavioural load remains unnecessarily high. Contrast this with an environment in which the very act of sitting down initiates deep work: visual clutter removed, noise dampened, ritualised cue like a hot beverage or specific playlist in place. The difference isn't just psychological. It's structural. One setup resists the habit; the other *enables* it.

This is why enduring habits are rarely built in hostile environments. A person may wish to adopt healthier eating patterns, but if their kitchen is dominated by ultra-processed convenience foods and their fridge offers no immediate alternatives, their commitment is functionally irrelevant. Here, design matters more than desire. A kitchen preloaded with accessible, high-quality ingredients silently nudges better choices. A set of pre-cut vegetables in clear containers is not just a health hack; it is a structural cue—one that speaks louder than willpower ever could.

We see similar dynamics in social environments. Behavioural contagion—the spread of behaviours through peer influence—is not a psychological side note; it's a primary force in habit sustainability. A person who adopts a writing routine is more likely to maintain it if surrounded by others who write. Fitness routines are more likely to persist in communal settings where the behaviour is normalised. The inverse also holds: habits seen as outliers in one's immediate social environment struggle to root. In that sense, a person trying to meditate daily in a high-conflict household or toxic workplace isn't failing—they're resisting gravity.

This brings us to an overlooked but critical point: *changing a habit often requires changing the architecture that surrounds it.* This architecture includes physical layout, spatial aesthetics, time structures, and interpersonal cues. The most effective habit redesigns begin not with the behaviour itself, but with the question: *What in this environment currently makes the behaviour unsustainable?*

This design orientation is used with remarkable effect in behavioural economics and public health. Consider the case of "choice architecture" in cafeterias. Simply placing fruits and vegetables at eye level dramatically increases consumption—*not because people became more health-conscious, but because friction to the better choice was reduced.* Similarly, seatbelt compliance increased not through moral campaigns, but by making the unbuckled state noisily uncomfortable. The environment did the behavioural heavy lifting.

For individuals, the implications are profound. A reading habit becomes more reliable when a book lives on the bedside table, not buried on a digital device. A fitness routine sticks better when clothes are laid out the night before, shoes placed by the door. These are not motivational tricks—they are *structural supports.* They cue behaviour without requiring cognitive strain. And under pressure—when motivation fades or fatigue hits—it is these cues that carry the habit forward.

Importantly, the reverse is also true: *removing negative cues is as powerful as adding positive ones.* A person trying to reduce compulsive scrolling may find success not by installing yet another app blocker, but by moving their phone charger to a different room. A person attempting to eat more mindfully might benefit more from using smaller plates, dimmer lights, or family-style serving—cues that subtly reframe consumption. These are not constraints; they are *liberations from cognitive overload.* They let the environment remember what we otherwise forget.

Of course, environments cannot solve everything. They are not substitutes for meaning or identity. A perfectly arranged home gym will not transform someone who fundamentally rejects movement. But for those with the desire—however fragile—*the environment is what keeps the desire alive long enough to become routine.* In that sense, structural support is not just convenience. It is continuity. It is what sustains the habit during periods of low energy, high stress, or emotional volatility.

This reframes the role of the individual. You are not just the user of your environment; you are its architect. This is an empowering, but also humbling, realisation. Many people live in environments designed by accident or inherited from others' preferences. Their daily contexts are more reflective of marketing, inertia, or architectural constraints than personal intention. But environments can be re-authored. They can be stripped of friction, rebalanced, and optimised—not for aesthetic perfection, but for *behavioural alignment.*

To do this well requires observation, honesty, and a kind of behavioural forensics. Ask: *Where do my habits most often fail, and what in the environment reinforces that failure?* Which spaces cue reactivity, and which invite focus? When do I feel most in alignment with my identity, and what environmental factors are present? The answers to these questions reveal not just individual patterns but the underlying structure that makes them persist.

Ultimately, designing environmental cues is not about engineering life into a sterile routine. It's about crafting a habitat where the behaviours that matter most are not only possible, but *probable.* Where resistance is replaced by flow. Where friction is replaced by fit. And where the self you intend to become is quietly cued by the space you inhabit.

Chapter 5
Behavioural Engineering – Rewiring Reactions

We often grant too much credit to intention and too little to the architecture of our reflexes. Much of what we do—our day-to-day behaviours, especially under pressure—doesn't emerge from deliberation but from default. We like to imagine we're steering the ship of choice, but more often than not, we're running scripts. When stress tightens the window for thought and emotion spikes, behaviour tends not to be selected—it's triggered. And it is here, in that unthinking space, that lasting behavioural change is either seeded or lost.

The real promise of behavioural design lies in a fundamental reframing: what if, instead of battling instinct with discipline, we redesigned the terrain on which instinct plays out? What if the path to better behaviour didn't rely on gritted teeth and sheer effort—but on smarter systems? This chapter proposes precisely that: a shift from control-as-force to control-as-structure. Discipline may still have its place, but it's an expensive resource, draining the very mental energy needed to endure. There's a more elegant alternative: engineer the context so that better reactions become automatic.

Central to this inquiry is a sharp distinction—one that's easy to overlook but transformative when grasped. Reaction is fast, conditioned, and shaped by prior experience. Response, by contrast, is reflective, chosen, and rooted in present values. Moving from the first to the second is what it means to exert agency. But this leap doesn't happen spontaneously. It must be designed into being, using principles as deliberate and rigorous as those used in constructing a building or coding a system.

The first structural principle is the design of interruptions. Behavioural loops—those familiar patterns of lashing out, scrolling mindlessly, falling into negative thought spirals—are seldom the result of reflection. They are procedural, automatic. To disrupt them, we must first break the momentum. This can be surprisingly physical: a strategically placed note, a tactile object, a sensory cue. Or it might be embedded in digital environments—friction layers that delay impulse gratification. Then there are embodied techniques: breath resets, posture shifts, micro-movements that signal a pattern break. What these interventions share is the creation of a pause—a wedge of time that interrupts automation and allows space for a different choice. Without such interruptions, behaviour change remains reliant on willpower alone, and that, as we've seen, is fragile.

The second principle is reframing. Whereas interruption halts the sequence, reframing alters its trajectory. It's not a denial of what's occurring but a recasting of its meaning. A criticism becomes information. A delay becomes preparation. A stressor becomes a cue. Reframing is not just for therapy rooms—it's a tool of design. Change the frame, and the behaviour often shifts with it. Not because you forced it to, but because you redefined what it was responding to. And meaning—quietly, powerfully—shapes action.

Next comes the search for leverage. Behavioural design is not a brute force exercise. It thrives on economy—doing the smallest thing that produces the greatest shift. That might mean altering the time of a task, reordering a routine, or slightly adjusting one's physical space. It doesn't take a total overhaul to trigger a cascade. Leverage points allow you to change the outcome without wrestling the whole pattern to the ground. They are quiet but powerful tools. In some cases, they even bypass resistance entirely—not by overpowering it, but by rendering it irrelevant.

What this chapter offers is not a set of hacks but an infrastructure. These are not passing tricks, but durable tools for reshaping how you behave under duress. We'll draw on examples ranging from personal transformation to organisational culture shifts—anywhere human systems falter and reactive behaviour takes over. We'll also explore the deeper philosophical underpinnings, from the Stoic distinction between what we control and what we don't, to neuroscience's evolving understanding of how brain patterns can be updated through practice.

Let's be clear, though—this is not a pursuit of sterile self-control. Emotion is not the enemy here. Nor is the goal to perfect oneself into frictionless efficiency. We are not robots, and any behavioural model that pretends otherwise collapses in the face of real life. What we are pursuing is far more human: the ability to choose, when it matters most. Not through strain, but through structure. And structure, unlike mood, holds.

Ultimately, this is the core claim: regulation is not merely a matter of personality. It's a design issue. Like a bridge engineered to flex under strain or a platform that guides the user subtly but surely, behavioural resilience is built. It doesn't require superhuman control—it requires thoughtful construction. If we're still operating on scripts encoded decades ago, shaped by old conditioning or cultural defaults, then trying to think our way into change will often fall short. The thinking must be translated into architecture—physical, cognitive, environmental. That is how new patterns take root.

Readers who take this seriously will leave not only with insight into why they do what they do—but with blueprints for building alternatives. The aim is not to erase reaction but to stretch the space between impulse and action just wide enough for agency to slip through. That gap—small, but critical—is where power returns to the individual.

So no, this isn't about willpower. That's the old model. This is about architecture. And architecture, unlike impulse, can be planned.

Default Settings and Mental Autopilot

There is a quiet mechanism embedded deep in the mind—a system so familiar that most people fail to recognise it. It governs how we brush our teeth, respond to emails, judge social cues, speak to ourselves, and interpret difficulty. It's not personality. It's not identity. It's *habitual cognition.* And unless examined and redesigned, it operates on autopilot. Much of what destabilises us psychologically is not dramatic trauma or high-stakes crisis. It is the unexamined loop of default reactions, thoughts, and behaviours that repeat unnoticed—and, over time, erode mental clarity, stability, and agency.

The premise of this chapter is not simply that we have habits of action, but that we also have *habits of thought.* These default mental settings—what we pay attention to, how we interpret uncertainty, where we place blame or credit—constitute the architecture of our internal life. While some defaults are adaptive, many are outdated, installed not by conscious decision but by early life experiences, social conditioning, or emotional survival. These settings shape our stress responses, our decision-making, and our interpretations of self-worth—often without consent.

Understanding mental autopilot requires acknowledging a hard truth: *much of what feels like free will is pre-programmed.* Neuropsychological research from the past two decades supports this idea. Studies in decision science and behavioural economics—from the foundational work of Daniel Kahneman and Amos Tversky to modern-day cognitive neuroscience—demonstrate that we often choose based on mental shortcuts known as heuristics. These shortcuts are not always flawed; they are efficient. But efficiency comes at a cost: *loss of conscious oversight.* What we sacrifice in critical reflection, we gain in speed—and not always wisely.

Take, for instance, the *negativity bias*—a default cognitive setting hardwired into the human brain to prioritise threat over safety, criticism over praise, and failure over success. In evolutionary terms, this was adaptive; early humans who ignored danger didn't survive long enough to pass on their genes. But in modern environments—especially those saturated by media, noise, and comparison—the same bias becomes maladaptive. It locks attention onto perceived risks, encourages hyper-vigilance, and undermines calm. What was once protective becomes corrosive.

Or consider *catastrophising*—a behavioural loop where the mind leaps to the worst-case scenario, regardless of evidence. This is not simply a bad habit. It is a mental autopilot function rooted in neural efficiency: better to be falsely alarmed a thousand times than to be unprepared once. But over time, this pattern exhausts the nervous system. It creates chronic tension, narrows creative thinking, and compromises decision-making. The loop reinforces itself: stress justifies the reaction, and the reaction generates more stress. The system sustains its own dysfunction.

The deeper problem lies not in the loops themselves, but in our lack of *awareness* that we are in them. This is what distinguishes conscious behaviour from cognitive automation. When you are on autopilot, you are not choosing—you are replaying. And replayed enough times, even damaging patterns begin to feel like personality. A short temper becomes "just who I am." Constant busyness becomes "just how life works." Resignation to mediocrity becomes "just reality." But none of these are facts. They are conditioned defaults—internal scripts running without updated input.

This chapter asks a critical question: *How do you know whether your thoughts are accurate—or merely automatic?*

To answer it, we must examine the three primary types of default loops that sabotage mental stability:

Behavioural Loops – These include compulsive checking, avoidance behaviours, chronic procrastination, and ineffective coping mechanisms such as excessive screen use, overworking, or emotional eating. The loop is simple: discomfort triggers behaviour, which produces short-term relief, reinforcing the pattern.

Emotional Loops – Recurrent emotional states that emerge from familiar triggers and predictable interpretations. For example, perceived rejection might automatically lead to shame, which reinforces isolation, which confirms the belief of unworthiness. The emotional feedback loop strengthens each time it completes itself without disruption.

Cognitive Loops – These operate at the interpretive level: how we explain things to ourselves. Mental filters like black-and-white thinking, mind reading, or personalisation distort incoming data to fit old conclusions. They preserve psychological consistency at the expense of accuracy and adaptability.

Crucially, *mental autopilot is not just personal—it is cultural.* Societal systems also run on default loops: productivity over wellbeing, speed over depth, reaction over reflection. We absorb these defaults unconsciously. For instance, many internalise that self-worth is tied to output, leading to habitual overworking. Others inherit the script that rest is laziness, making relaxation feel like guilt. These defaults are not innate. They are installed.

Yet change begins not with rejection, but with inspection. To interrupt autopilot, we must first *map its terrain.* That means identifying recurring triggers, tracking predictable patterns, and noticing what precedes a behavioural or emotional spiral. One of the most powerful interventions in behavioural psychology is the "cue-routine-reward" framework, first articulated by Charles Duhigg and further developed in habit research. It posits that most automatic behaviour follows a cycle: a cue triggers a routine, which delivers a psychological reward. Break the loop at the cue, or redesign the reward, and the pattern loses power.

However, we can go further than mere interruption. The goal is not only to stop what isn't working, but to *replace it with deliberate design.* Behavioural loops can be recoded. Emotional defaults can be recontextualised. Cognitive scripts can be rewritten. And when these shifts are small but precise, they begin to rewire not only the brain's responses but the self's narrative. You are no longer someone who merely reacts. You are someone who designs.

This is the work of *metacognition*—the capacity to think about one's own thinking. It is the opposite of autopilot. It requires effort, but not extravagance. The practice begins with noticing. Every moment of self-observation—every time you ask "Is this true?" or "Is this useful?"—is a step out of automation and into authorship. Over time, this authorship reshapes not only behaviour, but identity.

Indeed, the promise of behavioural architecture is not perfection, but *liberation.* When defaults are brought to light, they lose their grip. When loops are made visible, they can be redesigned. And when reactions become conscious responses, the individual regains the dignity of choice.

To do this at scale, however, requires infrastructure. Mental cues, emotional regulation strategies, and environmental supports must align. Just as engineers design bridges to carry weight, so too must we design systems to carry our intentions through stress, fatigue, and ambiguity. That begins by identifying the loops that sabotage stability—and refusing to let them run the show.

You are not your loops. You are the architect.

Designing Interruptions

In high-performance systems—whether engineered, biological, or behavioural—failure is rarely the result of a single dramatic flaw. It is usually the compounding effect of small, unexamined processes running without resistance. The human mind is no exception. In moments of stress, boredom, social tension or uncertainty, our brains revert to speed over discernment, defaulting to rapid, automatic responses that require little conscious thought but carry high cognitive and emotional costs. These are not decisions—they are impulses wearing the mask of intention.

Left unchecked, impulse becomes habit. Habit becomes identity. And identity—if built on automation rather than authorship—becomes a prison of patterned reaction. If the purpose of inner architecture is to design a mind capable of rebuilding itself, *then the capacity to pause—to interrupt—is foundational.* This subchapter explores how consciously designed interruptions can disarm compulsive behaviour, insert space between stimulus and response, and reinstate the mind as a site of deliberation rather than reflex.

Let us begin with a simple yet often ignored principle: *conscious behaviour begins with interruption.* Without a reliable mechanism for disrupting automaticity, even the best intentions are overwritten by cognitive momentum. Consider the smoker who lights a cigarette without awareness, the executive who checks their phone in the middle of a conversation, or the student who compulsively scrolls despite the looming deadline. These are not failures of discipline—they are failures of *design.* The problem is not only that the behaviour happens, but that it *happens before it can be noticed.*

Designing interruptions is not about willpower. It is about *interface engineering at the level of behaviour.* Just as a well-designed building includes fire escapes, load-bearing supports, and exit signage, so too must a well-designed life include psychological failsafes—deliberate pauses engineered into our behavioural architecture. These are not passive hopes. They are intentional structures.

In neuroscience, this space between impulse and action is called the *response window*—a fraction of a second when the brain's prefrontal cortex has an opportunity to override the amygdala's emotional charge. The wider this window, the greater the potential for rational choice. But the default human system narrows this window under stress. Therefore, interruption must be externally supported, not left to internal idealism. *We must build the pause into the system itself.*

So, what does it look like to design effective interruptions? There are three primary strategies—cognitive, behavioural, and environmental—and each plays a distinct role in expanding conscious space.

1. Cognitive Interruptions: Reframing in Real Time

At the cognitive level, the interruption must occur *within the mental narrative*—the story we tell ourselves in the moment of reactivity. This can be as simple as an internal question designed to destabilise the script:

– "What else could this mean?"
– "Is this reaction mine—or inherited?"
– "What outcome am I rehearsing without consent?"

These are not affirmations. They are *interrogations*—micro-pauses in the story-making process that give the rational brain a foothold. For example, Viktor Frankl famously asserted that "between stimulus and response, there is a space. In that space is our power to choose." But space must be engineered. It will not appear on demand unless it has been *trained in advance.* Mental rehearsal of cognitive interruptions—during calm, not crisis—conditions the mind to deploy them when it matters most.

2. Behavioural Interruptions: Repatterning the Body

While cognitive reframing is powerful, it often arrives too late in the cycle unless *embodied.* That is, the interruption must register in the nervous system. This is where physical pattern disruption plays a crucial role. Simple but intentional movements—changing posture, standing up, splashing cold water, touching a grounding object—can interrupt the physiological momentum of stress or compulsivity. In trauma therapy, this is known as *pattern completion*: redirecting energy to break the cycle of threat anticipation.

One particularly effective tool is *the 90-second rule*, introduced by neuroanatomist Dr Jill Bolte Taylor. She found that when an emotional trigger is activated, the resulting biochemical response lasts approximately 90 seconds unless it is re-triggered by rumination. This means that *if we can ride out the emotional surge with awareness and a grounding interruption*, we can prevent the emotion from becoming behaviour.

The takeaway? Most reactions are shorter than we assume. But unless we design something to *catch the fall*, we don't give ourselves the chance to test that.

3. Environmental Interruptions: Contextual Friction

Even the best internal strategy is no match for poor environmental design. Just as an architect designs buildings to guide flow and function, behavioural architecture depends on *environmental cues that either trigger or interrupt impulse.* One of the most underleveraged tools for behavioural change is *designed friction*—creating intentional resistance between an impulse and its execution.

Want to reduce digital distraction? Log out after every use. Turn devices to greyscale. Place your phone in another room. Want to eat less junk food? Store it in inconvenient locations. Want to curb reactive emailing? Use delay-send features or apps that ask "Are you sure?" before transmission. These are not gimmicks. They are the behavioural equivalent of traffic lights—engineered pauses that *insert choice where there was once compulsion.*

Research in behavioural economics supports this principle. The work of Richard Thaler and Cass Sunstein on *nudging* shows that small shifts in how choices are structured can dramatically alter outcomes without requiring coercion. The implication is profound: *we can design our environments to interrupt our worst patterns—without waiting for internal motivation.*

But a crucial insight follows: *interruptions are only useful if they redirect, not just delay.* A pause without reflection becomes stagnation. A disruption without redirection becomes avoidance. The true purpose of the interruption is to *recover authorship*—to insert a sliver of deliberate consciousness into the mechanical loop of stimulus and response.

This is where practice becomes identity. The more we build interruptions into our behavioural architecture, the more we become someone who pauses, someone who reframes, someone who notices. These are not traits—they are *trained capacities.* And when rehearsed consistently, they move from intervention to instinct.

To illustrate, consider the practice of *Implementation Intentions*, a concept developed by psychologist Peter Gollwitzer. This involves pre-committing to a specific interruption behaviour under a defined condition. For instance:

– "If I feel anxious before a meeting, I will take three deep breaths before speaking."
– "If I feel the urge to check social media, I will stretch for 60 seconds first."

The genius of implementation intentions lies in their simplicity: they install *micro-interruptions into pre-defined scenarios*, training the mind to insert awareness before action. Over time, they become second nature—not because the urge disappears, but because the default pattern has been rerouted.

However, interruption design is not without ethical considerations. In organisational and social systems, interruptions can be manipulated—used to delay accountability, gaslight intuition, or enforce compliance. Interruption is not inherently virtuous. Its power lies in *who designs it and for what purpose*. That is why we must distinguish between *disruptions that empower reflection and those that enforce suppression*. The former liberate. The latter control.

A well-designed interruption does not shame the impulse. It simply declines to obey it. It says, "You are allowed to exist, but not to drive." This is the core of conscious self-regulation—not denial, but deliberate delay.

Ultimately, what this chapter insists upon is that reactivity is not destiny. It is merely default. And defaults can be rewritten—but only if we are willing to treat interruption as a *design problem*, not a moral failing.

If you want to change your behaviour, don't just try harder. *Interrupt better.*

Response Over Reaction – Training Reflective Space Through Reframing

There is a profound difference between a reaction and a response. One is automatic, often unconscious—fired off by pattern recognition, emotional bias, or evolutionary defence mechanisms. The other is deliberate, considered, and chosen. One is the product of a conditioned past; the other is an act of authorship in the present. *In high-stakes moments—personal or professional—this distinction is not semantic. It is structural.* It determines whether we repeat inherited reflexes or exercise meaningful agency.

Modern psychology, cognitive neuroscience, and ancient philosophy converge on a striking truth: *the quality of our lives is largely determined by the space we create between what happens and what we do about it*. The larger that space, the greater our ability to direct our behaviour, regulate our emotional responses, and align action with long-term identity rather than short-term survival. This subchapter focuses on how to cultivate that space—not merely through restraint or awareness, but by mastering the cognitive tool of *reframing*.

Let us be clear: *reaction is not weakness—it is efficiency.* The human brain is designed to detect patterns, predict outcomes, and minimise uncertainty. When an event occurs, the brain doesn't start from scratch. It consults its archives: past experiences, emotional memories, social scripts, biases. Within milliseconds, a prediction is formed, and the body is primed to act accordingly. This is evolution's gift—and its liability. Because the faster the mind moves, the less likely it is to question whether its assumptions are still accurate.

Reframing is the disciplined disruption of this predictive loop. It is the skill of holding an experience at arm's length—not to deny its emotional charge, but to examine its possible meanings before locking into a narrative. And this is not a passive reflection. It is an act of mental architecture. A well-framed response becomes the psychological equivalent of a keystone arch: it redistributes weight, stabilises emotional load, and allows complexity to rest on clarity.

Consider a practical example. A colleague interrupts you in a meeting. Your immediate reaction is defensiveness: *They're undermining me.* If you act on this reflex—subtly withdraw, retaliate, or shut down—you reinforce a story about power, threat, and status. But what if, in that critical pause, you insert an alternative frame? *What if they're excited and just jumped the queue? What if they misunderstood the cue?* That simple cognitive pivot doesn't erase the discomfort—it transforms its direction. Instead of collapsing into certainty, you *create cognitive elasticity*, which allows your behaviour to adapt.

The Neuroscience of the Pause

In neurobiological terms, reactivity is governed by the limbic system—particularly the amygdala—which detects threat and mobilises a fight-or-flight response. Response, by contrast, requires activation of the prefrontal cortex—the seat of higher-order functions: planning, perspective-taking, impulse inhibition. The problem is not that the amygdala is wrong; it's that it is *early.* It reacts before the context has been fully interpreted. Reframing helps *slow the gap between stimulus and narrative*, enabling the prefrontal cortex to engage before the damage is done.

One powerful way to frame this distinction is borrowed from Viktor Frankl, the psychiatrist and Holocaust survivor who wrote: *"Between stimulus and response, there is a space. In that space is our power to choose our response. In our response lies our growth and our freedom."* This is not philosophy—it is strategy. The goal is to widen the space between what is felt and how it is processed, not by suppressing reaction but by interrogating its premises.

Reframing in Practice: Tactical Tools for Mental Recomposition

The practice of reframing is deceptively simple. At its core is a single question: *Is there another way to interpret this?* But effective reframing requires more than surface optimism. It demands *trained scepticism towards one's initial narrative.* Below are four reframing techniques rooted in empirical research and clinical application.

Temporal Reframing: Ask, *Will this matter in a week? A month? A year?* This zooms the lens of awareness away from urgency and into proportion. It challenges the mind's tendency to magnify the now and misallocate emotional resources.

Perspective Reframing: Ask, *What would I think if I were advising someone else?* This shifts cognition from first-person emotional bias to third-person analysis. Studies in cognitive distancing (Kross & Ayduk, 2011) show that this form of self-talk regulates emotion more effectively than suppression or distraction.

Intentional Reframing: Ask, *What value of mine is being activated or threatened right now?* This realigns the reaction with identity rather than ego. Often, our defensiveness masks a deeper concern—such as fairness, respect, or integrity. Identifying this anchor can convert reactivity into principled action.

Assumption Reframing: Ask, *What assumption am I making, and is it necessary or true?* This targets the hidden logic of our mental scripts. Often, we react not to the event, but to an assumption about what the event implies.

Each of these methods functions not as a trick, but as a *pause button on narrative momentum.* Reframing is not denial. It is inquiry. It doesn't weaken emotion; it contextualises it. And through that context, we earn the right to choose.

The Ethical Dimension of Response

Choosing response over reaction is not simply a matter of mental clarity—it is an ethical act. Reactions are contagious. An emotional outburst in one meeting can ripple across a team for weeks. A poorly handled disagreement in a family can calcify into decades of avoidance. A leader who cannot reframe criticism becomes a tyrant of tone. Therefore, *learning to insert reflective space is not just about personal growth. It is about cultural contribution.*

It also reframes power itself. In most social settings, the loudest person sets the tempo. But in well-designed inner architectures, *the most reflective person holds the power.* Not because they dominate—but because they regulate. Their presence introduces a different logic into the system: one that privileges *response time over reaction time.* This is especially critical in high-conflict environments, where rapid escalation is the norm. The capacity to interrupt the emotional contagion loop through deliberate reframing becomes a form of leadership.

Contrasts and Critiques: When Reframing is Misused

While reframing is a powerful tool, it is not a panacea. It can be abused to rationalise avoidance, to soften confrontation that is morally necessary, or to suppress legitimate feelings in the name of control. There is a difference between *reframing and refragging*—reinterpreting reality to avoid discomfort rather than understand it.

Moreover, not all emotional responses are overreactions. Some are *informationally valid.* Anger, grief, fear—these are not symptoms of irrationality. They are signals. Reframing must therefore be deployed with nuance, not to invalidate emotion, but to *translate it into clarity.* The question is not whether an emotion is appropriate, but *whether it is actionable.* Reaction dumps energy. Response directs it.

From Training to Trait: Response as Identity

The consistent application of reframing techniques does something remarkable over time: it reshapes our sense of self. We cease to see ourselves as the product of conditions and begin to operate as the *engineers of meaning*. Emotional sobriety becomes a norm, not an aspiration. We become the kind of person who slows down instead of escalating, who considers context before assigning blame, who steers emotion rather than being steered by it.

In this sense, *response is not merely a skill—it is an identity framework*. A person who responds over reacts is someone who values authorship over automation, interpretation over impulse. They no longer live at the mercy of emotional weather. They install a climate system.

Final Insight

The world doesn't need more clever reactions. It needs *conscious responders*—those who insert space, examine frames, and act from grounded clarity. In a culture obsessed with immediacy, urgency, and feedback loops, *response is a radical act*. It is the refusal to become whatever the world makes you in the moment. It is the declaration: I will interpret this, not be consumed by it.

The greatest power we possess is not what we feel first—but what we choose next.

Behavioural Leverage Points – Small Shifts, Outsized Impact

When people think about transformation—mental, behavioural, emotional—they often imagine radical overhauls: new careers, lifestyle resets, or psychological reinventions. But the science of complex systems—and the lived reality of sustainable change—points elsewhere. It tells us that transformation is rarely about sweeping acts. It is often about *targeting the right node within the system. Behavioural leverage points* are those precise, often underestimated, elements of conduct or context where a small adjustment yields disproportionate psychological and emotional gains.

This is not speculative theory. It's the logic underpinning architecture, medicine, systems design, and behavioural economics. The same principle that allows an engineer to stabilise a bridge with a few recalibrated tension cables also enables a person to reinforce mental resilience by modifying one keystone routine. When change feels hard, it is often because we are pushing on the wrong part of the system. *Behavioural leverage means locating the right hinge.*

In the context of mental fitness and cognitive clarity, behavioural leverage points are micro-adjustments—minute shifts in habit, timing, framing, or environment—that reduce friction, disrupt negative cycles, and amplify well-being. Crucially, these points do not demand exhaustive willpower or long-term behavioural revolutions. They require precision. That is the paradox: *to think small in order to go far.*

Let's begin by reframing how most people attempt change.

The Trap of Global Intentions

Many well-meaning attempts at personal improvement fail not because they lack sincerity, but because they lack precision. A person vows to "be more focused," "reduce stress," or "get healthier." These goals are laudable but structurally weak. They are *macro-intentions*—broad, amorphous desires that lack actionable entry points. They ignore the underlying architecture of habit: context, cue, reward, identity. Consequently, they default to willpower, which is both finite and volatile under stress.

Contrast this with the application of a behavioural leverage point. Instead of a vague goal like "get better at focusing," a leverage-based strategy might identify that the first 10 minutes of one's morning—currently spent in reactive mode, scrolling emails—is creating cognitive turbulence that lingers throughout the day. By modifying *that specific loop*—say, by replacing it with a scripted, intentional setup routine involving analogue planning or silence—one creates a shift with cascading benefits. Focus is not forced; it is structurally supported.

This is the art of behavioural leverage: *finding the one hinge that opens five doors.*

The Systems View: Feedback Loops and Point of Entry

The late systems theorist Donella Meadows, in her foundational work *Thinking in Systems*, articulated a hierarchy of leverage points within systems. The most powerful points are not the most obvious. Changing inputs has some effect. Changing feedback loops has more. Changing goals or paradigms has the most—but is also hardest. In human behaviour, the equivalent is this: modifying outcomes (e.g., "get up earlier") is weak leverage. Modifying internal scripts (e.g., *what does waking early signal about who I am?*) is powerful leverage.

For practical application, three categories of behavioural leverage points have high impact when intentionally adjusted:

Micro-Temporal Shifts – the *when* of a behaviour, not just the what

Environmental Anchors – the *where* of habit initiation

Cognitive Reframing – the *why* that underlies decision loops

Let's examine each.

1. Micro-Temporal Shifts: The Power of Timing

Most people overemphasise intensity and underestimate timing. Yet behavioural science shows that *when* you perform a task often matters more than *how well* you perform it. For example, studies in chronobiology and decision fatigue suggest that people are cognitively sharpest in the early part of the day—but only if that time hasn't been eroded by high-friction tasks. This makes the first hour of conscious attention one of the most powerful leverage points in the behavioural system. A 15-minute change here—reducing noise, deferring reactive work—can recalibrate the entire day's decision ecosystem.

Another micro-temporal leverage point is in the *transition phase* between tasks. Most people conflate "doing more" with "being more productive." Yet research in attention residue (Leroy, 2009) shows that the residue of the previous task impairs cognitive performance in the next. A simple transition protocol—like three minutes of journaling or intentional breathwork between meetings—acts as a cognitive reset. Tiny cost. Outsized gain.

2. Environmental Anchors: Structuring for Effortlessness

Environment is not neutral. It is a silent architect of behaviour. Most actions we call "habit" are in fact context-driven scripts activated by cues embedded in our surroundings. A bowl of crisps on the desk is not just food—it's a decision loop waiting to fire. A phone on the table is not a tool—it's an interruption system with an open invitation. This is why modifying environmental cues can yield exponential behavioural returns.

One of the most underutilised leverage points is *friction.* Behavioural economist Dan Ariely refers to this as *choice architecture.* Increase friction for behaviours you want to reduce (e.g., place the TV remote in a drawer; turn phone to greyscale) and reduce friction for those you want to adopt (e.g., place your journal open on your desk; pre-fill your water bottle the night before). The behaviour doesn't change because you will it—it changes because the system changes.

Leverage is not about doing harder things. It's about making better things easier to do.

3. Cognitive Reframing: Rewiring the Identity Layer

All behaviour is downstream of identity. Not just self-concept ("I'm a disciplined person") but *felt congruence*—the degree to which an action aligns with a person's story about who they are. One of the most effective leverage points is not behavioural at all—it's narrative.

Take the act of saying "no" to a social invitation. To a people-pleaser, this act may trigger guilt or identity threat ("I'm letting them down"). But if reframed through a values-aligned lens ("I am someone who protects depth over overcommitment"), the same act becomes coherent rather than conflictual. This is behavioural leverage via meaning. The act didn't change. The interpretation did—and so the emotional resistance diminished.

Practically, one can build *identity scripts* to reinforce desired behaviours. For example:
– "I'm the kind of person who protects mornings for deep work."
– "I close loops before opening new ones."
– "I defend the quality of my attention as a form of self-respect."

These are not affirmations. They are *constructive anchors*—cognitive cues designed to reduce narrative dissonance and stabilise decision-making under pressure.

Case Study: High-Performance Minimalism

Consider a CTO of a scaling tech firm dealing with cognitive overload, sleep fragmentation, and poor focus. He tries time-blocking, supplements, even a silent retreat. Nothing sticks. But with a behavioural strategist, he isolates one leverage point: *email checking behaviour.* Previously done every 7–10 minutes, unconsciously. Through deliberate restructuring, he checks only at set intervals—once mid-morning, once mid-afternoon. A simple change. But over three weeks, it improves focus, reduces anxiety, and creates space for strategic thinking. *No major overhaul. Just a hinge point discovered and leveraged.*

This is the philosophy of behavioural leverage: *small hinges swing big doors—if they are the right hinges.*

Caveats and Intellectual Integrity

Not every behaviour has a leverage point that can be accessed without deeper structural change. In cases of trauma, addiction, or neurobiological constraints, micro-adjustments alone may be insufficient. It is important to distinguish *low-effort leverage points* from the need for therapeutic or clinical intervention. Precision is not a substitute for complexity—it is a way of engaging it more effectively.

Moreover, leverage points require *iteration.* Not every shift will yield a visible effect immediately. But well-designed leverage experiments provide fast feedback. If there is no structural benefit within a defined window, abandon or refine. Leverage is not guesswork; it is adaptive design.

Closing Insight

We are taught to revere scale: bigger goals, broader strategies, sweeping resolutions. But sustainable mental architecture is rarely built on size. It is built on specificity. On knowing *where to push.* Leverage points offer that intelligence. They remind us that change does not require more force—but better design.

In high-performance cognition, the most powerful transformation often comes from the most overlooked details.

Let others chase discipline. You can chase design. Because once the system is aligned, effort becomes direction—not resistance.

Chapter 6
Cognitive Load Management – Stop Carrying What You Don't Need

The brain, for all its brilliance, was never built to function like a data server. It wasn't meant to juggle a dozen open loops, track endless to-do lists, or absorb the relentless flood of stimuli modern life insists on delivering. And yet, for many driven, high-performing individuals, that's precisely what it's being asked to do. The mind, once a tool for clarity and discernment, increasingly resembles a cluttered inbox—constantly pinging, barely triaged, always teetering on overload. So normalised has this state become that we've almost forgotten what cognitive ease feels like. The weight of constant input has settled into the background hum of daily existence. We accept mental fragmentation and chronic fatigue not as red flags, but as badges of modern ambition. They are no such thing. They are, rather starkly, evidence of a system buckling under poorly designed expectations.

Cognitive overload doesn't usually arrive with drama. It accumulates. Not through grand crises, but via the slow, relentless piling-on of micro-demands—each one small, seemingly inconsequential. A fleeting email. A half-formed decision. A note-to-self scribbled but never resolved. These fragments—unclosed loops—quietly chew away at our bandwidth. One by one, they don't seem much. Taken together, they degrade mental sharpness, dull emotional responsiveness, and corrode our capacity for long-range thought. It's not simply that they tire us out—they blur the edges of judgement.

What's needed here isn't another discussion about time management. That's the wrong lens. The real concern is bandwidth: not how much you can do in 24 hours, but how many *clean*, strategic decisions your mind can meaningfully support before its integrity starts to fray. Protecting that capacity isn't a matter of working harder—it's a matter of designing smarter.

Borrowing from systems theory, there's a principle known as load-bearing design: you engineer a structure to carry only the weight it's meant to. Any more, and failure becomes a matter of time. The brain demands a similar respect. And yet, rather than designing our mental processes to support clarity, most of us are trapped in a cycle of accumulating complexity. We add goals. Stack routines. Download tools. Integrate inputs. Rarely pausing to ask: *Is any of this essential?* In chasing marginal gains, we often neglect foundational coherence. What results is a mental ecosystem that may look efficient on paper—but collapses under ambiguity, freezes under stress, and reacts poorly to even modest internal friction.

Let's be clear: the issue isn't that cognitive load exists. Complexity is part of life, especially for those navigating demanding roles or responsibilities. The real problem is the absence of *intentional architecture*—a conscious approach to what earns a place in your headspace, what gets processed and resolved, and what should be discarded entirely. This chapter doesn't peddle surface-level hacks or inbox-zero dogma. Instead, it challenges us to rethink how we structure mental capacity in the first place.

And at the centre of it all, a truth that's both obvious and oddly overlooked: decision fatigue is not a moral failing. It's not a sign that you're undisciplined or weak-willed. It's a systems error. A failure of design.

Decision Fatigue Is a Design Flaw

It is now well-established in behavioural psychology that the human brain has a finite capacity for high-quality decision-making in a given timeframe. Pioneering research by Roy Baumeister and colleagues demonstrated that the act of making decisions—regardless of magnitude—draws on a common reservoir of cognitive energy. This is not a metaphor. MRI studies show that deliberative choices engage specific regions of the prefrontal cortex which, when overworked, reduce inhibitory control and bias individuals toward default behaviours. In other words: the more decisions you make, the less strategic and more reactive you become.

Modern life, however, is saturated with low-grade decisions. What to wear. Which email to respond to first. Whether to switch apps or keep writing. These decisions—each trivial in isolation—form an unrelenting sequence. The real cost is not the seconds they consume but the cognitive residue they leave behind. We are not tired from doing too much. We are tired from *deciding* about too much.

The high-functioning mind must be architected for *decision economy*. That does not mean outsourcing decisions wholesale. It means pre-designing certain categories of action so that willpower is reserved for contexts that *require* it. Consider Barack Obama's widely cited decision to reduce wardrobe variety while in office. The purpose wasn't fashion minimalism—it was cognitive conservation. By automating minor choices, he preserved clarity for the decisions that truly mattered. This same logic applies beyond politics: from morning routines to meal structures to digital workflows, the key is not rigidity but design. *Reduce discretionary choices where discretion is unnecessary. Reclaim mental focus for what matters most.*

This is not about living on autopilot. It's about reducing cognitive friction in service of deeper presence.

The Discipline of Letting Go

Mental clarity does not emerge from more effort. It emerges from *intelligent subtraction*. This is perhaps the most counterintuitive principle in modern cognitive design. Most people approach overwhelm by adding structure: more apps, more systems, more rules. But true cognitive relief rarely comes from addition. It comes from release.

Letting go—of commitments, narratives, unsolved problems, mental to-do lists—is not a spiritual suggestion. It is a cognitive imperative. Research in cognitive load theory, initially developed by John Sweller, demonstrates that working memory is tightly constrained in capacity. When overloaded, not only does task efficiency drop, but creative insight becomes virtually impossible. To think laterally, to synthesise ideas, or to generate novel strategies, the mind must first be unburdened.

The discipline of letting go, then, is not passive. It is an active practice of clearing bandwidth. This might involve closing unresolved cognitive loops (David Allen's GTD model), journaling for thought defragmentation, or conducting a weekly *cognitive audit*—a deliberate review of open tasks, unresolved tensions, and redundant inputs. The goal is simple: *unload what the brain is trying to track but doesn't need to.*

Importantly, letting go is not limited to tasks. It also applies to *mental attachments*: perfectionistic self-standards, unresolved interpersonal loops, and habitual worry patterns. These are cognitive parasites—processes that consume attention without producing value. The question is not "How do I do more?" but *"What am I still carrying that no longer deserves to be carried?"*

This chapter will offer frameworks for identifying cognitive excess and systematically pruning it—not to create emptiness, but to restore mental spaciousness. Because it is in the quiet space of a well-managed mind that clarity, innovation, and calm become accessible.

Designing Your Daily Bandwidth

Energy is not evenly distributed throughout the day. Neither is attention. And yet, most routines are structured as if we're operating at full bandwidth from morning to night. We aren't. Circadian rhythms, ultradian cycles, and environmental cues all modulate our cognitive capacity—hour by hour, sometimes minute by minute. The highest-functioning minds aren't those that work the longest. They're the ones that *match high-leverage tasks to high-bandwidth windows.*

Designing your daily bandwidth means aligning tasks to energy. It means scheduling analytical work when prefrontal activity is sharpest (typically mid-morning), placing creative thinking during alpha-wave phases (early morning or post-exercise), and allocating administrative or social tasks to natural cognitive troughs. It also means protecting your *recovery cycles*. Every 90 to 120 minutes, mental focus wanes—yet most people push through. The resulting fatigue is not just physical; it is strategic blindness.

This chapter will introduce practical methods for *energy mapping*, priority filtering, and recovery integration. It will show you how to build a rhythm—not a routine—for your mental work. Because cognitive performance is not about intensity. It is about *resonance*—the right task at the right energy state, supported by the right environmental conditions.

When bandwidth is protected and intentionality is restored, even complex mental work becomes fluid. You don't force focus. You *design for it.*

What This Chapter Offers

This chapter is not a productivity manual. It is a blueprint for *cognitive integrity*. You will learn how to:

Identify and eliminate micro-frictions that drain mental energy

Structure your environment to reduce unnecessary decisions

Practise targeted release of cognitive overload through intentional letting go

Build a bandwidth-aware daily schedule that optimises performance without burnout

Reframe cognitive clarity as a function of system design, not personal grit

You'll walk away with a more intelligent relationship to mental input, internal pressure, and decision quality. This is not about squeezing more from your mind. It's about *liberating it* from burdens it was never meant to carry.

Because true cognitive mastery is not achieved by carrying more. It's achieved by learning—systematically, precisely—what to carry, *and what to put down.*

The Mind as a Failing Hard Drive – How Unprocessed Data Reduces Mental Clarity

Modern minds are less plagued by ignorance than by excess. Information now arrives not in streams, but floods—unrelenting, unfiltered, and often uninvited. Emails, alerts, thoughts, conversations, ambient media, lingering memories—all entering the brain faster than it can organise or prioritise. *The result is not a smarter mind. It is a saturated one.*

Imagine a hard drive running close to full capacity. As available space diminishes, operations slow. Files take longer to retrieve. Corruption becomes more likely. System crashes are no longer anomalies but regular disruptions. This is not a metaphor. In cognitive science, the phenomenon of *mental fragmentation* shares striking parallels with failing storage architecture. The brain, too, has limits—not of knowledge, but of real-time processing. And like digital systems, it does not perform well under chronic load.

This subchapter explores a disquieting reality: *the human mind, left unchecked, begins to degrade under the cumulative weight of unprocessed inputs.* Clarity, creativity, and resilience are not merely traits. They are functions of cognitive hygiene. And hygiene begins with data management.

The Brain as an Active Processor—Not a Passive Vault

One of the most persistent myths about memory is that it acts like a file cabinet: we store information in a mental drawer and retrieve it when needed. But contemporary neuroscience dispels this illusion. The brain does not passively store—it *dynamically reconstructs.* Each act of remembering is a reprocessing of neural pathways, not a simple retrieval.

Which makes unprocessed information uniquely problematic. Unlike archived files on a hard drive, data left unresolved in the brain continues to draw cognitive resources. An unfinished task, an unanswered question, or a vague worry—all occupy what researchers call *attentional space.* The Zeigarnik effect, first identified in the 1920s, illustrates this well: people are more likely to recall incomplete tasks than completed ones. The implication is clear—mental resources are hijacked by the unresolved.

In other words, *the mind doesn't just remember data—it rehearses it.* And every unfinished mental thread becomes a hidden process running in the background, slowing down the entire system.

Mental Clarity Requires Regular Compression and Closure

One of the defining features of a high-functioning computer is its use of data compression and efficient file handling. Large, redundant, or outdated files are either archived, deleted, or systematically compressed. In mental terms, this is analogous to *meaning-making and closure.* Information, to be useful, must be integrated. That means contextualised, emotionally metabolised, and categorised—either for use or for dismissal.

Yet most modern minds do the opposite. We accumulate experiences without reflection. We consume information without synthesis. We store emotions without processing. *We open cognitive loops and rarely close them.* This is not a failure of willpower. It is a systemic absence of deliberate mental housekeeping.

Psychotherapists refer to this accumulation as "unfinished emotional business." Cognitive scientists might call it excess working memory load. Philosophers might describe it as spiritual noise. The label matters less than the function: *when we fail to metabolise what we take in, we begin to drown in our own cognitive backlog.*

Sleep plays a partial role here. During slow-wave sleep, the brain consolidates memories, prunes redundant synapses, and prepares neural real estate for new inputs. But sleep alone is insufficient. Without intentional waking practices—journaling, reflection, mental defragmentation—cognitive noise builds faster than the system can resolve it.

The Cost of Chronic Fragmentation: From Decision Paralysis to Existential Fatigue

The dangers of a saturated mind are not abstract. They manifest as reduced executive function: impaired decision-making, slower cognitive flexibility, heightened reactivity, and decreased creativity. More subtly, they manifest as *existential fatigue*—a state where the mind, bombarded with inputs, loses the signal entirely.

A person in chronic mental overload finds themselves unable to prioritise not just tasks, but values. They lose the ability to distinguish the urgent from the important, the relevant from the trivial, the factual from the emotional. Over time, this cognitive haze becomes the background condition of existence. *They are no longer thinking. They are merely sorting.*

The psychologist Barry Schwartz described this phenomenon in his work on "the paradox of choice." Too many options—whether products, paths, or even ideas—can induce paralysis rather than empowerment. But this insight doesn't only apply to shopping. It applies to how we manage our mental architecture. The unexamined mind doesn't just contain too much. It contains too much *undigested.*

Information Is Not Knowledge—And Emotion Is Not Processed by Time Alone

Another common assumption: that with time, the mind naturally organises itself. That information will "settle." That emotions will "fade." While partially true for trivial experiences, complex information and emotionally charged data do not self-organise. They require *cognitive engagement.*

Consider grief. It does not fade with time alone—it metabolises only through active integration. Similarly, professional feedback, relational conflicts, life-altering news—these inputs demand a processing mechanism. Left unaddressed, they become *ambient load*—emotions without anchors, ideas without frameworks, concerns without articulation.

This is why mental clarity is inseparable from reflection. Practices like journaling, dialogue, meditation, or structured review aren't aesthetic indulgences. They are *functional maintenance tasks*—ways of resolving incomplete mental loops before they calcify into background stress.

Cognitive Architecture: The Case for Intentional Input Design

One of the more overlooked strategies in cognitive optimisation is *input curation.* If unprocessed data is the root of mental overload, then reducing inflow is not laziness—it is intelligence. You do not solve a failing hard drive by cramming it with more files. You stop adding, and start curating.

This means evaluating not just quantity, but quality of inputs:

What kinds of information do you regularly consume?

Are your thought patterns primarily reactive or constructive?

Are you exposed to more signals than your reflection time can metabolise?

The minimalist mindset is not about austerity. It is about *bandwidth protection.* Strategic neglect is not an abdication of duty. It is a design principle. If clarity is the goal, *fewer high-quality inputs are more valuable than constant stimulation.*

From Data Saturation to Thoughtful Design: Practical Implications

The implications of viewing the mind as a failing hard drive are not merely diagnostic—they are architectural. To protect mental clarity, individuals must engage in systematic cognitive design. That includes:

Mental defragmentation routines – Daily or weekly practices to close open loops (e.g., the GTD "Mind Sweep," or structured journaling).

Emotion processing mechanisms – Contextualising difficult experiences through conversation, reflection, or therapy.

Information diet curation – Choosing inputs (books, conversations, platforms) that support clarity, not clutter.

Scheduled mental stillness – Building whitespace into the day, not as leisure, but as a necessary condition for signal detection.

Personal knowledge systems – Externalising key thoughts, insights, or frameworks into a second brain system (e.g., digital notes, Zettelkasten, or physical notebooks), *freeing up working memory.*

These are not productivity tactics. They are cognitive survival strategies. The mind, like any complex system, demands intervals of maintenance, decluttering, and architecture review. Without them, even the most intelligent individual becomes a victim of their own unprocessed mind.

Final Thought: Don't Optimise Your Capacity. Reclaim Your Clarity.

The modern mind doesn't need to hold more. It needs to hold less, *better.* The myth of infinite mental capacity must give way to the discipline of thoughtful processing. Because no matter how ambitious your goals, no matter how rich your knowledge—*you cannot think clearly in a system overrun by cognitive debris.*

Mental clarity is not a luxury. It is the precondition for wisdom. And wisdom begins when we stop carrying what we can't process—and start choosing what is truly worth storing.

Decision Fatigue is a Design Flaw – Explains how to reclaim energy through simplified decisions

There is a hidden tax on our mental lives—one paid not in currency, but in clarity. It's deducted from our best hours, often without consent, and leaves behind a peculiar exhaustion: not physical, not emotional, but decisional. That foggy mental depletion we feel after a morning of small choices—replying to emails, choosing what to wear, responding to notifications—is not incidental. It's a predictable outcome of a poorly engineered cognitive environment. *Decision fatigue is not a personal failure. It is a design flaw.* And unless we address it systemically, it erodes not only our efficiency, but our judgment, discipline, and ultimately, our self-trust.

The term "decision fatigue" entered public consciousness largely through the work of social psychologist Roy Baumeister, who demonstrated that human decision-making capacity is a finite resource. The more decisions one makes throughout the day, the more one's cognitive function deteriorates—particularly in terms of willpower and complex reasoning. But the deeper insight is this: *not all decisions are worth the cognitive cost they extract.* In fact, most aren't. The challenge is not simply to make better decisions. It is to reduce the number of decisions that require conscious effort in the first place.

The False Virtue of Endless Optionality

In modern culture, optionality is often mistaken for freedom. More choices, we're told, mean more autonomy, more agency, more fulfilment. Yet evidence from behavioural economics and cognitive psychology points in the opposite direction. The more options we face, the more energy we expend navigating them—and the less satisfied we become with whatever choice we ultimately make.

Barry Schwartz, in his foundational book *The Paradox of Choice*, argues that an overabundance of choice leads to analysis paralysis and post-decision regret. Whether comparing mobile phone plans or deliberating over life goals, the cognitive load created by optionality often exceeds our available bandwidth. *We are overwhelmed not by the magnitude of our challenges, but by the granularity of our micro-decisions.*

And crucially, not all choices deserve equal footing. The decision of whether to have oatmeal or eggs for breakfast should not demand the same evaluative resources as a career shift or ethical dilemma. Yet in the absence of structural design, the mind treats them with similarly exhaustive mechanisms.

Decision Quality Depends on Decision Architecture

Good decisions are not just the result of intelligence or experience. They emerge from systems—mental, behavioural, and environmental—that *prioritise decision energy for what matters most.* This is the essence of decision architecture: constructing a cognitive landscape that pre-decides the trivial, so that attention and deliberation can be preserved for the meaningful.

Steve Jobs famously wore the same black turtleneck and jeans every day. Barack Obama limited his wardrobe to blue or grey suits. These were not affectations of eccentricity. They were acts of *cognitive conservation.* In positions of high responsibility, where strategic decisions must be made under pressure, even minimal friction in morning routines is a tax too costly to justify.

For professionals managing high cognitive loads, *routine is not a restriction—it is a protective mechanism.* The disciplined application of structure reduces decision clutter, freeing attention for what cannot be systematised.

The Energy Cost of Frictionless Environments

Paradoxically, many modern tools designed to simplify life actually exacerbate decision fatigue. Consider the smartphone: it centralises communication, entertainment, scheduling, and productivity. But in doing so, it invites hundreds of micro-decisions per day—most of them trivial, none without cost. Should I respond to this message now? Should I read this news alert? Should I check my social media feed? Each swipe, each buzz, each notification is a fork in the cognitive road. And while any one decision seems negligible, their cumulative toll is substantial.

Cognitive scientist Daniel Levitin notes that "the brain's attentional system is configured to seek novelty." But in the absence of constraint, this feature becomes a liability. Constant digital stimuli hijack attention and fragment our decision-making capacity into shards—each too dull to penetrate anything deeply.

The solution is not withdrawal from technology. It is *deliberate constraint.* Simplifying digital environments—removing unnecessary apps, curating notification settings, batching communications—are acts of cognitive reclamation. They are the equivalent of installing filters on a firehose.

The Three Categories of Decisions—and Why Most Shouldn't Be Made

Not all decisions are created equal. For the purpose of mental design, we can group them into three broad types:

Non-strategic, repetitive decisions – These include what to eat, what to wear, when to work out. They carry low stakes but occur frequently. These should be automated through rules, defaults, or routines.

Mid-level logistical decisions – These involve scheduling, delegating, or planning. They require contextual judgment but not deep creativity. These should be *batched*, deferred, or made within predefined frameworks.

High-leverage, identity-shaping decisions – These involve values, commitments, and strategy. They deserve unfragmented attention and fresh cognitive bandwidth.

The tragedy is that most people spend the best hours of their day—their peak cognitive window—on Category 1 and 2 decisions, leaving Category 3 either rushed or postponed indefinitely. *This is not a time-management problem. It is an architectural flaw.*

The Ritual of Pre-Deciding

One of the most powerful antidotes to decision fatigue is the *ritual of pre-deciding*. Pre-deciding means choosing in advance what your defaults will be, so that in moments of fatigue, stress, or distraction, your behaviour still aligns with your priorities.

Examples of pre-deciding include:

Setting standard meal plans for weekdays

Creating uniform work schedules with fixed focus blocks

Establishing personal policies ("I don't check email before 10am" or "I don't accept meetings on Fridays")

Using templates for common responses or decisions

The aim is to *front-load your cognition*—to do the strategic thinking once, then let execution follow with minimal re-deliberation. This mirrors the concept of mental automation found in behavioural psychology, which suggests that willpower is not as effective as structure in maintaining behavioural integrity over time.

Choice Simplification Is Not Anti-Ambition

A common resistance to decision simplification is the fear that it may stifle spontaneity or reduce the richness of life. But this assumes that all choice is equally valuable. It isn't.

Simplifying low-value decisions doesn't impoverish your experience. It *protects* the capacity to fully inhabit the high-value ones. Just as a writer protects creative mornings by eliminating email during those hours, or a surgeon relies on protocols to preserve attention for complications, intelligent constraint is not a retreat—it is an investment.

As the philosopher Alain de Botton puts it: "The wisdom of life consists in the elimination of non-essentials." Simplicity is not a virtue in itself—it is a means to clarity. And clarity, in decision-making, is the highest form of cognitive power.

The Ethics of Decision-Making in Organisational Design

While much of this chapter addresses individual practice, the design flaw of decision fatigue also manifests systemically in organisations. Poorly designed workflows, unclear responsibilities, and lack of standard operating procedures create cognitive drag that compounds across teams. Employees burn through mental energy on decisions they shouldn't have to make.

Progressive organisations are now applying behavioural insights to decision design. This includes:

Clarifying roles to reduce decision overlap

Codifying team processes to reduce friction

Reducing tool sprawl and streamlining communication channels

Using checklists to standardise routine judgments

By *removing unnecessary choice*, organisations free up their most valuable asset: focused human attention.

Closing Loops, Not Just Opening Choices

There is something profoundly liberating about designing a day that *protects you from unnecessary decisions*. It creates a kind of psychological spaciousness—room for deep thought, creative insight, and responsive leadership. More importantly, it signals an understanding that *clarity is not a by-product of energy—it is a prerequisite for wise action.*

Decision fatigue will always exist in some form. But it need not define our cognitive landscape. When we accept that *not every decision is worth our attention*, we begin to reclaim the architecture of our lives. We choose not just what to do—but what deserves deliberation at all.

The Discipline of Letting Go – Reveals how release boosts creativity and clarity

If high performance demands intense focus, sustained clarity, and creative problem-solving, then *what we let go of* matters just as much—if not more—than what we hold on to. Yet in a culture that romanticises accumulation—of achievements, responsibilities, ideas, commitments—the act of relinquishment is often seen as weakness or failure. This is a costly misreading. Letting go is not an abdication of control. It is a strategic discipline: one that clears cognitive space, restores perceptual accuracy, and unlocks mental resources previously imprisoned by noise. *Letting go is not giving up. It is getting out of your own way.*

The human mind is not infinitely elastic. It cannot endlessly stretch to accommodate every task, thought, grudge, regret, or plan. Attention is finite. Working memory is narrow. Creative bandwidth is constrained. Much like a physical space, the mind becomes unusable when it is overfilled. *Mental clarity is not the product of adding more tools or tactics. It is the result of subtracting what obstructs coherence.* And it is here—at the nexus of restraint and liberation—that the discipline of letting go reveals its transformational power.

The Myth of Mental Hoarding

There's a silent cost to cognitive clutter. Old ideas we no longer believe. Emotional debts we've already paid. Projects we're no longer excited by. Unfinished ambitions we feel vaguely ashamed for abandoning. All of these linger in the background like unclosed tabs in a browser, draining processing power, slowing performance, and eroding focus. This phenomenon has been well-documented in neuroscience: the *Zeigarnik Effect* suggests that uncompleted mental loops tend to preoccupy the mind disproportionately. Unless consciously closed or released, they consume attention without delivering value.

Letting go in this context does not mean erasing memory or abandoning responsibility. It means *declaring cognitive bankruptcy on ideas, expectations, and tensions that are no longer serving your current mental economy*. Without this discipline, the mind becomes a museum of half-lived intentions—well-lit, meticulously catalogued, and largely useless.

Creativity Is Subtractive Before It Is Generative

Most creative blockages are not due to a lack of ideas. They are the result of interference. Overcommitted schedules. Outdated frameworks. Excessive comparison. Internal noise that drowns signal. The sculptor Michelangelo reportedly said he carved the statue of David by removing everything that was not David. While perhaps apocryphal, the point is instructive: *creative clarity emerges not from piling on more material, but from refining focus through intentional removal.*

Cognitive science supports this claim. Studies in the field of *working memory*—the short-term mental workspace where complex thinking happens—show that this space is sharply limited. Estimates suggest we can actively manage between four and seven independent pieces of information at once. This constraint means that *every irrelevant mental object we carry—resentment, distraction, stale assumptions—competes with potentially useful insight for attention.*

Letting go is therefore not a soft, meditative luxury. It is a functional necessity. In design, in writing, in leadership, the act of subtraction—of deliberately cutting what no longer fits the intent—is what enables elegance, precision, and coherence.

The Emotional Architecture of Holding On

But if letting go is so beneficial, why do we resist it? Because psychologically, holding on serves an illusion of security. We cling to relationships that drain us, narratives that limit us, and expectations that exhaust us, not because they serve us, but because they are *familiar.* The cognitive bias known as the *endowment effect*—our tendency to overvalue what we already possess—compounds this inertia. The longer we carry a belief or identity, the harder it is to discard it, even in the face of contrary evidence.

This emotional entanglement becomes most evident in identity-congruent habits. For example, the entrepreneur who continues pushing a failing product not because of market data but because their self-worth is fused with the original idea. Or the professional who refuses to abandon a prestigious role despite its mental toll, because doing so would feel like losing status. Letting go, in these cases, requires confronting discomfort—not just of change, but of who we are without the thing we release.

The deeper insight here is that *clarity requires courage.* Not the courage to add more, but the courage to release that which no longer serves our highest aim. In the words of Joseph Campbell: "We must be willing to let go of the life we planned so as to have the life that is waiting for us." Applied pragmatically, this translates to a constant reevaluation: not of whether we're winning, but whether we're still playing the right game.

The Neurocognitive Effects of Releasing Control

Neurologically, the benefits of letting go extend beyond metaphor. Mindfulness research consistently shows that practices focused on release—such as breathwork, focused attention meditation, or cognitive defusion techniques—are correlated with improved working memory, reduced stress reactivity, and heightened creative insight.

One landmark study published in *Cognitive, Affective, & Behavioral Neuroscience* found that participants who underwent mindfulness training were significantly better at redirecting attention from irrelevant stimuli. Their brains exhibited *decreased default mode network (DMN) activation*, which is associated with rumination and self-referential thought. In essence, *letting go reduced mental noise and made room for more deliberate cognition.*

Moreover, letting go of tightly held assumptions or goals can increase *cognitive flexibility*, a key predictor of problem-solving performance. When individuals are less psychologically attached to a particular solution or outcome, they are more likely to generate novel alternatives. In complex environments, this kind of mental elasticity is not just advantageous—it is vital.

Applied Strategies for Intentional Release

The question is no longer *should* we let go, but *how* do we do it deliberately? The following strategies, while deceptively simple, are powerful when applied consistently:

Scheduled Renunciation – Just as one might review finances or clean out physical spaces, set regular intervals to audit mental commitments: projects, goals, beliefs. Ask: *Does this still align with who I am becoming?*

Constraint-Based Design – Intentionally set limits—not just on time or input, but on the number of active goals or commitments allowed at once. Scarcity breeds selectivity, and selectivity protects clarity.

Cognitive Closure Rituals – Create mechanisms to *close open loops* mentally. This could include journaling sessions to reflect and release unresolved thoughts, or simple statements like "I am choosing to move forward without this."

Emotional Reframing – Practice detaching identity from outcomes. The goal is to internalise the idea that *ending something does not mean you failed at it; it means you are optimising for alignment rather than inertia.*

Redefining Productivity – Shift metrics of success from accumulation (tasks completed, items acquired) to coherence (does what I'm doing serve my current values?). This shift naturally deprioritises low-value efforts.

Cultural Tension: The Bias Toward Grit

Modern productivity culture often promotes persistence at all costs. "Don't quit." "Push through." "Finish what you start." While there is value in perseverance, this narrative becomes dangerous when it overrides discernment. Sometimes, letting go is not quitting—it is *graduating.* It is the mature decision to stop investing in something just because of how much time or ego you've already spent on it.

There is a subtle but crucial distinction here: *grit without clarity becomes masochism.* Staying the course is admirable only when the course still leads somewhere worth going. Otherwise, discipline becomes denial—of better options, of truer values, of evolving insight.

Strategic Release as a Cognitive Asset

Ultimately, the discipline of letting go should be seen not as a spiritual or emotional indulgence, but as a cognitive strategy. It is the mind's way of pruning its mental architecture to retain only what supports clarity, creativity, and coherence.

Just as elite athletes taper training to preserve energy for competition, high-functioning thinkers must periodically *shed ideas, assumptions, and burdens* to preserve focus for what actually matters.

Letting go, then, is not about detachment for its own sake—it is about *returning to signal.* It is about clearing the fog so that you can once again see the terrain of your own mind—and move through it with precision.

Designing Your Daily Bandwidth – Helps build daily routines that match energy cycles

Human productivity is not flat. It is not consistent from hour to hour, nor is it immune to fluctuation from sleep, mood, food, or stress. And yet, we continue to build routines, schedules, and professional expectations on the faulty premise that all hours are created equal. They are not. *Some hours are deep, others are shallow. Some hours are strategic, others administrative. Some are best for synthesis, others for output.* The failure to design around this variability doesn't just waste time—it actively distorts focus, creativity, and wellbeing. To work against your energy is to pay a cognitive tax for your own misunderstanding.

In that context, daily bandwidth is not merely a question of time management. It is *bio-aligned design.* It is about orchestrating your day so that what you are doing *matches what you are capable of doing well* at that time. This is not a luxury for the ultra-optimised. For knowledge workers, creators, leaders—anyone whose work depends on clear thought and consistent execution—*matching task complexity to cognitive availability* is a non-negotiable edge.

Energy is a Rhythm, Not a Resource

We often speak of energy as if it were fuel: something to be topped up with coffee, depleted by work, or restored through rest. But biologically, energy behaves more like a rhythm than a tank. It rises and falls in *predictable ultradian cycles*—typically 90–120 minute waves in which cognitive performance waxes, peaks, and then wanes. Ignore these rhythms, and you may power through with effort, but at the cost of clarity and later fatigue. Align with them, and you'll find surprising ease, creativity, and retention.

Numerous studies in chronobiology and occupational psychology support this. Anders Ericsson's famous research on elite performers showed that top violinists, athletes, and chess players all worked in 90-minute sessions, followed by deliberate rest. They intuitively respected the cadence of effort and recovery. Yet in modern work culture, this biological architecture is often ignored. The result is not only burnout, but blunt thinking—people working longer but solving less.

Designing daily bandwidth is, at its core, about respecting your brain's architecture more than your calendar's demands.

The Myth of Uniform Availability

One of the most pervasive illusions in time management is that every hour is fungible. That a task postponed to the afternoon is equivalent to doing it first thing. But in reality, *when you do something often matters more than how long it takes you to do it.* A two-hour task tackled during your cognitive prime may only require 45 minutes. The same task, attempted at 3:30pm after a heavy lunch and a series of meetings, might take twice as long with half the clarity.

This misalignment is particularly acute for high-stakes thinking: strategic planning, writing, coding, problem-solving. These tasks require what Cal Newport calls *deep work*—a state of distraction-free focus that only a few hours of the day can reliably support. Misplacing these tasks—slotting them into fragmented, low-energy blocks—is not just inefficient. It's a design flaw.

To correct it, you must first identify your *chronotype*—the pattern by which your alertness rises and falls. Morning people (larks) hit their stride early; night owls peak in the afternoon or evening. Most adults fall somewhere in between. The aim is not to force yourself into a single ideal template, but to *observe and then defend your peaks.* Anchor your cognitively intensive work to these natural highs, and protect them from unnecessary meetings, shallow emails, or errands that can be offloaded to your mental valleys.

Energy Budgeting Over Time Blocking

Traditional productivity systems rely heavily on time blocking: mapping out tasks in hourly segments. But what these systems often fail to accommodate is the mismatch between the cognitive demand of a task and the available bandwidth at that time. Energy budgeting offers a corrective.

Rather than asking, *Do I have time for this?*, a better question is: *Do I have the right kind of energy for this?* Categorise tasks not just by priority or urgency, but by *mental load*—strategic (high-focus), procedural (medium-focus), and automatic (low-focus). Then distribute them across your day accordingly.

This approach is especially valuable in professional environments where multitasking, context-switching, and "time famine" are chronic. By shifting focus from quantity of hours worked to *quality of energy invested*, you create conditions for better output with less cognitive residue.

Design as Energy Conservation

Cognitive load theory, drawn from educational psychology, teaches us that the brain can only handle a limited number of active elements before performance degrades. In practical terms, this means that *mental overhead—decision-making, switching contexts, managing unfinished loops—drains energy disproportionately.* Effective daily design, then, becomes a question of minimising friction:

Reduce choices: Pre-decide meals, clothing, and routines where creativity is not required.

Batch tasks: Group similar energy-level activities to avoid cognitive switching costs.

Automate repetition: Use systems or software to handle recurring tasks (email filters, calendar rules).

Eliminate ambiguity: Create checklists or protocols for complex but frequent tasks.

None of these measures are revolutionary. But their compound effect is dramatic: *they preserve your bandwidth for the work that only your mind can do.* That preservation is not indulgence—it's stewardship.

Real-World Application: High-Performance Routines

Elite performers across disciplines—CEOs, athletes, academics—already practice bandwidth design, often without naming it as such. Consider Barack Obama, who famously wore only grey or blue suits during his presidency to reduce decision fatigue. Or Maya Angelou, who wrote from hotel rooms, removing herself from distractions. Or Jack Dorsey, who themed each day of the week at Twitter to avoid constantly re-evaluating priorities. These are not quirks. They are *architectural choices* made in service of conserving clarity.

The same principles apply at more modest scales. A software developer might reserve 9am–12pm for uninterrupted coding and refuse meetings during that window. A teacher might avoid grading papers late at night, recognising that analysis requires fresher attention. A writer might build their day around a two-hour window of flow and treat the rest as administrative terrain. The point is not uniformity—it's *intentional match.* The right task. The right time. The right energy.

Navigating Constraints: Adaptive Design

Of course, not everyone controls their calendar. Parents, shift workers, frontline professionals—many operate within externally imposed structures. But even here, design is possible. You may not control *when* you work, but you can often shape *how* you work within the available constraints.

For instance, if you know your afternoon slump hits at 2pm, schedule low-responsibility activities then, or use that time for physical movement. If your most creative ideas come after your evening walk, ensure a notebook or voice memo app is always within reach. *Design does not require perfection. It requires pattern recognition followed by better alignment.*

What's most important is resisting the myth that optimal performance comes from willpower alone. What matters more is *environmental compatibility*. Most burnout does not come from too much work. It comes from working badly—fighting your own biology, ignoring your natural rhythms, and forcing output during your least available hours.

Closing Loops and Cognitive Hygiene

Designing daily bandwidth also includes recovery and loop closure. Every decision, message, or task left unfinished consumes background energy. Ending the day with an intentional cognitive shutdown—reviewing tasks, making a brief plan for tomorrow, and mentally closing work mode—signals the brain that it can *stop holding the thread.*

This practice is supported by research from organisational psychologist Dr Sabine Sonnentag, whose work shows that detachment from work during off-hours is a key predictor of long-term performance and wellbeing. Bandwidth, then, is not just created by good mornings. It is preserved by good endings.

Final Reflection

To design your day is to *respect the architecture of your own attention.* It is not about squeezing more into your schedule. It is about aligning action with capacity, so that your effort is not only productive but sustainable. It is not how many hours you work, but how well those hours reflect your available clarity, energy, and intent.

Ultimately, the discipline of bandwidth design is not about productivity in the narrow sense. It is about *protecting your ability to think clearly, act decisively, and recover fully*. It is about building a life that functions at your mental prime, more often than by accident. The reward is not just more output. It is the return of your attention to what deserves it most.

Chapter 7
Values as Beams – The Hidden Framework of Meaning

Some structures announce themselves with confidence—cathedrals, bridges, towers that reach skyward as if built to be admired. But others, the most critical ones, stay hidden. In architecture, it's the unseen steel beams tucked behind plasterboard that quietly shoulder the load, keeping the entire edifice upright. You don't notice them until they fail. Psychological life works much the same way. Beneath our routines, our choices, even our resilience under duress, lies a subtler scaffolding: our values. These are not ornamental. They are structural. Strip them away—or fail to set them properly—and what looked stable on the surface begins to crack under pressure.

This chapter shifts focus with intent. We step away from the mechanics of behaviour and turn towards something more elemental: the question of meaning. Not "What are you doing?"—that's a surface-level inquiry—but "Why are you doing it?" And more precisely: "According to which internal architecture?" Here we are not concerned with actions in isolation, but with the deep-running tensions—or harmonies—between one's behaviour and their chosen (or unchosen) value system. Because, and this must be said plainly, the absence of clear, deliberately chosen values isn't just a missed opportunity for insight. It is a silent structural flaw—one that only reveals itself under load.

In a world increasingly obsessed with optimisation, we've become adept at tweaking the visible layers: refining habits, gamifying productivity, even "hacking" our own psychology. And yet, astonishingly few people pause to ask whether all that fine-tuning is happening atop a foundation they actually believe in. The result is a peculiar kind of dissonance: people who are highly disciplined, yet directionless. Efficient, yet existentially adrift. Their systems work—but for what? The engine hums, but it isn't clear where the vehicle is going, or why.

That dissonance is not minor—it is the quiet drag on our vitality, the subtle friction that saps joy from achievement. And it's entirely avoidable, provided we're willing to dig deeper. This chapter is an invitation to do just that: to uncover, clarify, and consciously select the values that will form your internal load-bearing framework. Not abstract ideals scribbled on a workshop flipchart, but lived principles—tested, aligned, and resilient enough to hold weight over time.

Here, values are not treated as slogans or aspirations. They are treated as engineering elements. They give shape and coherence to one's mental structure, offering both orientation in uncertainty and strength in adversity. When your behaviour is tethered to these deeper elements, consistency no longer requires force. It becomes structural integrity.

And so, what follows is not a sentimental appeal to "live your truth," nor a philosophical musing on ethics for its own sake. It's a practical inquiry into stability. Because when values are aligned and embedded, they act not only as compass but as ballast. They steady the mind, clarify priorities, and absorb shock when life tests the load.

Without them, one may build fast—but rarely will it last.

Meaning Is Not a Luxury—It Is Infrastructure

Many associate values with vague platitudes: honesty, kindness, hard work. The word has been so diluted in public discourse that its relevance often feels rhetorical rather than structural. But to dismiss values as idealistic is to fundamentally misunderstand how meaning is constructed in the human mind. *Values are not beliefs—they are priorities.* And priorities shape perception. They tell us what to care about, what to ignore, what to fight for, and what to release. Without them, decision-making becomes reactive, identity becomes diffuse, and behaviour becomes noisy.

The emerging fields of existential psychology and meaning-centred therapy (notably the work of Viktor Frankl, Paul Wong, and Irvin Yalom) underscore this point: individuals who experience their lives as meaningful are not necessarily those with the most comfort or success, but those with a coherent alignment between what they do and what they believe matters. In short, meaning is not something we find—it is something we *frame*. And values are the framing tools.

To design a life without values is like building a bridge without load distribution. It may look functional—until too much weight is applied.

Designing a Meaning-Centric Life

The modern professional is over-informed but under-aligned. Productivity systems, self-help doctrines, and career playbooks flood us with strategies to do more, be more, respond faster. But rarely do these systems begin with the most basic question: *what matters enough to structure your life around?* Without that clarity, the pursuit of goals becomes erratic or externally driven—leaving people efficient, but not anchored.

This chapter introduces a rigorous, not romantic, approach to designing a meaning-centric life. It treats value selection as a form of psychological architecture: something to be drawn deliberately, reinforced structurally, and tested against real-world tension. You'll be invited not just to list your values, but to evaluate their integrity: *Are these values lived or merely stated? Do they hold under pressure, or do they collapse into convenience?*

A life designed around conscious values is not merely more principled. It is more *coherent.* Your habits become extensions of your priorities, your relationships reflect your internal architecture, and your energy is directed with greater fidelity.

When Values Conflict: Structural Cracks

But alignment is not always elegant. Sometimes the most instructive moments are not when values support one another—but when they compete. What happens when ambition clashes with integrity? When loyalty interferes with truth? When individual freedom comes at the cost of community responsibility? These moments are not philosophical riddles—they are lived tensions.

Structural engineers know that stress accumulates most intensely at points of intersection. The same applies in our lives: when competing values meet under pressure, *cracks form where design was assumed, but never verified.* This chapter provides readers with tools to identify these fault lines and navigate value conflict with clarity, not avoidance.

Drawing from decision science and moral psychology, we explore techniques such as *value hierarchy mapping*, reframing internal dissonance as a design signal rather than a failure, and learning to distinguish between core values and adopted ideals. The aim is not to eliminate conflict, but to ensure that *when trade-offs are made, they are made consciously, not unconsciously inherited from cultural or familial scripting.*

This is not just ethical hygiene—it's structural literacy.

Minimalist Values for Maximum Clarity

Just as minimalist architecture seeks structural elegance by reducing the unnecessary, the clearest lives often stem from *a small set of deeply integrated values*. Simplicity in values doesn't mean simplicity in thought—it means prioritisation. Many people fail not because they lack values, but because they are trying to live by too many, simultaneously and without hierarchy. The result is internal confusion masked as conscientiousness.

This chapter advocates for *selective clarity*: the intentional process of identifying *no more than three to five core values*, and then designing daily choices, long-term goals, and social boundaries around them. These values become the equivalent of architectural beams: few, but load-bearing. Chosen correctly, they provide guidance in ambiguity, resolve in crisis, and consistency across context.

To illustrate this, we examine the lives of thinkers and leaders who built their work around minimalist but powerful value frameworks. From the principled economy of Angela Merkel's leadership, to the clarity-driven decision-making of Stoic philosophers, to the austere ethical rigour in the writings of Simone Weil—these figures show that intellectual and moral strength is not found in complexity, but in *coherence.*

Why This Chapter Matters Now

This chapter is particularly timely. We live in an era saturated by choice and paralysed by comparison. The global shift toward remote work, the erosion of traditional career scripts, and the decentralisation of institutions have handed individuals more autonomy than ever before. But autonomy without internal structure quickly devolves into noise. As sociologist Zygmunt Bauman warned, the freedom to choose without guidance creates not liberation, but anxiety.

In this landscape, values are not relics of moral tradition. *They are structural technologies for navigating ambiguity.* They offer a way to build psychological stability in environments where external consistency can no longer be relied upon. Whether you are designing a career, a company, or simply your next month, values act as orientation points that stabilise your internal compass.

You do not need a map if you have a true north.

What You Will Gain

By the end of this chapter, you will have:

A clear definition of what values are—not as abstract ideals, but as concrete design tools

A method for identifying and selecting your core values with intellectual and emotional rigour

A strategy for navigating value conflict without collapse or paralysis

A framework for minimalist value alignment that simplifies your decisions, sharpens your focus, and strengthens your behavioural architecture

More importantly, you will begin to *experience your values not as aspirational statements, but as structural realities*. They will shape not just what you believe, but how you design your time, your habits, and your identity.

This chapter is not about becoming virtuous. It is about becoming *structurally sound.*

From Performance Values to Living Values

Distinguishing between internalised principles and performative posturing

There's a peculiar kind of dissonance in modern life that goes unnoticed until the pressures of contradiction push it to the surface: people espouse values they do not live. The dissonance isn't always malicious or even conscious. It's often the by-product of well-intentioned social adaptation—a desire to belong, to impress, to affirm that one is "on the right side" of an issue. But behind this adaptation lies a deeper question of structural integrity: *Are your values truly your own—or are they merely behavioural performances that win applause but erode coherence?*

This subchapter dissects one of the most subtle yet critical tensions in contemporary behavioural architecture: the divide between **performance values** and **living values**. One functions as social theatre. The other operates as psychological scaffolding. The difference between the two is not semantic—it is existential. Living according to values you haven't internalised is like building a house on rented land. Eventually, you'll be evicted by inconsistency.

The growing sophistication of personal branding, social media signalling, and ideological affiliation has blurred the boundary between moral posturing and moral embodiment. But if we are to design a life that holds under pressure—a core premise of this book—then distinguishing between values we *broadcast* and those we *embody* is not optional. It is structural maintenance.

The Danger of Performative Coherence

Performance values arise from the outside in. They are constructed in reaction to social context. Whether driven by reputation management, ideological group-think, or professional incentive, they are curated to serve an external narrative—*this is who I want you to think I am.* There is nothing inherently unethical about this. All humans are, to some extent, performative. But the problem arises when the performance *replaces* the practice.

The danger is twofold. First, performative alignment creates a brittle self-concept. Because it's anchored to audience approval, it is vulnerable to context collapse. What happens when you're no longer rewarded for expressing a particular value? Do you still live it? If not, the value was never structural—it was *ornamental.* Second, the over-adoption of performance values creates cognitive congestion. When your stated identity is inflated with values that don't guide your actual choices, internal conflict becomes inevitable. This is not failure—it is misalignment.

The phenomenon is not merely cultural or social; it has neuropsychological correlates. Studies in cognitive dissonance (Festinger, 1957) and moral licensing (Monin & Miller, 2001) show that individuals who publicly commit to virtuous values often reduce their actual investment in those values. *The expression of the value is mistaken for the execution of it.* A person who claims to value honesty but routinely avoids difficult conversations isn't necessarily a hypocrite—they may simply never have interrogated whether that value was ever truly integrated.

The Anatomy of a Living Value

Living values operate from the inside out. They are not statements—they are constraints. They limit your options, not expand your applause. Unlike performance values, living values impose *real behavioural cost.* They shape decisions even when no one is watching. They are often inconvenient. Sometimes they are painful. But because they are *structural,* they produce coherence, not contradiction.

Living values can be identified by their *traceability.* That is: can you point to concrete, consistent behaviours that reflect the value in action? For instance, someone who claims to value sustainability but makes no meaningful change in their consumption or energy use likely holds a performance value. But the individual who quietly reconfigures their purchasing habits, redesigns their commute, and accepts limitations to align with environmental responsibility—*without broadcasting it*—is likely embodying a living value. The difference lies not in the rhetoric, but in the rigour.

Values, to qualify as *living*, must meet at least three criteria:

Behavioural Consistency: The value is reflected across multiple areas of life, even when inconvenient or invisible.

Emotional Resonance: The value evokes personal meaning or psychological necessity—not just ideological alignment.

Cognitive Integration: The value influences decisions, not just discussions.

The philosopher Charles Taylor writes that a moral framework is not a set of abstract commitments but a *background that makes sense of experience*. Living values function precisely in this way. They give your decisions texture, your conflicts direction, and your compromises clarity. They do not float above life—they hold it together.

Institutionalised Performance: A Broader Perspective

This tension between living and performance values is not limited to individuals. It is institutional. From corporations that trumpet diversity without structural inclusion, to educational systems that profess critical thinking while rewarding conformity, organisations frequently confuse *stated values* with *operational ones*.

This misalignment is not accidental—it is systemic. Organisations are rewarded for coherence in communication, not coherence in culture. The result is a proliferation of performative codes of ethics, mission statements, and public commitments that are not reflected in internal policy or decision-making structure. The term "values-washing" has emerged in business ethics circles to describe this phenomenon: *the adoption of moral branding without moral infrastructure*.

For individuals navigating such systems, the risk is internalising the performance without building the architecture. That is: mistaking *exposure to value discourse* for *actual value development.* Working for a purpose-driven organisation does not automatically confer purpose. Living in a value-saturated culture does not mean you've built value alignment. *The signal is not the structure.*

Transitioning from Performance to Living

So how do you shift? What does it take to move from performance values—those that reflect external expectation—to living values, which reinforce internal coherence?

The transition begins with subtraction. Identify values you claim, but which do not meaningfully shape your decisions. This is not a moral failure; it is architectural refinement. Many individuals discover that they have adopted values aspirationally—as ideals to be admired, rather than integrated. The key is not to discard these values wholesale, but to question their legitimacy: *Do I actually live this, or do I just like the idea of living it?*

Next comes reinforcement. Choose a small number—three to five—of values that feel both meaningful and behavioural. Then, construct daily and weekly commitments around them. If you value curiosity, where in your schedule is time set aside for open-ended exploration? If you value compassion, how often do you initiate conversations with people you disagree with? The point is not to moralise your behaviour—it is to *ground your values in visible routines.*

Lastly, reflect in conflict. The most revealing test of a value is not whether you celebrate it, but whether you protect it *when it costs you.* Living values will force you to say no to opportunity, end relationships, or resist conformity. These moments are not regrettable—they are *proof of structure.*

Ethical Implications: Integrity vs. Impression

There's an ethical cost to performance values that extends beyond personal dissonance. In social spaces—especially online—the proliferation of performative virtue creates *a distorted moral ecology.* It rewards appearance over alignment, statement over sacrifice. And in doing so, it undermines trust in the very values it claims to elevate.

When everyone claims to value everything, values become noise.

To restore moral clarity—whether in institutions, teams, or individual lives—requires elevating *the integrity of quiet action over the currency of public affirmation.* This is not a call for stoicism or secrecy. It is a call for *structural humility*: the ability to build one's life around values that are lived more than they are labelled.

Final Thought: A Blueprint Worth Building

From a behavioural engineering perspective, internalised values are not just ethical—*they are efficient.* They reduce decision fatigue, clarify boundaries, and increase psychological resilience. When you know what you won't compromise, many choices make themselves.

But this efficiency is only unlocked when the values are *real.* Not rehearsed. Not inherited. Not performative. Real.

And real values don't need to be shouted to be strong. Like structural beams, their purpose is not to be seen. *It is to hold the weight of your life without buckling under pressure.*

Designing a Meaning-Centric Life Teaching Purpose-Based Mental Design

Modern life presents a paradox. Never before have individuals had more access to choice, yet never have so many reported feeling lost within it. We can optimise our calendars, measure our biometrics, and micro-adjust our productivity routines. But efficiency without direction is simply acceleration into meaninglessness. What we lack is not data or even motivation. What we lack is *coherence.* We are building faster than we are designing. And what's missing from the design is not complexity, but purpose.

This subchapter addresses a foundational error in how modern life is often architected: *we design for output without first designing for meaning.* Most people attempt to solve existential dissatisfaction with tactical tools—more goals, better habits, clearer priorities. But tactics are downstream from values. Without an intentional centre of gravity, the system of one's life becomes structurally unanchored. It may function, but it will not hold.

To live a meaning-centric life is to reverse-engineer the architecture of your mind. It is to start not with what you can do, but with *why doing matters to you in the first place.* This is not philosophical indulgence—it is strategic necessity.

The Cost of Value-Agnostic Design

The dominant mode of self-development today is performative optimisation. It is driven by metrics, moulded by trends, and validated through comparison. It rewards visibility over substance, achievement over alignment. And it frequently leads to exhaustion disguised as ambition.

The psychologist Viktor Frankl, who developed logotherapy based on his experience surviving Nazi concentration camps, argued that "life is never made unbearable by circumstances, but only by lack of meaning and purpose." Yet meaning is not found—it is *constructed*, through conscious alignment between one's values and one's behaviours.

When meaning is not explicitly designed into one's life structure, life becomes defined by reactive loops. People chase what others pursue, defend what they've never questioned, and perform success without experiencing significance. *The danger is not failure—it is unexamined momentum.*

Mental Architecture Begins with Structural Purpose

Designing a meaning-centric life requires a fundamental reorientation: rather than pursuing tasks and hoping meaning will emerge from achievement, we must begin with the premise that *purpose is a prerequisite to sustainable action.* Without it, effort collapses into entropy.

The analogy here is architectural. Just as a building requires weight-bearing beams to withstand time, stress, and expansion, so too does a mind require structural values to endure complexity, failure, and contradiction. These values are not goals. They are not strategies. They are *anchors*—chosen commitments that define what is non-negotiable in how you live, not just what you do.

In practice, this means interrogating your current commitments through a value lens. Ask not only what fills your calendar, but what fills your character. Where in your daily, weekly, or annual rhythm do you see evidence of your deepest commitments? Are they present, or are they aspirational but absent?

Designing for meaning begins with noticing what you are unintentionally building.

Purpose Is Not Passion—It Is Pattern

One of the most misleading tropes in modern discourse is that meaning arises from discovering a singular "passion." This is both reductionist and misleading. Passion is transient, often emotionally driven, and rarely capable of sustaining long-term effort. Purpose, by contrast, is durable. It is not discovered—it is *constructed,* out of pattern recognition across time.

Purpose emerges from the intersection of three elements: identity (who you are becoming), contribution (what you give), and coherence (how it fits together). When designing for meaning, the goal is not to find a singular pursuit that explains everything, but to *construct a system of living where your actions reinforce a coherent sense of why you matter.*

This involves mental design choices such as:

Choosing depth over breadth: Not doing more, but doing what aligns most

Prioritising principle over preference: Holding to integrity even when it costs

Accepting trade-offs consciously: Letting go of "everything" to do the *essential*

These are not productivity decisions. They are existential ones. And they are design decisions.

Realignment Requires Subtraction Before Addition

A meaningful life is often built less by adding than by subtracting. It's tempting to think we can find purpose by accumulating new inputs—more projects, new relationships, fresh pursuits. But if your internal architecture is cluttered with unexamined assumptions, social scripts, or identity debris, no addition will bring clarity. Meaning requires internal space.

One of the most underutilised tools in meaning-centric design is *ethical subtraction*. What roles, habits, or identities no longer serve your values? What inherited beliefs create internal contradiction? Many people carry psychological obligations that were never chosen—scripts from parents, cultures, institutions, or ideologies that no longer align.

Letting go of these is not a rejection of one's past. It is the *completion* of it. Only then can new structures be built that reflect present truth rather than inherited momentum.

Designing for meaning is as much about release as it is about construction.

Case Example: Alignment as Behavioural Consistency

Consider an executive who claims to value family, integrity, and creative freedom. On paper, these are admirable. But in practice, she works eighty-hour weeks, misses most of her children's milestones, withholds difficult feedback to avoid discomfort, and hasn't engaged in a creative project in five years.

Here, the dissonance is not between value and desire—it is between *stated values and lived patterns*. The resolution is not more ambition. It is realignment. Through purposeful design—restructuring time commitments, defining boundaries, and renegotiating her work identity—she can bring her life into alignment with what she claims to value. The effect is not only emotional clarity, but *structural coherence.*

Living meaningfully is not about grand gestures. It is about repeated congruence.

When Meaning Conflicts with Efficiency

There is a deeper tension that must be acknowledged: designing for meaning sometimes conflicts with conventional measures of efficiency. Slowing down to consider value alignment may reduce short-term output. Saying no to projects that violate core values might constrain growth. But the trade-off is *integrity*. And integrity, over time, is not only morally preferable—it is strategically more sustainable.

Living a meaning-centric life does not mean rejecting ambition. It means anchoring ambition in values that are resilient under pressure. That's not idealism—it is *systemic wisdom.*

Meaning-Centric Design Is Mental Engineering

To design a meaning-centric life is not to pursue abstract self-improvement. It is to build a system of mental structure where:

Your identity has depth because it is not reactive

Your habits have clarity because they are value-driven

Your time has structure because it reflects what matters

This is not a final state. It is an ongoing discipline. As life conditions change, meaning must be re-evaluated, not assumed. Design is iterative. But the more your system is built on explicit principles, the less you will need to rely on willpower to remain in alignment.

Ultimately, *a meaningful life is not something you find—it is something you are willing to build deliberately, defend consistently, and refine regularly.*

Final Insight: The Architecture of a Meaningful Mind

What distinguishes a meaningful life is not dramatic moments of purpose, but the *invisible scaffolding of aligned design.* Every calendar choice, every boundary honoured, every principle protected adds structural weight to the framework of identity. Over time, this design builds a life that feels less like it's being survived and more like it's being stewarded.

The central question is not "What should I do?"
It is "*What kind of system would make my values unavoidable?*"

That is the work of meaning-centric design. And it is not philosophical garnish. It is the foundation of resilience, clarity, and peace in an increasingly disorienting world.

When Values Conflict: Structural Cracks

Addressing Conflicting Values and Alignment Strategies

We tend to speak of values as if they are inherently harmonious—fixed moral anchors that guide our decisions with clarity and resolve. But in practice, personal values often collide in unpredictable and destabilising ways. The tension is not a sign of weak character; it's evidence of complexity. The more thoughtful and multidimensional a person becomes, the more likely they are to carry competing commitments that, while individually virtuous, pull them in divergent directions.

This is not merely an internal inconvenience. *Unresolved value conflict creates structural instability in identity.* People become exhausted not by the absence of values, but by the silent war between them. The individual who values both freedom and security may oscillate endlessly between autonomy and attachment. The professional who values excellence and wellbeing may find herself caught in cycles of overachievement followed by burnout. The conflict is not abstract—it is structural. And without conscious alignment, the friction becomes architecture: something that silently shapes every choice, every reaction, every form of avoidance.

This article examines the under-recognised phenomenon of *value conflict*—not as a psychological footnote, but as a primary source of incoherence in behaviour, identity, and life design. It also offers tools for resolving these conflicts through reflective design, alignment strategies, and a more nuanced understanding of integrity.

Value Conflict: Not a Flaw, But a Fracture Point

Most people assume that once they've "defined their values," the hard part is over. They expect clarity, coherence, perhaps even moral confidence. Instead, they are often met with contradiction. The value of independence clashes with the need for intimacy. The drive to lead can undermine the desire to serve. The pursuit of truth may conflict with loyalty to community.

This is not a rare dysfunction—it is a structural feature of mature minds. As moral psychologist Jonathan Haidt has shown, people don't operate with a single, unified value system. They juggle multiple moral matrices simultaneously, often inherited from different social contexts: family, education, religion, profession, culture. The result is a patchwork of overlapping priorities, many of which are incompatible in practice.

The mistake is assuming that personal integrity means rigidly honouring all values at all times. That is not integrity—it is naïveté. True integrity requires *the willingness to navigate value conflict with conscious trade-offs*, rather than unconscious repression.

The Hidden Cost of Unaddressed Value Clashes

Conflicting values, when ignored, create subtle forms of psychological wear-and-tear. The most immediate cost is decision fatigue. When values contradict and no hierarchy is established, each new choice feels like a referendum on identity. Even small decisions—like whether to take on a new project or take a day off—

become emotionally charged, because they represent a tug-of-war between loyalty and rest, ambition and preservation.

But the deeper cost is internal fragmentation. The self begins to split—not in a clinical sense, but in a structural one. People start to compartmentalise their lives in order to preserve contradictory values. The executive who values both transparency and diplomacy may speak differently in private and public settings. The educator who values intellectual freedom and institutional loyalty may avoid hard conversations to preserve both roles.

This self-splitting leads to behavioural incoherence, which in turn breeds cynicism: *"I say I value X, but my life reflects Y."* Over time, the mind adapts not by resolving the conflict, but by normalising the fracture. The result is a slow erosion of trust in the self.

All Values Are Not Created Equal

One of the most liberating insights in the design of a coherent value structure is this: *you are not obligated to honour all your values equally, all the time.* Values are not a flat list; they are a hierarchy. And a hierarchy that is not consciously ordered will be subconsciously imposed by circumstance, fear, or habit.

This is where structural design becomes essential. Just as an architect must decide which beams are load-bearing, we must decide which values are primary. This does not mean discarding the rest. It means designing *principled prioritisation.*

Take the classic conflict between compassion and truth-telling. Do you spare someone's feelings, or do you say what needs to be said? The answer depends on *which value you have chosen to hold as structurally primary in this situation.* For a therapist, compassion may be the design principle. For a journalist, truth may be non-negotiable. Both are valid—*but not simultaneously, in equal measure.*

The goal is not moral perfection. The goal is internal *predictability*—to know, in advance, what principle you are willing to let guide you when the values clash.

The Ethics of Trade-Offs

When confronting value conflict, it is tempting to resolve it through rationalisation: to explain away the tension, or reframe one value to fit another. But true alignment requires *acknowledging the loss embedded in each trade-off.*

If you choose autonomy over belonging, there will be loneliness. If you choose justice over harmony, there will be conflict. If you choose wellbeing over productivity, there will be limits to recognition. These are not signs of failure—they are the ethical costs of clarity.

Mature mental design involves *ethical accounting*: not only making choices, but acknowledging what you are giving up by making them. This prevents unconscious resentment from forming and allows one to live with integrity, even in complexity.

Strategies for Structural Realignment

The following are not tactics, but *design disciplines*—ongoing practices that help resolve or reframe value conflict before it hardens into paralysis.

1. Periodic Value Re-Auditing
Values are not static. As roles, contexts, and life stages change, so must the hierarchy of values. A principle that once felt essential may now be a legacy priority—retained out of habit, not alignment. Reviewing values on a seasonal or annual basis prevents structural rigidity from taking root.

2. Situational Anchoring
Instead of holding all values universally, assign contextual primacy. For instance, in your family system, maybe patience takes precedence. In your creative practice, perhaps truth overrides harmony. This form of "value zoning" enables nuanced behavioural consistency.

3. Principle-Stretch Testing
Imagine a hypothetical situation in which two of your core values come into direct conflict. Play out how each would guide your action. Then ask: *Which one would I feel more at peace honouring—even if it led to discomfort?* This reveals the underlying structure of your value system.

4. Integration Through Language
Many value conflicts are linguistic artefacts. For example, people may frame values as opposed when they are not. "Freedom vs. commitment" may seem like a binary, but reframing commitment as *self-authored allegiance* rather than constraint may dissolve the tension.

Language is not neutral—it encodes our assumptions about compatibility.

Case Study: The Educator and the Whistleblower

Consider a senior academic who values institutional loyalty, intellectual honesty, and psychological safety for her students. Over time, she becomes aware of systemic discrimination within her university's admissions process. Speaking out would honour truth and protect students—but it would violate loyalty to her colleagues and potentially undermine the reputation of the school.

If she has not *pre-designed her value hierarchy*, the decision becomes paralysing. But if she has clarified that institutional loyalty is secondary to intellectual integrity, then while the decision remains difficult, the path forward is structurally coherent. The conflict may remain externally—but *internally, she does not fracture.*

This is the purpose of mental design: not to eliminate difficulty, but to *prevent moral ambiguity from becoming personal incoherence.*

Final Reflection: The Architecture of Coherence

A value conflict is not a sign that something is wrong with you. It is a signal that your internal architecture is due for inspection. The most aligned lives are not those without conflict, but those where *the structure of identity is strong enough to absorb contradiction without collapse.*

If you are to live a meaningful life, you must be willing to make principled sacrifices. You must be willing to say: *This value matters more than that one in this moment—not because the other is unimportant, but because structure requires prioritisation.* That is not moral compromise. That is moral engineering.

And that, in the end, is how structural cracks become reinforcements—*not through avoidance, but through deliberate design.*

Minimalist Values for Maximum Clarity

Encouraging the Selection of Core Guiding Values

The modern individual is over-informed and under-aligned. In a culture that celebrates choice, plurality, and constant evolution, there is an unspoken burden: *the proliferation of personal values.* We are encouraged to stand for justice, freedom, compassion, growth, discipline, curiosity, loyalty, excellence, and more. The impulse is admirable. The outcome is often debilitating.

What was meant to offer moral orientation frequently becomes a fog of competing principles. As people attempt to honour a dozen noble values simultaneously, they dilute their capacity to honour any one with depth or consistency. It's not that they lack integrity—it's that they lack *design.* The mind, like any system, cannot function with too many primary directives. Overcommitment to too many values is not a strength of character. It is a form of *ethical clutter.*

This subchapter argues for a minimalist approach to values—not in the sense of asceticism, but in the service of *strategic clarity.* By deliberately selecting and operationalising a small number of core values, individuals can build internal coherence, reduce decision fatigue, and develop a more legible life architecture. Far from being reductive, *value minimalism is liberating.* It replaces moral confusion with structural integrity.

The Paradox of Abundance

The assumption that more values equal greater moral sophistication is intuitively appealing. But from a systems design perspective, the opposite tends to be true. In cognitive science, the concept of "cognitive load" refers to the limits of working memory when handling complex inputs. When too many competing variables are introduced, the system slows, defaults, or breaks.

The same applies to personal values. When an individual tries to simultaneously optimise for a dozen ethical priorities, they inevitably encounter conflict. Should I prioritise honesty or kindness? Should I pursue ambition or presence? Should I preserve security or embrace risk? Each value might be valid—but if they are not clearly ranked, behaviour becomes erratic. The individual feels torn between parts of themselves, not due to a moral failure, but because *their values were never designed to function together.*

Minimalist value architecture solves this by moving from a catalogue of ideals to a hierarchy of commitments.

From Catalogue to Compass

People often treat values like a vision board: a collection of aspirational concepts that feel good to associate with. But values are not ornaments. *They are instruments of navigation.* And a navigational system that tries to point in all directions is functionally useless.

The discipline of minimalist values begins with a question that most people avoid because it demands real clarity: *Which values are you willing to consistently inconvenience yourself for?* Not which ones you admire, or which ones you post on social media. Which ones will you protect under stress, even when it costs you?

These are your *operative values*. They deserve primacy not because they are the only values that matter, but because *they are the ones that shape your actual decisions*. They are your internal operating system.

Choosing 3 to 5 operative values may feel like a betrayal of the rest. But it is actually an act of responsibility. You are saying: *These are the beams I will build my identity on. The others, while worthy, must remain peripheral to avoid structural overload.*

Case Study: From Role Confusion to Value Clarity

Consider a high-performing executive who feels pulled in multiple directions. She values excellence, family, impact, authenticity, and generosity. These are not contradictory values on paper—but in practice, they clash constantly. She stays late to demonstrate excellence, but misses dinner with her children. She gives to colleagues but compromises her own bandwidth. She's authentic in meetings but fears the political cost of transparency.

This is not a character flaw. It is a *design flaw.* She has too many "first principles." And without a clear value hierarchy, the system cannot prioritise.

After a deliberate reassessment, she chooses *presence, integrity, and contribution* as her operative values. Excellence and generosity are still important, but they are routed through these anchors. She decides to define contribution by her ability to lead without self-erasure. She reframes excellence as *depth, not breadth.* She sets boundaries that honour presence as a form of love, not luxury.

Suddenly, her decisions gain clarity—not because life is simpler, but because *her values are no longer competing for her loyalty.* She has given them an order. That order gives her freedom.

The Neuroscience of Simplicity

From a neuroscientific perspective, value overload contributes to chronic stress. The brain's executive function—responsible for planning, weighing options, and self-regulation—is a finite resource. When constantly tasked with reconciling ambiguous priorities, it fatigues faster.

This explains why people often revert to default behaviours when tired or overwhelmed. When values are not clear, the system defaults to impulse, habit, or external scripts. In contrast, a streamlined value set acts like cognitive shorthand: it reduces deliberation, improves reaction quality, and preserves energy for high-stakes decisions.

This is not a rejection of complexity. It is an embrace of *designed simplicity*, in service of complex lives.

Minimalism is not Reductionism

Critics of minimalist values sometimes argue that the world is too nuanced for such pruning. They fear that narrowing values risks flattening the richness of ethical life. But this is a misunderstanding.

Minimalism in this context is not about rejecting depth. It is about *creating depth through focus*. When you prioritise a small number of values, you gain the space to explore them more fully. You get to ask: *What does integrity mean in practice? How do I embody presence, not just perform it?* You move from aesthetic to application.

It is also worth noting that minimalist values do not mean moral rigidity. They can be re-evaluated over time. The values that serve you at 30 may not fit the demands of 50. What matters is that you always know *which values are doing the steering*—and you've chosen them consciously.

Crafting Your Core: Practical Framework

If you're unclear where to begin, consider this triadic framework:

Define What Anchors You – Which value grounds you when life is chaotic?

Define What Guides You – Which value helps you make the difficult call?

Define What Elevates You – Which value pushes you to grow, even when it's hard?

These three roles—anchor, guide, and horizon—can help you select operative values that serve both stability and aspiration.

Avoid selecting values that are overly abstract (e.g., "happiness") or socially conditioned (e.g., "success") unless you can operationalise what they *mean* in your life. Precision matters. So does personal relevance.

Minimalist Values in a Complex World

We live in an era saturated with ethical branding. Corporations, influencers, institutions—everyone signals values. The line between marketing and meaning is increasingly blurred. In such an environment, having a *quiet, personal, internally consistent value system* is not just rare. It is radical.

Minimalist values give you something the noise cannot: clarity. And clarity, in a disoriented world, is power.

When you know what you stand for, you no longer need to signal it. Your decisions speak for you. Your boundaries speak for you. Your presence speaks for you.

This is not about becoming morally perfect. It's about becoming structurally coherent.

Final Reflection: Building Less to Live More

The individual who aligns their life to five values lives more deeply than the one who subscribes to fifty. Why? Because they are not divided by moral multitasking. They are not second-guessing every action, paralysed by internal contradiction. They have fewer principles—but they *live them fully*.

Minimalist values are not about less meaning. They are about *less noise*. They are the discipline of choosing, the courage to commit, and the wisdom to know that clarity is not a given. It is something you *design*.

And like all good design—it disappears, quietly, into the structure of a well-lived life.

Chapter 8
Emotional Load-Bearing – Designing for Inner Storms

Contemporary praise for the mind often centres on its agility—its ability to juggle tasks, troubleshoot swiftly, iterate endlessly. But beneath this sleek surface, there's an older, often overlooked architecture: one concerned not with information processing, but emotional endurance. It's not your mental dexterity that determines whether you hold together in a storm—it's how well your emotional scaffolding can carry the weight. And all too often, we discover, too late, that it can't. Not because we are weak, but because no one ever taught us how to build for pressure.

This chapter does not float in abstraction. It is about engineering—emotional engineering. Not metaphorical, not symbolic, but practical and psychological. The kind of deliberate, sometimes unglamorous work that creates a structure capable of holding sadness, rage, fear, disappointment—without letting it corrode the rest of your system. Emotional resilience, in this context, isn't a gift or a slogan. It's a discipline. It's structural.

Most people never consciously choose their emotional frameworks. They inherit them—through family norms, social conditioning, cultural scripts, or survival instincts. They suppress emotions, call it coping, and carry on. They mistake repression for regulation, silence for control. Vulnerability becomes threatening, not because it is inherently dangerous, but because their system was never designed to house it safely. And then, when the inevitable happens—loss, heartbreak, betrayal—the system cracks. Not because the emotion is too much, but because the structure is too thin.

This chapter isn't here to soothe. It's here to lay out blueprints. How do you store grief in such a way that it doesn't seep into every conversation? How can you create rituals that metabolise emotional volatility without paralysing momentum? How do you practise vulnerability that doesn't destabilise you—but strengthens your internal architecture instead?

Let's begin where many go wrong: the confusion between compartmentalising and containing. On the surface, they may look alike—keeping strong under pressure, carrying on despite chaos. But their long-term effects could not be more different. Compartmentalising tucks emotion into hidden corners, sealed off and ignored. It's tidy, for a time. Functional, even. But it's function purchased at the cost of wholeness. Containing, by contrast, doesn't bury. It holds. Acknowledges. Makes space. It creates a boundary—not to exile feeling, but to honour it. The compartmentaliser fractures slowly. The container fortifies.

Ironically, it is the compartmentaliser who is often rewarded—especially in high-functioning, high-stakes environments. These are the professionals who keep calm, never crack, remain "objective." They make it through the fire—but carry its smoke in their lungs. Slowly, the weight becomes ambient. A tightening around the eyes. A shrinking of empathy. A flatness in creativity. When emotion is pushed too far underground, it doesn't disappear. It metastasises.

Now, consider the individual who contains. They feel deeply, yes—but they've built rooms inside themselves for grief, for rage, for reflection. They don't collapse in tears at the first sign of stress. Nor do they smile through silent suffering. They pause, they process, they allocate. Their strength is not the absence of emotion—it's the architecture that supports its weight.

That architecture often includes what might be called internal sanctuaries. Not sanctuaries of avoidance, but of processing. For some, it's prayer. For others, a blank notebook. For soldiers, it's the after-action review; for therapists, a ritual of reflective supervision. These practices are not indulgences. They are structural clearings—places where difficult emotion can be absorbed, sorted, stored, and moved through. Without such spaces, emotion leaks. With them, it transforms.

And then there is the question of vulnerability. Not the Instagram kind. Not tearful overexposure masquerading as depth. Real vulnerability—the kind that is calibrated, intentional, and deeply connected to internal stability. Too often, it's misunderstood as fragility. In truth, when designed carefully, it becomes a pillar of psychological strength. Not only does it permit authentic connection, but it dramatically reduces the energy cost of emotional disguise. Pretence, after all, is exhausting.

But—and this is key—vulnerability, to be constructive, must be designed. What do you share? When? And with whom? Do you speak to process, or to manipulate? Is your openness a compulsion, or a choice? The emotionally mature individual does not overshare in the name of "realness." They open up with intention. Every disclosure is placed within a broader emotional strategy.

This strategy is not performative. It is clarifying. It reduces guesswork in relationships. It eliminates the need for defensive detours. In personal terms, it lets pain find its place—not as an intruder, but as a contributor to depth. Pain, processed wisely, becomes structure. Left to fester, it becomes corrosion.

Emotional load-bearing, then, is not about always appearing composed, nor about perpetually "letting it all out." It's about constructing an emotional infrastructure with load ratings. Knowing your limits. Reinforcing your supports. Designing for pressure, not pretending it won't come.

You'll encounter frameworks throughout this chapter—not sentimental mantras, but genuine tools. Ways to ritualise emotional upkeep, to structure reflection, to retain coherence when the internal weather turns violent. You'll explore techniques for storing emotion without freezing creativity. For channelling anger without wreckage. For remaining yourself—intact and recognisable—even when your inner world feels undone.

We draw from diverse sources: trauma research, systems design, psychotherapy, leadership case studies, and the quiet wisdom of those who live with emotional integrity under unthinkable strain. These individuals differ in age, context, temperament. But what unites them is not what they feel—it's what they've built inside themselves in order to feel well. Their stability is no accident. It is authored.

And that, ultimately, is the point. Every person lives within an emotional architecture. The question is: did you inherit yours, or did you design it? Did it emerge by default—or was it constructed, layer by intentional layer, to withstand time and tension?

Much of this book has explored cognition, behaviour, identity. All useful, all important. But if the emotional substrate remains unstructured, the whole scaffolding is vulnerable. No theory holds under prolonged emotional weight unless it's been built for such strain.

So here's the ask: not to feel more, but to feel better. Not to chase catharsis, but to cultivate structure. This chapter is your drafting table. Not a diary, but a design lab. Here, you learn not only how to endure emotional storms, but how to build homes that can hold them.

By the final section, you won't be immune to sorrow, anger, or loss. But you will know how to bear them—with deliberate grace, and without architectural collapse.

The Myth of Emotional Mastery – Replaces Control with Endurance as the Goal of Emotion Management

There is perhaps no greater misconception in the domain of self-development than the pursuit of *emotional mastery*. The term is seductive. It evokes images of composed leaders, unflinching warriors, serene yogis—individuals who appear untouched by chaos, immune to emotional turbulence. But behind this ideal lies a dangerous illusion: that human progress depends on our ability to *control* what we feel. This idea is not only psychologically misleading—it is structurally unsound.

The modern self-help canon frequently equates maturity with the ability to override emotion. Anger must be extinguished. Grief must be 'processed and moved on from.' Anxiety must be hacked. Vulnerability must be optimised. The language shifts slightly across schools—whether stoicism, mindfulness, biohacking, or military conditioning—but the central myth remains unchanged: that mental excellence requires emotional suppression, sublimation, or sterilisation. That mastery is achieved through dominance over the emotional body.

But mastery, in this rigid sense, is a false summit. It breeds repression, not resilience. And it ultimately erodes the mind's capacity to respond with humanity, nuance, or creativity. The truth—less palatable but far more powerful—is this: *psychological strength is not about controlling emotion, but about enduring it wisely.*

Endurance, not control, is the real engine of emotional intelligence.

Emotion is Not a Problem to Be Solved

Emotions are not interruptions to rationality. They are *data*, deeply encoded with evolutionary intelligence. Fear alerts us to risk. Guilt points toward ethical dissonance. Grief honours attachment. Anger signals perceived injustice. While these signals can be distorted or disproportionate, they are rarely meaningless. And yet, the common reflex is to treat emotions as mechanical failures—to 'fix' them when they arise, or to silence them before they interfere.

This tendency is reinforced by a culture that idolises productivity and penalises perceived instability. Workplaces reward stoicism. Social media celebrates curated optimism. And even mental health discourse often missteps—encouraging people to label, medicate, or reframe their emotions before they've been properly witnessed.

The deeper cost of this control paradigm is that it creates a kind of internal censorship. Individuals become fluent in performing steadiness while privately disassociating from the full bandwidth of their feelings. The result is not clarity but *compression*—a narrowing of the emotional spectrum, a flattening of affect, and a long-term tax on psychological elasticity.

To move beyond this, we need to reconsider what emotional maturity truly entails. Not the elimination of suffering, but *a capacity to hold suffering without collapse.*

The Architecture of Emotional Endurance

Endurance is not passive. Nor is it endurance for endurance's sake. It is an *active skillset*—psychologically demanding, biologically taxing, and ethically rigorous. At its core lies the ability to:

Feel fully without being consumed

Name without collapsing into narrative

Respond without denying what is present

This is difficult because emotional endurance runs against our default programming. The human nervous system is wired for avoidance of pain. Most people recoil reflexively from discomfort—by intellectualising, numbing, projecting, or bypassing. These are not signs of weakness but survival mechanisms. Yet, unless reconditioned, these reflexes keep us perpetually reactive.

To endure emotion skilfully is to sit inside its storm system without flinching or fleeing. To *allow the wave* without needing to accelerate its exit. To experience the ache of shame or the disorientation of grief and still make conscious choices about how to engage with the world. In endurance, there is no panic. There is space.

Consider Holocaust survivor and psychiatrist Viktor Frankl, who endured the most inhumane of circumstances yet famously asserted that "between stimulus and response, there is a space. In that space is our power to choose our response." That space is not a gift—it is built. And it is built through disciplined emotional presence.

Control is Brittle. Endurance is Adaptive.

The belief in emotional control often produces brittle people. They are stoic until they snap. Calm until collapse. Their emotional 'mastery' is conditional: it works when circumstances cooperate, but it shatters under cumulative load. Control lacks *adaptive range.* It creates psychic rigidity—requiring the world to remain predictable to maintain composure.

Endurance, by contrast, is structurally flexible. It accepts that the world will be volatile. It anticipates emotional turbulence and integrates rituals, relationships, and philosophies to metabolise it. The emotionally enduring person does not avoid intensity—they *design for it.* Their aim is not to suppress but to *sustain internal coherence* across highs and lows.

In systems theory, resilience is defined not as resistance to change, but as the *capacity to absorb disturbance and reorganise while retaining core purpose and structure.* Applied psychologically, this suggests that we should train less for control and more for *capacity*—not "How do I stop feeling this?" but "How do I hold this without losing my clarity, values, or rhythm?"

The False Virtue of Emotional Stoicism

Cultural narratives around control often disguise themselves as virtue. "I don't let things get to me." "I'm not emotional." "I move on quickly." While these statements can reflect true integration, they more often reveal emotional avoidance. The suppression of emotional responsiveness may look like strength but often reflects habituated disconnection.

This disconnection has costs. It narrows empathy. It inhibits creativity. It limits relational intimacy. The emotionally controlled individual may function efficiently—but often at the cost of depth. By refusing to feel, they forfeit the very signals that make human life rich and ethically awake.

Moreover, the aspiration to 'master' emotion invites a dangerous dualism. It frames the self as an executive manager, and emotion as a subordinate force to be disciplined. But this division is not real. Emotion is not 'other'—it is part of cognition. Emotion influences memory, decision-making, perception, and moral reasoning. Any attempt to control it as though it were external is not mastery—it is misunderstanding.

Tools That Build Endurance (Not Suppression)

So what does it mean, in practice, to train emotional endurance? While the tools are varied, their architecture is consistent: *expand capacity, not control.* This includes:

Slow processing rituals (e.g., reflective journaling, dialogue with trusted interlocutors, somatic scanning)

Emotional pacing (recognising load limits and sequencing exposure)

Containment strategies (creating deliberate space for emotional digestion rather than default expression)

Reframing without repression (seeing emotion through broader meaning lenses without denying its presence)

These practices shift the goal from termination to *containment with continuity.* The aim is not to 'feel better' but to *feel wisely and stay functional*—to think while grieving, to move while afraid, to love while uncertain.

Philosophical Reorientation: Emotion as Terrain, Not Obstacle

Philosophically, this subchapter invites a reorientation: stop thinking of emotion as a force to overcome, and begin seeing it as terrain to navigate. Like a storm system over a mountain range, emotion is inevitable, sometimes intense, occasionally destructive—but *never permanent.* Emotional endurance asks: can you traverse the terrain without rerouting your life around it?

The most enduring minds in history were not those who 'conquered' emotion, but those who *partnered with it thoughtfully*—Seneca writing through grief, Mandela transmuting anger into political clarity, Maya Angelou turning personal trauma into cultural resonance.

They didn't 'master' their emotions in the control sense. They integrated them. They endured without fragmenting. And in doing so, they turned emotion from a liability into a luminous part of their cognitive and ethical range.

Emotional Excellence is Not Perfection—It is Design Integrity

In the architecture of selfhood, emotional endurance is load-bearing. It is what keeps the identity upright when the winds of uncertainty, fear, or loss rise. Those winds will come. They always do. The question is not whether you can stop them. It is whether you've built internal systems that can hold shape amidst their pressure.

True emotional excellence is not perfection. It is *design integrity under strain.* It is showing up—present, responsive, honest—even when your internal weather is unsettled. And that integrity is what makes endurance not just psychologically sound but *morally significant.* It allows us to be dependable even while processing sorrow. It allows us to lead without pretending invulnerability. It allows us to *stay human in complexity.*

In replacing the myth of control with the practice of endurance, we are not lowering the bar—we are raising it. We are asking not for performance but for *presence under pressure.* And that presence, when refined, becomes the quiet force that undergirds wisdom, empathy, and meaningful change.

Compartmentalising vs. Containing – Teaches Healthy Emotional Storage and Processing

There is a quiet but dangerous flaw embedded in many models of mental resilience: the belief that strong people keep emotions neatly locked away in psychological boxes. This notion—often reinforced by leadership culture, certain therapeutic approaches, and popular narratives of stoic endurance—confuses suppression with strategy, and avoidance with maturity. At the heart of this confusion lies the misunderstood practice of *compartmentalisation.*

Compartmentalisation is often presented as a tool of mental hygiene: put your feelings aside, stay on task, don't let emotional 'mess' bleed into functional spaces. In limited cases, this can be useful. But what happens when compartments become permanent? When the mind fragments itself in order to function? When emotional truths are pushed into cold storage, never to be revisited or integrated? Over time, this strategy degrades mental clarity, relational depth, and emotional health.

By contrast, *containment* offers a far more sustainable alternative. Where compartmentalisation slices the mind into isolated silos, containment provides coherent, bounded space *within the self* to hold discomfort, process it safely, and then release it without rupture. In architectural terms, compartmentalisation is a locked cellar; containment is a reinforced chamber with oxygen flow. Both conceal. Only one breathes.

This chapter explores the fundamental difference between the two, why it matters, and how intelligent emotional design is not about denying feelings—but about designing safe, durable, and intentional ways of holding them.

The Illusion of Emotional Separation

Compartmentalisation, as a psychological strategy, involves the mental segregation of thoughts or feelings from the rest of one's conscious experience. It is often automatic—an evolutionary residue of our brain's need to reduce overload in crises. Soldiers in war zones compartmentalise grief to stay alert. Emergency doctors do the same to maintain clinical effectiveness in trauma wards. In these environments, compartmentalisation can *save lives.*

But outside acute stress contexts, this strategy backfires. When people regularly section off sadness, anger, fear, or doubt and return to them rarely—if at all—those unprocessed emotions don't disappear. They compound. What was once self-protective becomes self-defeating. *Mental silos become emotional landmines.*

Consider the professional who blocks out resentment toward their employer to remain productive. Or the parent who shoves aside burnout for the sake of family function. Or the friend who bottles grief behind a socially acceptable mask. They may appear stable. But the cumulative tension often shows up elsewhere: unexplained anxiety, chronic fatigue, outbursts, apathy, or even physical illness.

Psychologically, the mind does not delete what it avoids. It merely buries it deeper. And buried emotions, like faulty wiring behind a wall, compromise structural integrity over time. *The cost of long-term compartmentalisation is internal incoherence.*

Containment: A More Sophisticated Design

Where compartmentalisation enforces separation, containment enacts *integration with boundaries*. A contained mind does not exile emotion; it builds inner architecture capable of holding it—consciously, temporarily, and safely—until the individual is ready to process it.

This distinction is not merely semantic. It reflects different neural, emotional, and behavioural outcomes.

In containment:

Emotions are acknowledged, not denied.

Space is created intentionally, not reflexively.

The individual retains access to emotional data without being overwhelmed by it.

Containment trains the capacity for *emotional ambidexterity*: to feel deeply *and* function effectively. Not by shutting down one's emotional system, but by ensuring it doesn't flood task-relevant cognition. It is the mental equivalent of a well-designed dam: water is not ignored—it is channelled and regulated.

A practical example might involve someone experiencing relational grief while also needing to lead a project at work. Instead of numbing or suppressing the grief (compartmentalisation), they *contain* it—acknowledge its presence, give it symbolic space (perhaps a journal entry, a moment of quiet), and consciously 'shelve' the intensity with an agreement to revisit it after the work is complete. The difference is consciousness and consent, not concealment.

Containment is not the denial of feeling—it is the dignified delay of its full engagement.

The Neuroscience of Holding Space

From a neurobiological perspective, emotional containment requires significant cognitive resources. The brain's prefrontal cortex—responsible for executive function—acts as a regulator of the limbic system, where emotions originate. When we consciously hold space for a feeling without acting on it, we are engaging *inhibitory control*: a process involving the dorsolateral prefrontal cortex and anterior cingulate cortex. This takes effort. It requires awareness, energy, and practice.

In contrast, compartmentalisation often bypasses the frontal lobe entirely. It is more akin to dissociation—a limbic system 'freeze' response. Quick, clean, and unconscious. But biologically costly in the long run. It weakens neural pathways responsible for emotional regulation and reduces affective tolerance—the ability to stay present with uncomfortable states.

Containment strengthens these pathways. The more an individual practices containment, the greater their affective range and emotional flexibility. They become less likely to react impulsively or shut down under pressure, and more capable of making meaning in the midst of complexity.

This is not emotional suppression—it is emotional sophistication.

When Containment Fails

Containment is not infallible. Like any structure, it must be maintained. When overwhelmed by cumulative stress, trauma, or emotional overload, even the most skilled individuals can find their containment breaking down. What's essential is recognising the early signs: rumination, sleep disruption, emotional volatility, or somatic symptoms.

This is where containment differs once again from compartmentalisation. A compartmentalised mind often lacks internal visibility. It doesn't notice the pressure until it explodes. A contained mind, by design, monitors its own thresholds. It is proactive rather than reactive.

In healthy containment, the individual learns to offload the emotional load *consciously and safely*—through therapy, trusted relationships, somatic practices, or solitary rituals. The emotion is not archived indefinitely; it is *cycled through intentionally.*

Ethical Implications of Compartmentalised Cultures

On a societal level, the promotion of compartmentalisation has dangerous moral consequences. Institutions—military, corporate, governmental—often valorise emotional detachment as professionalism. But this detachment can lead to ethical numbing.

A police officer who is trained to suppress empathy may later fail to discern ethical lines in the field. A CEO who blocks out concern for workers in the name of efficiency may rationalise inhumane policies. A surgeon who numbs themselves to suffering may misread the humanity of the person under their scalpel.

Containment, by contrast, *maintains access to feeling without sacrificing function.* It allows people in positions of responsibility to stay emotionally connected to the impact of their actions, without being paralysed by it.

In a world that increasingly demands both compassion and competence, containment is not a luxury—it is a professional imperative.

Building Containment Capacity

Containment can be trained, just like strength or stamina. But it requires intention. Among the most effective approaches:

Reflective practices: Daily journaling, structured self-inquiry, or narrative processing that makes emotional experience explicit.

Ritualised space-holding: Time-bound routines (such as 15-minute emotional check-ins) to release stored feelings regularly.

Symbolic anchoring: Objects, gestures, or mantras that remind the self of containment boundaries ("This belongs here, not everywhere").

Co-regulation: Trusted relationships in which feelings are held communally, not discharged chaotically.

None of these eliminate the need to feel. They simply give feeling a *functional structure*—one that supports endurance rather than erodes it.

Closing Insight

Emotions do not become dangerous because they are intense. They become dangerous when they are *unstructured.* Compartmentalisation may offer short-term relief, but over time, it fragments the psyche. Containment, by contrast, creates coherence. It allows the self to be *whole and stable even in pain.*

The difference is not just psychological—it is architectural. One strategy builds walls. The other builds space.

To live as a mentally resilient human being is not to feel less. It is to feel wisely, spaciously, and with design.

Building Safe Internal Spaces – Offers Grounding Rituals for Emotional Resilience

A person's resilience is often misjudged by their ability to push through hardship, suppress feeling, or maintain composure under duress. But true resilience is not the absence of emotional disturbance—it is the *presence* of a stable internal structure in which distress can safely unfold. It is not the mind's armour that determines resilience, but the quality of the *spaces within it.*

In the architectural sense, we do not weather storms by hardening the air—we build strong rooms to hold it. Likewise, emotional resilience is best conceived not as an unshakable willpower but as a *designed capacity for safe emotional processing.* These inner spaces—psychological sanctuaries we construct and maintain—serve as holding environments for difficult feelings, unresolved questions, and unspoken fears. Without them, we are at the mercy of emotional weather. With them, we develop a durable capacity for *grounded presence.*

This article explores the nature of internal safety, its critical function in emotional design, and the grounding rituals that build and maintain it. These are not self-help slogans or abstract ideals, but *concrete psychological architectures*—backed by science, refined by philosophy, and urgently needed in the pace-bound, overstimulated lives of high-functioning individuals.

Emotional Safety Begins Internally

When we speak of feeling "safe," we often think of external conditions: environments free from threat, people we can trust, or routines that foster calm. These are foundational. But internal safety is something different—and deeper. It is the felt sense that *whatever arises within us can be faced without disintegration.*

This is not a given. For many, especially those raised in emotionally invalidating or unpredictable environments, the inner world is not a safe place. Feelings trigger panic. Thoughts spiral. Vulnerability is equated with collapse. In such cases, the absence of internal safe spaces is not merely inconvenient—it is *debilitating.*

The solution is not to suppress these states, nor to flood them with blind catharsis. It is to build the *mental infrastructure* in which they can exist without becoming overwhelming. In trauma psychology, this is sometimes referred to as developing a "window of tolerance"—the range within which a person can experience emotional intensity without shutting down or becoming dysregulated. But that window must be built intentionally. It is not opened by accident.

To feel deeply and remain functional is not a gift of temperament—it is a practice of design.

From Panic Rooms to Processing Rooms

The metaphor of a "panic room" is useful here. Many people develop internal equivalents: rigid, locked-down states they retreat to when feelings threaten to overwhelm. These mental panic rooms are constructed out of repression, avoidance, or over-control. They offer short-term security, but long-term restriction. The problem is not that people lack places to hide from emotion; it's that they lack *spaces to be with emotion safely.*

By contrast, a psychologically safe internal space functions more like a *processing room.* It is open—but not exposed. Bounded—but not sealed. It allows emotion to arise, be named, be felt, and eventually be released or integrated. Importantly, this space does not require external permission. It does not depend on whether a spouse understands, a therapist is available, or a circumstance resolves. It is *inwardly governed.*

What builds this space? Practice. Deliberate, repeated rituals that cue the mind toward grounded openness. These rituals serve as *mental architecture*—walls, doors, and windows for our inner experience. Without them, emotional life becomes unstructured. And unstructured emotion, especially under pressure, leads to chaos.

Rituals as Emotional Architecture

To speak of ritual in the context of emotional resilience is to speak of *predictable, symbolic acts that structure internal reality.* These acts are not superstitions or habits—they are designed interventions that anchor the self in the midst of flux.

Neuroscientifically, ritual engages the basal ganglia (associated with habit formation), the prefrontal cortex (governing regulation), and limbic circuits (linked to meaning and emotion). When these systems fire together, the brain receives a clear message: *you are safe, you are present, you are held.*

Among the most effective rituals for building internal space are:

Time-Bound Emotional Check-Ins: Setting aside 10–15 minutes each day to name, notice, and journal about emotional states. The container of time makes this feel finite, rather than infinite.

Somatic Grounding Practices: Using breathwork, body scans, or touch-based techniques (such as placing a hand over the chest) to anchor emotion in the body. This signals the nervous system that intensity can be metabolised, not feared.

Symbolic Safe Space Visualisations: A practice drawn from trauma therapy, where individuals construct a vivid inner image of a safe place (real or imagined), and mentally return to it during stress. Over time, this creates a neural anchor of safety.

Closure Rituals: At the end of a difficult day or experience, small symbolic gestures (e.g., writing something down and discarding it, washing hands intentionally, lighting a candle) signal emotional transitions. These rituals demarcate space and give emotion a natural endpoint.

None of these require hours of spare time. What they require is *precision and intention.* Like well-designed architecture, it is not size that matters—it is structure.

Philosophy and the Design of Inner Spaces

The ancient Stoics, often misunderstood as unemotional, were in fact practitioners of finely tuned internal design. Marcus Aurelius spoke of creating an "inner citadel"—a place within where reason, reflection, and virtue could withstand the storm of outer events. The Buddhist tradition, too, emphasises the cultivation of mental space through mindfulness, recognising thoughts and feelings as passing weather systems within the sky of awareness.

These traditions agree on a central point: *The mind is not just something we have—it is something we must maintain.* Safe internal spaces are not automatic. They must be *built, revisited, and cared for like any meaningful structure.*

In contemporary psychology, this is echoed in the work of thinkers like Donald Winnicott, who argued for the importance of "holding environments" in human development—not just externally in childhood, but internally throughout adult life. The self needs to be held, especially when it hurts. If that holding is not provided from outside, it must be engineered from within.

The Modern Crisis of Uncontained Emotion

In a digital age, the crisis is not a lack of access to feeling—it is a lack of containment. Social media rewards emotional exposure without process. Productivity culture discourages stillness. The speed of modern life punishes internal spaciousness. In this context, emotional safety is not merely therapeutic—it is *radical.*

To build safe internal spaces today is to opt out of constant reactivity. It is to declare, silently but powerfully, "I will not be flooded. I will not bypass. I will hold what arises—carefully, honestly, and on my own terms."

This is the essence of emotional maturity: *to make space for discomfort without collapsing or contaminating the world around you with it.*

Final Reflection

A person does not become resilient by being unfeeling. Nor by performing composure. They become resilient by *knowing where, when, and how to feel—intentionally and safely.* This requires more than will. It requires *design.*

Safe internal spaces are not indulgences for the overly sensitive. They are structural necessities for the mentally durable. They prevent emotional overload from becoming existential collapse. They allow grief to soften rather than harden, anger to clarify rather than distort, and fear to speak without shouting.

To build these spaces is to affirm that our inner life matters—that it deserves structure, respect, and stewardship. It is to live not at the mercy of emotion, but in mature relationship with it. And in a culture that rewards speed and surface, this inner spaciousness may be among the most valuable assets a human being can cultivate.

Let the world be loud. Your mind, if well designed, need not be.

The Power of Designed Vulnerability – Shows How Planned Openness Reinforces Internal and Relational Strength

Vulnerability, when misinterpreted through the lens of cultural conditioning, often wears a costume of fragility. In boardrooms, classrooms, clinics, and even families, it is frequently coded as a liability—an exposure of internal weakness, a dangerous crack in an otherwise impermeable facade. Yet, in reality, *vulnerability is not the opposite of strength.* Rather, when *consciously structured*, it becomes one of its most potent reinforcers.

Modern neuroscience, relational psychology, and even leadership theory converge on this: sustainable resilience and authentic connection are not born from perfect control or pristine self-containment. They emerge from a willingness to *be seen*, to *risk emotional exposure*, and—critically—to *do so with intention.* This is not raw confession. Nor is it emotional impulsivity. It is *designed vulnerability*—a deliberate, measured act of openness that expands personal integrity and deepens relational trust.

To design vulnerability well is to exercise *architectural intelligence over emotion.* It is to know *what to share, when, with whom, and why*—and to do so not for validation, but for clarity, congruence, and human truth. This subchapter will examine how this form of openness—so often feared or mishandled—can become a strategic, stabilising force both within the self and across the fabric of our relationships.

Vulnerability Without Design: The Collapse of Containment

Before exploring the benefits of intentional vulnerability, it is essential to distinguish it from its misused or misperceived forms. Vulnerability without context, boundaries, or reflection becomes emotional dumping. It creates discomfort rather than closeness, confusion rather than clarity. In psychological terms, it breaches containment—unloading unresolved emotion onto others in the hope they will process it for us.

This is common in digitally mediated spaces, where the performance of vulnerability (think trauma disclosures on social media) often lacks reciprocal structure. Instead of generating authentic connection, it commodifies pain. In such environments, the signal of vulnerability is stripped of depth. It becomes a spectacle.

In personal and professional contexts, premature or disproportionate vulnerability can be perceived as a *threat to stability*, particularly in high-functioning environments. Colleagues or partners may withdraw, not out of coldness, but because the expression feels *invasive rather than invitational.* When vulnerability is not attuned to timing, trust, or mutual understanding, it *isolates* rather than connects.

This is why *designed vulnerability* matters. Without form, vulnerability is an emotional flood. With form, it becomes *an intelligent transmission of truth.*

The Architecture of Designed Vulnerability

So, what does it mean to *design* vulnerability?

It means understanding it not merely as a feeling to release, but as a signal to calibrate. The best-designed vulnerability involves a paradox: you disclose *from a place of groundedness, not desperation.* You do not ask to be rescued. You reveal in order to *be real.*

There are three central pillars of designed vulnerability:

Intentionality – Vulnerability must serve a purpose. Whether that purpose is to clarify an internal tension, strengthen relational trust, or model authenticity in leadership, it should never be arbitrary. Ask: *What is this vulnerability in service of?*

Contextual Intelligence – Who are you sharing with, and what is the relational bandwidth between you? In an intimate partnership, deeper vulnerability may be appropriate. In a team setting, a more measured version may be required. Without this calibration, even truth can become misaligned.

Containment – Designed vulnerability respects boundaries—both yours and others'. It does not spill endlessly. It does not expect others to fix, absorb, or rescue. Instead, it shares openly *with full ownership of emotional responsibility*.

Designed vulnerability, then, is not about weakening your defences. It's about *removing them selectively and skillfully*.

The Internal Strength of Strategic Openness

From a developmental standpoint, vulnerability is essential for integration. Parts of the self that remain hidden from conscious awareness cannot be metabolised. They fester in the dark, becoming distorted. When you give voice to previously silenced truths—through writing, speaking, therapy, or relational dialogue—you initiate a process of psychological cohesion.

This practice strengthens internal resilience for several reasons:

It reduces cognitive load: The act of withholding significant internal truths—especially painful ones—demands mental effort. Designed vulnerability *lightens that burden*. By naming what was unnamed, the brain reallocates energy from suppression to reflection.

It disarms shame: As Brené Brown's research has demonstrated, shame thrives in secrecy. When expressed in safe, structured environments, vulnerability dismantles shame's power. It reframes perceived weakness as *human complexity*.

It fosters identity clarity: Voicing one's emotional truths, especially those that contradict the persona or social performance, allows for an integrated self-concept. You stop living as a fragmented self, and begin living as *a congruent one*.

These are not romanticised claims. They are well-supported by data from affective neuroscience and clinical psychology. Openness, when guided by structure and safety, *literally rewires how we process emotion, relate to others, and evaluate risk.*

Relational Trust as a Product of Strategic Disclosure

Relationally, designed vulnerability is the fast-track to earned trust. Not performative trust—built on image or role—but *earned trust*, built on perceived congruence and reliability.

Leaders who admit to uncertainty without collapsing into indecision build loyalty. Partners who name discomfort without blaming create emotional bandwidth. Teachers who share struggle without self-pity become more credible, not less.

Why? Because designed vulnerability communicates *self-awareness and courage.* It reveals not just emotional truth, but psychological stewardship. You are not at the mercy of your feelings—you are in *relationship* with them.

Moreover, designed vulnerability is reciprocal in its effect. When you model it well, you create a microclimate where others feel safer to do the same. This produces *mutual attunement*, a critical component in psychologically safe teams, partnerships, and communities.

Counterarguments and Ethical Considerations

To engage fully with this concept, we must also engage its limits.

Critics may argue that vulnerability, even when designed, creates unnecessary risk—particularly in competitive professional environments. There is merit to this caution. Not all systems reward honesty. Not all contexts are safe. Disclosing trauma to a transactional manager may lead to disadvantage, not empathy.

Hence, the emphasis on *design.* Strategic vulnerability is not radical transparency. It is not confession for its own sake. It is not about being emotionally naked with everyone. It is *about discerning which truths, when expressed, serve alignment rather than exposure.*

There is also the ethical dimension. Vulnerability must never be used manipulatively. Weaponised openness—such as strategic self-disclosure to engineer sympathy, evade accountability, or control narrative—violates its foundational principle: *truth in service of connection, not control.*

Authenticity without integrity becomes performance. And performance, no matter how moving, corrodes trust if misused.

Practical Applications: Designing Your Vulnerability Architecture

To implement this form of emotional architecture, one must begin by mapping their *current relationship to vulnerability*. Ask:

What truths am I withholding that, if spoken clearly, would increase my congruence?

What parts of myself feel unsafe to reveal? Why?

In which relationships am I under-sharing out of fear? In which am I over-sharing out of habit?

Next, establish *vulnerability protocols*. These are internal guidelines that govern your openness:

Create safety *before* disclosure. Choose trusted contexts.

Share from the scar, not the wound, when possible. Don't outsource healing through exposure.

Use language that owns emotion rather than projecting it.

When possible, preface vulnerability with a frame: "I'm sharing this because it matters to me—and I trust this space."

These practices may seem mechanical at first. But over time, they become intuitive. And the payoff is profound: relationships based on trust, not performance; leadership based on presence, not image; and an inner life marked by coherence, not compartmentalisation.

Closing Insight

The paradox of strength is that it often emerges most visibly *through intentional softness*. The more robust your internal scaffolding, the more safely you can allow truth to move through it. Designed vulnerability does not weaken—it *fortifies*. It does not distract—it *distills*. And it does not diminish your capacity—it *amplifies it.*

To be emotionally intelligent in the modern world is not to master stoicism or engineer a polished façade. It is to design a way of being that accommodates risk without recklessness, truth without collapse, and openness without regret.

Designed vulnerability is not about letting everything out. It's about *letting the right things through, in the right way, at the right time*—and becoming more human, not less, because of it.

Chapter 9
Mindset as Architecture, Not Attitude

There's a core misconception embedded in the way popular culture encourages us to approach mindset. It's often cast as something fleeting—like a pep talk you give yourself over coffee, only to watch it evaporate somewhere between a missed deadline and your fifth unread message. In this portrayal, mindset behaves more like a passing mood than a cognitive framework. You're either radiating "growth mindset" vibes today, or you've somehow failed at inner strength. The implication? If your inner world wavers, it's on you. A personal failing. A lack of discipline.

This narrative, though widely accepted, is intellectually shallow—and structurally misleading.

The idea of mindset has been compressed, reduced to slogans and shallow affirmations, when in truth it began as something far more layered. It's time to restore that dimensionality. Mindset is not a tone you adopt to impress yourself or others. It's not mood lighting. It's load-bearing. A form of mental architecture, grounded not in good intentions but in design—crafted, revisited, strengthened over time. It holds up under pressure precisely because it wasn't built in haste.

This chapter takes a deliberate turn away from the optics of positivity. No more sugar-coating chaos with upbeat clichés. Instead, we'll explore mindset as structural: a living, breathing internal system that organises your thoughts, interprets your environment, and gives shape to emotional endurance. It's not reactive. It's pre-emptive. More foundation than façade.

The essential point is this: mindset isn't something that flickers on when you feel inspired, then fades with fatigue. It is the cognitive architecture that decides what even registers as inspiration in the first place. It shapes how you filter experience, what interpretations you lean towards, and which assumptions quietly govern your choices—often long before you realise you're making any.

When mindset is misunderstood as a performance, people try to *will* themselves into clarity. They chase a kind of mental aesthetic: focus, grit, optimism. But they do so without addressing the framework that makes such clarity sustainable. What they need is not more motivational fuel—but a better engine.

The work of shaping mindset, then, is not about fixing your feelings. Nor is it about reaching for endless positivity like some psychological panacea. It is about claiming agency over the internal space where interpretation happens—where beliefs form, where resistance sets in, and where resilience is either cultivated or squandered. It's less "try harder" and more "build better."

And like any form of design, this requires principles. It demands that we examine our defaults, revise inherited cognitive scripts, and make deliberate decisions about how our internal structures function—not just under ideal conditions, but when stress hits, when ambiguity looms, when certainty wobbles.

A resilient mindset doesn't pretend chaos is beautiful. It just has a place to put it. It creates room for complexity without demanding resolution at every turn. It grants you enough psychological altitude to observe what's unfolding without being swallowed by it.

So this chapter is not here to offer comfort. It's here to hand you the blueprints. To help you see mindset as something you construct and inhabit—not something you chase. To understand that beneath the noise of daily thought is a deeper system that filters, absorbs, and often defines your perception of the world and of yourself. And that this system can be designed. Rethought. Reinforced.

Because in the end, it's not about choosing positivity. It's about choosing your architecture.

Why Architecture Is a Better Metaphor Than Attitude

Attitudes are surface phenomena—socially visible, quickly shiftable, and largely reactive. Architecture is deeper. It is preconditioned by materials, context, constraints, and long-term intentionality. One can fake an attitude for a job interview. One cannot fake the structural integrity of a building.

This distinction matters. If mindset is treated as attitude, it becomes susceptible to erosion by daily mood swings, environmental triggers, or social comparison. But if it is approached as internal architecture, it invites design—through intentional cognitive choices, thought rituals, and flexible self-talk structures that can be sustained even under psychological duress.

Consider a storm. The question is not whether the storm will come—it always does. The question is: *What have you built to endure it?*

Where many self-help models attempt to teach storm evasion, this chapter concerns itself with storm endurance. It introduces mindset as a deliberately engineered shelter—made not from denial, toxic positivity, or affirmations alone, but from real psychological materials: reappraisal, cognitive distancing, value anchoring, and temporal reframing.

Adaptive Thinking Is Not an Optional Upgrade—It Is a Survival Mechanism

At the core of this architectural view is the necessity of *adaptive thinking.* Our environments—technological, interpersonal, and existential—are in constant flux. A rigid mindset, no matter how seemingly confident, is brittle. It fractures under stress. In contrast, *a well-designed mindset incorporates mechanisms of flex*, allowing it to shift without collapse. This is cognitive agility, not ideological fluidity.

Therapeutic disciplines such as Cognitive Behavioural Therapy (CBT), Acceptance and Commitment Therapy (ACT), and Dialectical Behaviour Therapy (DBT) offer tools for this kind of design. These are not mere interventions for pathology; they are *design blueprints for the psychologically well.* For instance:

CBT trains thought awareness and restructuring—*replacing distorted cognitive inputs with more realistic alternatives.*

ACT teaches acceptance of discomfort alongside value-guided action—*building tension-tolerant structures within the self.*

DBT emphasises dialectical flexibility—*holding two seemingly opposing truths at once without disintegration.*

Taken together, these modalities form a toolkit for mental architecture that is both emotionally resilient and intellectually rigorous.

"This Is Temporary, but I Am Not": Anchoring Through Impermanence

One of the foundational design principles of a strong mindset is *anchoring in impermanence.* This may seem paradoxical. Isn't stability the goal? In truth, *what grants real internal stability is not denying change but designing for it.* Just as great architecture anticipates weather, decay, and human movement, mindset must account for emotional flux, unexpected loss, and relational dislocation.

The phrase "This is temporary, but I am not" becomes a stabilising mantra. It is not spiritual optimism. It is a cognitive anchor: the situation is transient, but the self remains the primary builder. This belief creates what Viktor Frankl described as an inner freedom—*a space between stimulus and response where one's power to choose resides.*

When internalised, this perspective transforms the meaning of challenge. A setback is no longer a reflection of fixed identity. It becomes a *material*—something that, once processed, can be integrated into the design. It also protects against the erosion of self-definition by external volatility.

This approach is not passive. It does not encourage blind endurance. Instead, it is *active framing*: building mental structures that allow discomfort to exist without defining the self.

Mindset as a Constructable Space: Implications for Daily Life

The idea that mindset is a buildable space has real-world consequences. It shifts responsibility not just inward—but forward.

Instead of waiting for motivation or clarity to arrive, one begins to *construct the conditions under which these emerge.*

A professional navigating burnout doesn't just try to "stay positive"—they redesign workflow expectations, integrate cognitive breaks, and use reframing to decouple self-worth from productivity metrics.

A student struggling with performance anxiety doesn't rely on generic encouragement—they build an internal narrative architecture grounded in effort, not identity, and learn to manage physiological signals through grounding techniques.

A parent managing emotional overload doesn't suppress it—they architect space for containment through rituals, emotional processing strategies, and value-based decision rules.

These are not theoretical gestures. They are applied examples of what it means to view mindset as infrastructure—not decoration.

Moving Beyond Motivation: The Myth of "Feeling Ready"

One of the most pervasive myths about mental functioning is that good mindset follows good mood. This belief leads many to wait—wait for inspiration, for energy, for clarity—before taking meaningful action. But designed mindset reverses the order: *you take action to build clarity, not the other way around.*

Mindset is not about *feeling ready*. It is about *building readiness conditions*—mental environments that support forward movement, even when emotions lag behind. This is the architecture of self-trust. Over time, it rewires the association between discomfort and paralysis. It teaches: *I can move before I feel perfect.*

In this sense, designed mindset reclaims emotional sovereignty. It acknowledges the presence of fear, doubt, and fatigue without granting them executive control. It builds space around them—space large enough for action to still occur.

What This Chapter Offers

In the pages that follow, this chapter will introduce the reader to actionable design strategies for building such a mindset space:

It will explore how *adaptive thinking* is taught, not inherited—and how to train cognitive flexibility using evidence-based therapeutic tools.

It will unpack the principle *"This is temporary, but I am not"* as a cognitive foundation for enduring high-ambiguity phases in life.

It will challenge the myth of mindset as mood and redefine it as an *environmental architecture*, capable of being engineered by those willing to build deliberately, rather than wait passively.

Critically, the chapter will treat mindset not as an abstract virtue, but as *an operational system*—one that interacts with behaviour, environment, values, and language. It is not about being mentally tough. It is about *being mentally well-designed.*

There is no "perfect mindset." There is only one that *fits the complexity of your current landscape*—and evolves with you. That is the mindset worth building.

Beyond Positivity: The Myth of the "Right Mindset"

One of the most pervasive intellectual hazards in the modern psychological discourse is the casual overuse of the phrase "right mindset." It's offered as a universal remedy: the antidote to failure, fear, procrastination, grief, stagnation. But like any poorly defined ideal, it does more to obscure than clarify. *The language of mindset has been flattened into motivational cliché—over-simplified, context-agnostic, and largely unexamined.* In practice, it functions less like a cognitive tool and more like a vague prescription written in neon font.

This chapter does not reject mindset as a construct. It rejects the hollowed-out version that saturates popular media, corporate onboarding slides, and self-help seminars. It challenges the illusion that there is a singular, universally "correct" mental posture that guarantees success or resilience. This isn't just intellectually dishonest—it's psychologically corrosive. By examining where the concept of "the right mindset" breaks down, we can begin to reconstruct something far more useful: *mindsets that are context-responsive, ethically coherent, and psychologically adaptive.*

The Cult of Positivity and Its Hidden Costs

"Just stay positive." "See the opportunity in every setback." "Reframe failure as feedback." These ideas are not inherently wrong. But when used indiscriminately, they become detached from nuance, ethics, and lived experience. *Positive thinking, when prescribed as a moral imperative, quickly turns into an instrument of denial.*

Psychologists have long noted the phenomenon of "toxic positivity"—the pressure to maintain an upbeat disposition even when it conflicts with reality. This isn't just emotionally disingenuous; it's neurologically costly. Studies in affective neuroscience suggest that emotional suppression, particularly in high-stakes or high-stress environments, *activates stress circuitry more intensely* than honest emotional acknowledgment. In other words, when you pretend to feel what you don't, you don't merely hide your discomfort—you amplify it.

Moreover, positivity as a default response can delegitimise complexity. Consider grief. Or systemic injustice. Or existential doubt. These are not problems to be reframed into silver linings. They are conditions that call for courage, clarity, and constructive endurance—not a grin and a gratitude list. *To treat all suffering as a perspective issue is to deny its depth.*

The Performative Mindset Economy

Mindset, once a construct grounded in rigorous psychological research—most notably Carol Dweck's work on "fixed vs. growth" orientations—has been appropriated into a performance metric. We are now encouraged to *display* the right mindset, often more than we are taught how to authentically develop one. This performative culture, especially prevalent in workplaces and online platforms, reinforces an invisible hierarchy: those who seem mentally unshakeable are rewarded with trust, leadership, and visibility. Those who reveal uncertainty, ambivalence, or mental fatigue are advised to "work on their mindset."

But performative mindset culture fails a fundamental test of integrity: it asks individuals to *appear* resilient rather than *be* resilient. In doing so, it generates internal dissonance. When outward positivity is demanded and inward conflict is suppressed, the result is psychological incongruence—often a precursor to burnout or emotional disengagement. In short, *pretending to have the "right mindset" can erode the very psychological robustness it claims to promote.*

Context Matters: The Problem with One-Size-Fits-All Mindsets

Any mindset—however well-intentioned—is only as effective as its alignment with context. This is where the myth of the universally "right" mindset collapses. Resilience in a startup founder looks different than resilience in a trauma survivor. Optimism in a first-year university student functions differently than in a terminally ill patient. The assumption that one type of mindset—a blend of optimism, perseverance, and positivity—should be universally applied is not only naive; it's anti-human.

More precisely, *mindsets must be designed in conversation with context.* Cognitive flexibility, not cognitive rigidity, is what enables a person to shift strategies when circumstances demand it. A surgeon in an emergency setting must suspend empathy momentarily to execute under pressure. A therapist, by contrast, must foreground attunement and psychological presence. Neither is more correct. They are *fit-for-purpose.*

This idea echoes what political theorist Isaiah Berlin once called the distinction between *monist* and *pluralist* worldviews. Monism seeks a single truth or ideal; pluralism accepts that multiple, often conflicting values can be valid simultaneously. Most popular mindset rhetoric is monist—it claims there's one optimal way to think. But real life is pluralist. It demands agility. *The most effective mindsets are those that evolve, not those that harden into ideology.*

The Ethical Dimensions of Mindset Prescription

The insistence on cultivating a "right mindset" also carries ethical implications. Who defines what the right mindset is? In many corporate settings, the desired mindset aligns suspiciously well with productivity metrics: resilient, adaptable, enthusiastic about change. While these traits are often beneficial, they are not morally neutral. *Framing these traits as universally virtuous obscures the power dynamics at play.*

For instance, an employee resisting an unrealistic deadline might be told they need a better mindset. But what if their resistance is ethical, not psychological? What if the real problem is structural exploitation, not personal attitude? When mindset language is used to deflect from systemic issues, it becomes a form of gaslighting—*a way to recast legitimate grievance as personal inadequacy.*

Similarly, in education, children from under-resourced backgrounds are often encouraged to adopt a growth mindset without comparable attention to material inequality. The implicit message: "If you fail, it's your mindset." This obscures structural disadvantage and overemphasises individual responsibility. *Mindset, in such contexts, becomes a tool of quiet compliance.*

Redefining Mindset: Toward Psychological Adaptability

Rather than pursuing a mythical "right mindset," we should be cultivating *psychological adaptability*. This is not a personality trait but a cognitive skill set: the ability to recalibrate mental frameworks in response to shifting environments, new information, and emotional complexity.

This includes:

Meta-cognition: awareness of one's own thought patterns and their biases

Reframing: the capacity to reinterpret events from multiple perspectives without distorting them

Value-based navigation: making decisions anchored in chosen, stable values rather than transient emotional states

Distress tolerance: the ability to hold psychological discomfort without defaulting to denial or premature closure

These are not always "positive" qualities. Sometimes they involve tolerating ambiguity, confronting painful truths, or choosing the less comforting option. But they are sustainable—and more importantly, *they are honest.*

The Language of Precision: Moving Beyond Binary Labels

A final, crucial point: the language we use to describe mindset shapes how we live it. Words like "right," "positive," or "strong" carry implicit judgments. They imply that deviations are failures. By contrast, more precise language—such as "context-appropriate," "value-aligned," or "ethically consistent"—invites reflection rather than performance.

It is not that optimism, perseverance, or confidence are unhelpful. It is that they should be *options in a broader repertoire*, not commandments to be obeyed regardless of circumstance. Just as architects choose materials based on climate, terrain, and function, so too must individuals build mindsets that fit the contours of their lives.

The invitation, then, is not to abandon mindset thinking, but to *upgrade its architecture*. To replace vague ideals with intentional structures. To stop asking, "Do I have the right mindset?" and start asking, *"What mental structure do I need to build for this particular reality—and how can I build it with integrity?"*

Designing for Adaptive Thinking – How Flexible Cognition Becomes a Mental Architecture

A brittle mind, like a brittle structure, fails not at the margins but at its core. It is rigidity—not weakness—that most often precedes collapse. In volatile environments, whether personal, professional, or societal, the most critical cognitive asset is not intelligence, motivation, or confidence. It is adaptability. Yet, despite its fundamental importance, adaptive thinking remains one of the least cultivated capacities in conventional education, organisational training, and even mainstream self-development.

Adaptive thinking is not simply reacting well to change—it is the architecture that allows us to remain structurally intact while redesigning ourselves from within.

To think adaptively is to perceive context with clarity, to shift mental models without abandoning coherence, and to maintain integrity without demanding control. And unlike temperament or intelligence quotient, adaptive thinking is not fixed—it is trainable. What follows is not a motivational suggestion but a structural imperative: *cognitive flexibility must be designed, not left to chance.* Drawing on contemporary psychology, evidence-based therapies, and philosophical insight, this chapter outlines how to construct a mind that bends without breaking—and why doing so is not just useful, but urgent.

The Psychology of Rigidity and Why It Fails

Cognitive rigidity often masquerades as certainty. It clings to routine, resists contradiction, and prioritises closure over inquiry. At its core lies a fear: that dissonance signals failure, that ambiguity denotes weakness, that change threatens identity. But reality is rarely static, and those who organise their thinking around fixed scripts eventually encounter what systems theorist Donella Meadows called "paradigm boundaries"—the invisible walls beyond which their inherited assumptions no longer apply.

Clinical psychology provides a clear account of what happens when rigid thinking meets dynamic environments. In cognitive behavioural therapy (CBT), for example, unyielding thought patterns are often identified as *cognitive distortions*—beliefs like "If I can't do it perfectly, I shouldn't do it at all," or "If something bad happens, it's a sign I'm failing." These rigid schemas fuel anxiety, depression, and burnout, not because the world is too harsh, but because the mind is too narrow to interpret it constructively.

Psychological flexibility, by contrast, is the central construct in Acceptance and Commitment Therapy (ACT), an approach that teaches individuals to hold thoughts lightly, clarify values, and act in alignment—even when discomfort is present. Rather than controlling internal experiences, ACT practitioners train individuals to observe them, disentangle from them, and reorient behaviour with intentionality. *This is not passivity—it is conscious adaptation.* The goal is not to feel better, but to live better, regardless of how one feels.

Designing Thought: From Architecture to Practice

The word "design" is not incidental. Like any form of architecture, adaptive thinking must be structurally planned, functionally tested, and periodically revised. It requires foundational principles, not ad hoc strategies. Three pillars form the basis of this design:

Cognitive Flexibility – the capacity to revise beliefs, perspectives, and interpretations without psychological fragmentation. This includes the ability to hold competing truths, delay closure, and shift mental lenses deliberately.

Context Sensitivity – the discernment to recognise which mindset or response is most appropriate in a given environment. Without this, flexibility becomes chaos. With it, adaptability becomes precision.

Value Anchoring – stable internal priorities that serve as ballast in the face of shifting circumstances. Flexibility does not mean rootlessness. It means adjusting the superstructure without uprooting the foundation.

To train these capacities is to move beyond information consumption and into *cognitive craftsmanship*. A designed mind does not simply adopt new beliefs when old ones fail; it *builds new interpretive scaffolds*—models that can flex under uncertainty without collapsing into relativism or contradiction.

Case Study: Adaptive Thinking in High-Stakes Environments

Consider the case of surgeons in high-pressure emergency settings. During a critical operation, a previously successful protocol may suddenly prove insufficient. A rigid adherence to precedent could cost a life. An effective surgeon must integrate evolving data (vital signs, visual feedback, team communication), reassess strategy in real time, and *execute a cognitive pivot* without panic or ego. This is not instinct; it is trained adaptability. Over years of practice, such professionals internalise the principle that *correctness is dynamic*, not fixed.

Similarly, in military decision-making, adaptive thinking is formally trained under the doctrine of "mission command"—a philosophy that empowers frontline leaders to deviate from original plans in response to real-time shifts, as long as their actions remain aligned with the overarching intent. Rigid execution of orders is no longer seen as discipline—it is often seen as failure to adapt to the complexity of modern battlefields. *The most reliable operators are those who think structurally, not reactively.*

Techniques from Cognitive Therapies that Foster Flexibility

Contemporary therapeutic frameworks offer practical tools for training adaptability in everyday thinking. These are not life hacks—they are *mental mechanisms*. Each offers a discipline of perception, interpretation, or behavioural alignment.

Cognitive Defusion (ACT): Instead of trying to eliminate negative thoughts, individuals learn to observe them as mental events—not truths. Saying "I'm having the thought that I'm failing" creates space between self and belief. This design feature separates content from identity, allowing more flexible responses.

Socratic Questioning (CBT): A method of interrogating assumptions. Questions like "What evidence supports this thought?", "What alternative explanations are there?", or "What would I tell a friend in the same situation?" destabilise automatic beliefs and activate prefrontal reasoning—moving the thinker from reactivity to reflection.

Reattribution Training (Schema Therapy): Teaches individuals to consider external, unstable, and specific causes for distressing events—thereby avoiding the "globalising" distortions that trap people in hopelessness. This reframes setbacks as problems to solve, not identities to adopt.

Dialectical Thinking (DBT): Encourages holding two seemingly opposing truths simultaneously—e.g., "I am doing my best, and I need to do better." This reduces black-and-white thinking and reinforces psychological nuance, particularly useful in interpersonal conflicts.

Each of these practices serves one purpose: *to loosen the grip of certainty and build the capacity for structured change.*

Philosophical Grounding: Flexibility as Virtue, Not Compromise

Philosophers have long recognised the power—and peril—of rigidity. Ancient Stoics spoke of *prohairesis*, the inner faculty of judgment that remains under our control even when events are not. But contrary to modern caricatures, Stoicism was not about emotional suppression—it was about mental adaptability rooted in virtue. Marcus Aurelius wrote not about dominating one's mind but about tuning it to nature's rhythms.

Similarly, pragmatist philosopher William James argued for "the will to believe" not as blind optimism, but as an *openness to possibility* in the absence of certainty. He believed the most vital intellectual capacity was *the ability to act under uncertainty without retreating into dogma or paralysis.*

These thinkers offer a consistent message: adaptive thinking is not weakness or indecision. It is disciplined openness. *It is the ability to design thought in alignment with both truth and purpose.*

Barriers to Adaptation: Why We Resist Mental Flexibility

Despite its benefits, adaptive thinking is often misperceived as indecisiveness or lack of conviction. In reality, what most resists adaptation is not intellect but ego. The attachment to previous identities, beliefs, or social postures makes mental flexibility feel like self-betrayal. Moreover, many educational and cultural systems reward consistency over evolution. Politicians are punished for changing their minds. Employees are labelled "unstable" if they question organisational orthodoxy. This creates a paradox: *our most adaptive minds are often punished in rigid systems.*

The solution is not to conform to such systems but to outgrow them—to develop internal architectures robust enough to *absorb contradiction without losing coherence.* This is a higher order of thinking: one that regards change not as a deviation from the self but as a function of growth.

The Architecture You Build, Not the Attitude You Perform

In closing—not with cliché, but with clarity—adaptive thinking is not a mood to summon or a trait to inherit. *It is an inner architecture you construct deliberately.* Like any sound structure, it must be tested under load, refined over time, and anchored in stable foundations. Its components—flexibility, context sensitivity, value alignment—are not motivational slogans. They are *engineering decisions.*

To build such a mind is not easy. But neither is living in one that fractures under strain. Rigidity may offer the comfort of predictability, but adaptability offers the power of longevity. And as any seasoned builder will tell you: the structure that bends is the one that endures.

"This Is Temporary, but I Am Not" – Encourages Impermanence-Based Mindset Stability

The modern mind is under constant siege—not only from the velocity of change in the external world but from the psychological demand to remain perpetually in control of it. From economic volatility to cultural flux, from rapid technological advancement to personal upheaval, stability can feel like a myth or a luxury afforded to others. And yet, beneath this churn lies a powerful, often misunderstood truth: *the capacity to endure is not built on certainty but on clarity*. When we learn to internalise the transience of circumstances while remaining anchored in a durable sense of identity, we design a mindset that does not collapse with the shifting weather of our lives.

The phrase *"This is temporary, but I am not"* is not a motivational slogan; it is an architectural principle for mental resilience. It is an invitation to rethink stability—not as the absence of difficulty, but as the capacity to contextualise difficulty within a larger, enduring framework of self. When adopted deeply, this principle alters how we process adversity, regulate emotion, and engage with uncertainty. It reframes endurance not as brute resistance, but as intelligent adaptation. This is not about positivity. It is about design.

The Fallacy of Permanent Emotion

One of the most common distortions in human cognition is the affective forecasting error—the assumption that our current emotional state will persist far into the future. When overwhelmed, we project that overwhelm onto tomorrow. When stuck, we assume stuckness is our new baseline. But neuropsychological research suggests that even intense emotions—grief, shame, elation—tend to decay more rapidly than we anticipate. The brain is inherently dynamic; its neurochemical landscape is built for flux.

Yet, because emotion feels immersive, we mistake it for permanence. This is particularly evident in depressive cognition, where the dominant narrative becomes not "I feel low today," but "*I am someone who will always feel this way.*" The distinction between *state* and *trait* collapses, and identity fuses with momentary pain.

To counter this collapse, we need to recover a core psychological faculty: *temporal framing*. That is, the deliberate contextualisation of present experience within a larger temporal arc. Cognitive-behavioural therapies, particularly those influenced by Acceptance and Commitment Therapy (ACT), teach individuals to notice and name thoughts and feelings without fusing with them. One might say, "I am experiencing self-doubt," rather than "I am a failure." This language is not semantic triviality—it is structural design. It reinforces the self as an observer of experiences, not merely a container for them.

Designing for Mental Continuity

In architectural terms, permanence is not synonymous with immobility. A well-designed structure is not static—it flexes. Think of a suspension bridge engineered to sway in heavy wind. Its strength is not in rigidity, but in elasticity governed by intelligent constraint. Mindsets must work the same way. Psychological endurance is the product of designed flexibility, not dogged resistance.

This is where impermanence becomes a feature, not a flaw. When we accept that emotional states, social roles, ambitions, and even identities are in constant evolution, we stop requiring that the world conform to a false narrative of fixedness. Instead, we build stability into the self—not as an unchanging monument, but as a flexible framework that adapts without fracturing.

In practice, this might look like designing "mental anchors" that hold firm amid change. These can be core values, personal philosophies, grounding rituals, or structured self-reflections. The point is not to resist change, but to hold fast to that which does not change arbitrarily. A sense of purpose, for example, can remain stable even when jobs, relationships, or contexts shift. *It is this continuity of principle—not of environment—that creates psychological integrity over time.*

Historical Parallels and Philosophical Echoes

This view of impermanence as a source of strength is not novel, but it is urgent. In Buddhist philosophy, the concept of *anicca*—the principle that all conditioned phenomena are transient—is a central path to liberation. The Stoics, too, advocated for *premeditatio malorum*—the anticipation of difficulty not as pessimism, but as a mental rehearsal for resilience. Marcus Aurelius wrote: "*You have power over your mind—not outside events. Realise this, and you will find strength.*"These are not antiquated spiritual musings. They are precise psychological strategies: shift locus of control inward, contextualise loss, accept change, and respond with agency.

In modern psychological terms, this translates into fostering a *growth mindset* (Dweck), *psychological flexibility* (Hayes), and *emotional granularity* (Barrett)—concepts that, while secular in language, echo these ancient insights. What these perspectives share is a commitment to *equipping the individual with inner architecture robust enough to house temporary chaos.*

Impermanence as a Design Constraint

From a systems-thinking perspective, constraints are not limitations—they are tools. Architects, composers, and engineers all recognise that creative stability emerges not despite limitations but because of them. Likewise, designing for mindset stability requires acknowledging the constraint of impermanence—not denying it, but building with it in mind.

Consider the example of a trauma survivor. One of the most damaging sequelae of trauma is the internalisation that the pain is now part of the self—etched permanently into identity. But trauma-informed approaches, such as those developed by Bessel van der Kolk or Gabor Maté, emphasise reprocessing the narrative: that the event happened to you, but it is not *you.* This shift allows the individual to hold the experience in memory without collapsing the self around it. The pain becomes part of the structure, but no longer defines it.

In professional contexts, the same logic applies. A project may fail. A career path may shift. A market may collapse. If one's identity is over-attached to any single outcome, then volatility becomes existential. But if identity is designed around enduring competencies or purpose—rather than fluctuating titles or metrics—then the individual can pivot without psychological disintegration.

Impermanence becomes a design constraint for a more flexible, intelligent self—not a threat to selfhood itself.

Beyond Positivity, Toward Psychological Realism

It is important to note that the embrace of impermanence should not be confused with denial, toxic positivity, or passive resignation. Stability is not achieved by pretending everything is fine. It is achieved by admitting that not everything will be—but *you will be*, because your sense of self is constructed with more than one room. You can contain grief and hope. You can acknowledge fragility and still act with conviction. This is not a contradiction. It is adulthood.

There is a profound difference between controlling emotions and holding them. When we insist on control—on fixing everything immediately, on reaching clarity without discomfort—we often amplify suffering. But when we *hold* emotions within a designed structure of understanding and perspective, we allow them to pass *through* us rather than define us.

This, ultimately, is the quiet power of "This is temporary, but I am not." It is not a call to ignore the weather. It is a reminder that you have built shelter—internally. That your identity, crafted with care and anchored in principle, is not held hostage by any single storm.

Closing Insight

Every architect knows that a strong foundation must be laid before the building rises. But not every architect remembers that the building must also be designed to shift—seasonally, structurally, even culturally. The same is true of the mind. Designing a mindset for permanence in an impermanent world is not just an intellectual exercise—it is an ethical one. You owe it to yourself to become a stable force in a volatile world. But that stability must be designed, not declared. It must be built from the acceptance of change, not the denial of it.

And that begins with an unassuming but powerful mental statement: *This is temporary. But I am not.*

Mindset Is a Space You Build, Not a Mood You Find – Defining Mindset as a Constructable Inner Environment

At some point in the last two decades, the term *mindset* was quietly diluted. Once a concept rooted in structured cognitive frameworks and behavioural design, it now circulates in wellness circles as a near-synonym for mood. "Shift your mindset," "adopt a growth mindset," "stay in the right headspace"—phrases that promise transformation, often without explanation or rigour. But mindset is not a mood. It is not a feeling state to be summoned by positive thinking. It is a mental architecture—constructed deliberately, iteratively, and with constraints. Just as a building must be designed to bear weight, withstand weather, and serve a purpose, so must a mindset. It is a system, not a sentiment.

This distinction is not semantic. It is structural. When mindset is treated as a mood, we judge its health based on how we feel in the moment. But when mindset is understood as a constructable environment, its function becomes long-range: to shape thinking, perception, and behaviour over time—*even when emotional conditions are poor*. It is precisely when we don't feel like being patient, generous, or focused that our mindset—if well-designed—can still produce those behaviours. This is not because we feel aligned, but because we've engineered alignment.

The Architecture of Mental Framing

To build a mindset is to construct a cognitive frame through which experience is interpreted and action is taken. Framing is not a passive lens; it is a living system that gives meaning to events. This principle is well documented in behavioural science. The same situation—rejection, loss, failure—can be interpreted as threat, challenge, feedback, or irrelevance depending on the mindset framing it.

Consider two individuals receiving identical feedback at work: "This project didn't meet expectations." One person spirals into self-doubt, interpreting the statement as an indictment of their capabilities. Another interprets it as a precise data point—a cue to adjust tactics without absorbing identity-level damage. The emotional response is downstream of the mental frame. The difference is not sensitivity; it is structure.

In cognitive-behavioural therapy (CBT), this phenomenon is operationalised through the practice of cognitive restructuring—the active redesign of maladaptive thought patterns into more accurate, functional ones. But even outside therapy, this approach remains applicable: individuals who build their mindset consciously can insulate themselves against the volatility of mood or external feedback. They do not deny emotion. They design around it.

Mood Is Weather; Mindset Is Shelter

The danger of conflating mindset with mood lies in their radically different temporal natures. Mood is transient. It is affected by sleep, blood sugar, ambient noise, unresolved conflict. It comes and goes. Mindset, if designed properly, does not. It persists. It shapes not only what we think, but *how* we think.

Take, for example, professional athletes. At elite levels, performance rarely hinges on skill gaps. It hinges on mindset—on whether the athlete can remain composed, adaptive, and strategic in high-stress moments. These qualities do not emerge from mood. They emerge from years of cognitive design: mental rehearsals, scenario planning, inner dialogue scripting. Mindset, in these cases, becomes a *performance environment* built and maintained under pressure.

What's true for athletes is true, in scaled form, for the rest of us. Whether you are preparing for a medical exam, delivering a board presentation, navigating divorce, or building a company, your success is less contingent on momentary emotional clarity than on whether you've built an internal space designed for clarity, regardless of emotion.

Mindset as a System of Constraints and Intentions

In architectural terms, good design is not merely aesthetic; it is functional. It anticipates needs. It accounts for load-bearing pressures. The same applies to mental design. A functional mindset is not merely aspirational; it is *load-tested.* It must withstand periods of fatigue, ambiguity, and conflict. To do so, it must be constructed not with vague affirmations, but with intentional constraints.

Constraints, in this context, are not restrictions on freedom—they are design principles that create reliability. For example:

A mindset built around the principle *"I do hard things even when I don't feel like it"* creates behavioural reliability under motivational deficit.

A mindset grounded in *'My identity is not dependent on approval"* produces durability in the face of criticism.

A mindset that holds *"Learning matters more than performing"* supports resilience after public failure.

These are not beliefs that can be plucked off an Instagram feed. They must be rehearsed, built into language, reflected in decision-making, and reinforced through action. *The test of mindset is not how it feels when things go well, but how it functions when they don't.*

Real-World Case Study: Adaptive Mindset in High-Stakes Environments

Let us consider a relevant domain where mindset-as-space is operationalised with precision: spaceflight. NASA's astronaut training includes not only physical endurance and technical mastery but intensive mindset design. Astronauts are taught cognitive protocols for operating under extreme uncertainty, isolation, and systems failure. The mindset designed for them is not "stay positive," but "follow protocol under pressure," "trust systems over panic," and "reduce scope to immediate controllables."

This framework is architected through mental simulations, scenario-based repetition, and value alignment. The result is not emotional detachment—it is durable mental space that enables clarity in crisis. For astronauts, mindset is not an accessory; it is infrastructure. This same principle holds for physicians in trauma wards, military strategists in hostile zones, or crisis negotiators mediating high-tension situations. In every case, mood cannot be relied upon. Design must be.

Philosophical Echoes: Stoicism and Inner Engineering

This concept also finds deep roots in philosophy. The Stoics, notably Epictetus and Marcus Aurelius, made no demand for optimism or cheerfulness. Instead, they encouraged designing the mind to withstand insult, loss, and chaos. The key Stoic insight was not suppression—it was *structure*. The Stoic mindset was not about feeling invulnerable, but about constructing a mental system wherein *one's values remained intact under duress*. Seneca's reminder that "we suffer more in imagination than in reality" is not a plea for positive thinking—it is a prompt to redesign the imagination.

Modern-day thinkers like Naval Ravikant and Nassim Taleb echo this sentiment. Ravikant speaks of building internal "equanimity engines," while Taleb discusses "antifragility"—systems that get stronger under stress. In both cases, the theme is clear: *construct mindset environments that not only absorb chaos but improve from it.* That requires not just awareness but architecture.

The Role of Repetition and Reinforcement

If mindset is space, then rituals are the carpentry. No mindset, however well designed in theory, will endure without reinforcement. This is where practices like journalling, reflection, affirmations (if precise), and values-based reviews come in—not as spiritual accessories, but as *structural maintenance.*

Psychologist James Clear, in his research on habit formation, notes that identity is shaped through repeated action. When you act in alignment with a mindset, even under stress, you reinforce it. When you bypass it, you undermine its architecture. The implication is clear: mindset must be lived to be stable. It must be practiced in small, granular moments—choosing patience in traffic, choosing composure during conflict, choosing curiosity over defensiveness.

The great challenge, and opportunity, is that these moments are design opportunities. Each response is a brick. Each ritual, a beam. Each value decision, a cornerstone.

Practical Implications: Building Your Own Mental Space

To move from theory to application, begin with two anchoring questions:

What emotional states most frequently destabilise my thinking?

What structural mindset design would allow me to think clearly in those states—regardless of them?

Then ask: *What rituals, language patterns, and value principles can I embed to make that design hold—especially under stress?*

This is the essence of mindset-as-architecture: it is *intentionally created*, not passively experienced. And like architecture, it must be revised, inspected, reinforced, and sometimes redesigned altogether. But when built well, it provides not only mental shelter but also cognitive agility. You can move freely within it—not because the world is safe, but because your inner space is sound.

Chapter 10
Identity Reconstruction – Who Are You Without the Old Walls?

At any given moment, each of us is the outcome of structures—some we've deliberately shaped, many we've simply absorbed. Identity is often romanticised as something to be uncovered, like a long-lost artefact buried beneath years of memory, pressure, and role-playing. The prevailing myth suggests that beneath our obligations, traumas, triumphs, and the myths handed down by family or culture, lies an authentic self just waiting to be unearthed. But let's be candid: identity isn't discovered. It's assembled. More specifically, it's constructed out of the ideas, narratives, and assumptions we never think to interrogate.

Those unexamined elements—the ones we inherit, repeat, and wrap ourselves in without resistance—form the structure we mistake for the self. They are quiet, habitual, and—more often than not—socially rewarded. So we leave them unchallenged. We call them "me."

This chapter begins where most self-help narratives tend to trail off. Not with the euphoric notion of finding oneself, but with the more difficult, more rigorous work of reconstructing. We're not digging for the so-called "real you." We're drafting. We're drawing up blueprints. We're tearing down inherited walls and choosing which ones deserve to be rebuilt.

The guiding premise is unapologetically architectural: identity is not essence, but edifice. It's a structure we inhabit. We move through it, maintain it, sometimes get stuck in its corners. And, as with any long-standing dwelling, there comes a point when its layout no longer serves. When its foundation cracks. When the interior starts feeling more like confinement than comfort. Renovation becomes inevitable. Sometimes, demolition is the wiser path.

The question—"Who are you without the old walls?"—is not some abstract, candlelit enquiry fit for a mindfulness retreat. It's a hard-nosed design challenge. A structural audit. It demands we examine the origins of our inner architecture. What was constructed in fear? What was borrowed for approval? What was installed hastily, under pressure, and has never been re-evaluated?

Consider the roles you've mastered. Are they reflections of your nature—or relics of what others once needed from you? Consider the beliefs you've long held. Were they chosen, or merely absorbed because questioning them would have disrupted too much comfort or kinship? And your personality—does it truly represent your disposition, or is it a polished survival strategy, honed through repetition and mistaken for authenticity?

These questions don't concern self-esteem or self-acceptance in the conventional sense. They are far more structural. They're about authorship. About whether you are the architect of your identity—or merely the occupant of a blueprint you never realised you could revise.

To step into this kind of inquiry is not easy. But it is liberating. Because once you recognise that identity isn't a truth to be found, but a structure to be designed, you reclaim the creative agency you may have unknowingly handed over years ago. And from that reclaimed space, something honest—perhaps for the first time—can begin to take shape.

Identity as a Designed, Layered System

Most models of identity still presume a core essence—something stable and discoverable, like the soul of a narrative protagonist. But psychology, sociology, and behavioural science increasingly converge on a more dynamic model: identity as a layered, adaptive construct. James Marcia's identity status theory, for instance, suggests that individuals move through stages of exploration and commitment, shifting identity across domains (e.g. career, belief systems, gender roles) over time. The work of Dan McAdams adds narrative structure to this—our sense of self is largely the result of the *stories we tell about ourselves*, stories that are edited and retold in light of new experience.

Yet, if we accept identity as layered and narrative-based, then it follows that it is also *designable.* Not in the superficial sense of "crafting a persona," but in the deeper, more serious sense of constructing inner coherence. The question is not "Who am I really?" but "Who have I been rehearsing to be—and why?" In this view, selfhood is not a static artefact but a site of continual iteration. We are the sum of our practiced beliefs, filtered memories, reflexive values, and social contracts. To reconstruct identity, then, is to engage in deliberate reconfiguration.

But that demands something frightening: demolishing the old walls.

Letting Go of Familiar Blueprints

Much of what we consider "ourselves" is, upon scrutiny, inherited pattern. If you were raised to equate success with achievement, you may mistake rest for laziness. If you were praised for being "the responsible one," you may fear flexibility as chaos. If you learned early that vulnerability invites rejection, stoicism may become a self-defining virtue. These aren't natural truths. They're reinforcements—emotional architecture calcified over time.

The task, then, is not to shame these walls. Many kept you safe. Many allowed you to belong. But safety and belonging are not the same as flourishing. When these structures begin to feel cramped, outdated, or dissonant, they must be examined not with guilt, but with discernment. And if needed, with disassembly.

This is the difference between storytelling and *storybuilding*—the latter is a future-focused practice. It recognises that while your past informs your foundations, it need not dictate the floorplan. Storybuilding asks: *What kind of person am I becoming? What values am I constructing into the walls of my decisions? What kind of inner space do I want to inhabit?* These are questions of both freedom and responsibility.

You Are Both Builder and Dweller

One of the most powerful mindset shifts a person can make is the recognition that they are not merely the product of their identity, but its architect. This is not motivational sentiment—it's cognitive reality. Consider neuroplasticity: the brain's demonstrated capacity to rewire itself in response to thought, behaviour, and environment. The implications are staggering. You are not trapped in an old version of yourself. You may have habituated to it, but you are not bound to it.

The concept of *being both builder and resident* of the inner world is central to modern therapeutic frameworks, including Acceptance and Commitment Therapy (ACT), Internal Family Systems (IFS), and narrative psychology. In each case, the individual is invited not merely to observe their identity, but to engage in its redesign. ACT, for instance, centres on "value-based action"—the idea that identity stability comes not from self-description, but from *self-direction.* IFS invites dialogue between competing inner parts, allowing for a more complex, yet coherent sense of self. Narrative psychology frames identity as a draftable manuscript. Each model, in its own language, affirms the same truth: *you are not finished.*

But taking on the role of builder is demanding. Unlike dwelling passively within an identity, building requires intentional choices about what to keep, what to upgrade, and what to let go. It means taking ownership of previously outsourced decisions—about morality, ambition, purpose, even personality. It means no longer hiding behind the excuse of "this is just who I am."

The Psychological Cost of Reconstruction

Identity work is not intellectually tidy. It is emotionally destabilising. Letting go of an identity—particularly one that has social currency—often triggers grief, alienation, or fear. The risk is not hypothetical. People have lost communities, jobs, even families for revising their core beliefs or stepping outside prescribed roles. This is why many hesitate to begin. But the cost of *not* doing the work is far greater: an inner life that feels misaligned, performative, or stifled.

Modern identity theory increasingly recognises the phenomenon of *false coherence*—where individuals present a unified, consistent self externally, while experiencing deep fragmentation internally. This psychological incongruence can manifest as burnout, anxiety, or existential depression—not because something is "wrong" with the person, but because they are trapped in an identity that no longer fits. Reconstruction is not indulgence. It is integrity work.

What This Chapter Offers

This chapter provides a structured yet flexible approach to identity reconstruction. It will guide you through the layered process of drafting the new self—not as a spontaneous reinvention, but as a designed system. You will learn how to distinguish inherited roles from chosen values, how to shift from passive storytelling to active storybuilding, and how to take ownership as both architect and resident of your internal world. Along the way, we will examine historical perspectives, psychological frameworks, and contemporary case studies that illustrate how identity can be reshaped—ethically, consciously, and courageously.

If previous chapters helped you understand the frameworks of thought, emotion, and value alignment, this chapter asks you to consolidate those learnings into a deeper proposition: *Who are you now willing to become, and what will you construct to hold that version of yourself?*

This is not a call to abandon your past. It is an invitation to unburden yourself from its architectural tyranny. The stories that once defined you may still be part of your scaffolding, but they need not dictate your skyline. What matters now is what you build next—and how intentionally you inhabit it.

The Collapse of Roles – Navigating Identity Voids After Major Life Changes

The human identity is often scaffolded by roles—titles we wear like architecture around our sense of self. Parent. Partner. Professional. Provider. Patient. These are not merely functions; they are scripts. We perform them daily, unconsciously measuring our worth, structure, and direction through them. And while roles help stabilise our social navigation, their collapse—whether through divorce, redundancy, illness, ageing, migration, or even personal awakening—can feel like a psychic free fall. When a core role dissolves, what often follows is not just a loss of routine but a profound disorientation: *If I am not this anymore, then what am I?*

This is not a modern predicament. Throughout history, rites of passage—from initiation rituals to mourning practices—have served as communal scaffolds for identity transitions. But in today's individualistic and accelerationist cultures, we are often left to navigate these dislocations alone. The result? People emerge from loss or change not just grieving a person or position, but grappling with the disappearance of the internal architecture that gave their days coherence. *Identity voids are real—and they are not psychological side effects, but structural crises.*

To understand this, we must move away from viewing roles as mere garments we choose to wear. Roles are environments we inhabit. They are mental and emotional habitats that tell us where to stand in relation to others, how to make decisions, what to prioritise, and even how to feel. A mother's role, for example, is not limited to parenting tasks; it informs values, daily rhythms, emotional expectations, and long-term planning. When such a role collapses—through children leaving home, through estrangement, or even through a shift in internal meaning—the vacated space is not neutral. It is filled with echoes, with the phantom habits of a former life, with identity inertia.

The psychology of role loss is layered. Cognitive dissonance often emerges first—an internal conflict between the self-concept we've internalised and the external reality that no longer validates it. A once-respected executive, after sudden redundancy, may continue to think in terms of departmental structure, deadlines, or hierarchy, even as their days grow unstructured. This dissonance creates friction, often mistaken for laziness or depression, when it is more accurately the mind's search for a new operating system. Here, the question is not whether one is resilient, but whether the internal tools for reconstruction exist.

Many therapeutic models address grief or trauma, but fewer offer blueprints for identity redesign in the absence of external role markers. And yet, this is one of the most important transitions a person can make: the move from *being defined by a role* to *defining oneself independently of roles*. Doing so is not an act of negation, but of architecture—rebuilding selfhood with deeper intentionality.

The first insight to accept is this: roles are not identities; they are structures housing parts of identity. When a role collapses, we can mourn its scaffolding without mistaking it for the whole building. But this requires internal differentiation—recognising what part of ourselves was contingent on external validation, and what part remains stable regardless. This distinction is not always intuitive. Social psychology shows that people tend to over-identify with their most socially rewarded role, even when it does not reflect their deeper values. A public intellectual may feel adrift not because they no longer think deeply, but because no audience is listening. The internal self still exists—but its feedback loop has gone quiet.

Second, we must normalise the void. Just as architecture requires empty space for light and flow, so too does psychological reconstruction require phases of internal emptiness. The void after role collapse is not evidence of brokenness, but a necessary clearing. This period often feels barren because we've been conditioned to equate productivity with purpose. But in reality, it is a fertile ground. It is in this state that alternative values, suppressed aspects of self, and new directions can be perceived—often for the first time in years.

Third, we must turn from storytelling to *storybuilding*. Storytelling relies on coherence with the past; it seeks to make linear sense of what has already happened. Storybuilding, by contrast, is a design discipline. It starts not from memory, but from vision. This is where narrative therapy, design thinking, and existential psychology converge. The future self is not found—it is constructed. And the materials of this construction are not always dramatic reinventions; often, they are quiet recognitions of long-ignored desires, latent strengths, or nascent philosophies.

Consider the case of someone who has retired after four decades in a demanding corporate environment. The social narrative around retirement is often framed as reward: rest, leisure, the fruits of labour. Yet many retirees experience not relief, but despondency. Their productivity engine has stalled. Their calendar, once full, is now adrift. But beneath the superficial narrative of "free time" is a more elemental challenge: *How do I validate my value when no one is measuring it anymore?* This is the heart of identity reconstruction—learning to live without performance as proxy for worth.

In practical terms, rebuilding after the collapse of a role demands a two-pronged approach: inner excavation and external experimentation. The inner work involves clarifying which values were inherent to the role and which were projections. It also involves grieving—not just the loss of status or routine, but the loss of certainty. The outer work involves prototyping new roles—not in the formal sense, but in lived micro-experiments. A former manager might volunteer in a mentoring capacity, not to recreate hierarchy, but to explore influence without positional power. A parent with an empty nest might take up artistic practice—not for skill, but for the reactivation of self-expression unbound by relational duty.

This is where design principles offer surprising resonance. Architects do not begin with decoration; they begin with function. In identity reconstruction, the question becomes: *What must my life now contain for it to feel worth inhabiting?* Not what title, not what role—but what rhythms, what relationships, what guiding ideas. Once those anchors are identified, the aesthetics—the external form of life—can follow. This inversion of the usual identity process (from outside-in to inside-out) is both radical and restorative.

Critically, the collapse of roles can also be an invitation to shed identities that were never fully ours to begin with. Many people live decades in roles inherited from cultural expectation, family projection, or economic necessity. Their collapse, painful as it is, can act as an unmasking. In the debris of the old role, one might find not emptiness but possibility—the space to author a self no longer dictated by legacy scripts.

This requires, above all, a shift in mindset: from *Who am I now?* to *What do I want to build?* This question reframes the identity void as a studio rather than a graveyard. It asks not for immediate answers but for enduring questions, the kind that guide a life beyond transient titles. What am I curious about? Where do I want to contribute? What type of experience makes me feel alive, not just relevant?

Psychologists, sociologists, and philosophers alike remind us that identity is not a fixed object. It is processual, narrative, layered—and deeply influenced by context. When that context shifts, the self must be redesigned accordingly. But if approached with clarity, courage, and a degree of creative experimentation, the collapse of roles does not have to signal dissolution. It can mark the beginning of *intentional selfhood*—a kind of authorship that is both more agile and more enduring than any role we've ever played.

The world will keep trying to label us. To pin us to titles, statuses, and timelines. But we do not have to accept every label as a life sentence. Sometimes the walls fall not to trap us in rubble, but to give us back the sky.

Drafting the New Self – Identity as a Layered, Designed Process

It is an illusion—comforting but misleading—that identity is something we *discover.* As if hidden in the folds of memory or beneath personality traits, waiting to be unearthed like a fossil. In truth, identity is something we *construct.* And like any act of design, it demands deliberate choices, structural thinking, and frequent revision. To live well in the modern world—a world defined by rapid change, shifting roles, and eroding traditions—we must learn not merely to express ourselves, but to *draft ourselves*, layer by intentional layer.

This subchapter is not about finding yourself. It is about becoming the architect of yourself.

The very phrase "Drafting the New Self" suggests a departure from identity as essence or inheritance. It reframes selfhood as *designed space*—conceptual, behavioural, and narrative territory we shape over time. This framing is not just semantic. It changes the fundamental question we ask from "Who am I?" to "What am I building—and why?" The shift is profound. The first question implies fixity and origin. The second implies process, agency, and direction.

Why does this distinction matter? Because most identity crises are not born of weakness. They are born of outdated blueprints. We continue to build lives upon assumptions that no longer serve us: that careers define character, that beliefs should remain static, that maturity means finality. But identity, when lived consciously, is not a final product. It is *a living document*, and like any good design, it evolves to meet context.

In this view, the self is not a monolith. It is modular. It is formed by layers—some inherited, some chosen, some imposed, and some aspirational. Each of these layers has its own narrative logic, emotional gravity, and behavioural influence. A person may, for instance, carry an inherited identity of being "the reliable one" in their family, a chosen identity of being a mentor at work, and an aspirational identity of becoming a more expressive artist. These layers are not contradictions; they are *dimensions*. Trouble arises not when we have many layers, but when those layers remain unexamined—or worse, in conflict.

The process of drafting the new self, then, begins not with reinvention, but with *audit*. What identities have we inherited without question? Which roles have hardened into cages? Which stories do we keep telling about ourselves that no longer ring true? And—perhaps most urgently—what parts of ourselves have we underdeveloped out of fear, neglect, or social conditioning?

In psychological terms, this is the process of identity differentiation. It aligns with Erik Erikson's theory of psychosocial development, particularly his assertion that healthy identity formation involves not mere role absorption but *synthesis*. In adulthood, especially in transitional periods, synthesis becomes an active discipline. The goal is no longer coherence with the past, but coherence with our evolving values and desired futures.

Here, the design metaphor becomes practical. Architects begin not with aesthetics, but with *function*. What is this space for? Who must it serve? What should it withstand? Likewise, in personal identity drafting, we must ask: *What kind of life do I want this self to support?* A person who wants to lead must design for responsibility, clarity, and integrity. A person who wants to explore must design for flexibility, openness, and risk tolerance. Identity is not the costume we wear to play a part—it is the infrastructure that shapes the parts we can play at all.

Crucially, identity design is not solitary. It is relational. We do not build ourselves in vacuums, but in conversation—with family systems, cultural norms, peer feedback, and historical forces. This presents both a challenge and an opportunity. The challenge is that many of our inherited identity layers come with embedded expectations—about gender, class, race, or professional conduct. These expectations can calcify, becoming invisible walls that delimit what feels "acceptable" to be. The opportunity is that *relationships can also be mirrors and scaffolds*. They can help reflect who we are becoming, not just who we have been. Thoughtfully curated relationships act as psychological co-designers: people who see, support, and sometimes challenge the drafts we present.

But let us be clear: identity design is not branding. It is not performance. It is not about curating a palatable version of yourself for social approval. Quite the opposite—it often involves relinquishing social comfort in favour of personal alignment. This is not the self as product. This is the self as *principled architecture*—constructed to endure, to flex, to house meaning across time.

How, then, does one practically draft a new self? There is no one model, but several disciplines converge here: narrative psychology, values clarification, design thinking, even somatic therapy. One effective method involves three iterative phases: excavation, articulation, and integration.

Excavation means discerning what identity content you've absorbed passively—from parents, schooling, culture—and holding it up to scrutiny. For example, you might realise you've internalised the belief that being busy equals being valuable. Or that expressing vulnerability is weakness. These scripts, often unconscious, form identity defaults. Drafting the new self means bringing them to consciousness and asking: *Do I still believe this? Do I want to keep living as if it's true?*

Articulation is the generative phase—where you begin defining new identity elements not as aspirations alone, but as design principles. Let's say someone wants to move from being "the fixer" in relationships to being "the clear communicator." This identity principle can then shape behavioural choices, boundaries, and even the tone of voice they cultivate in difficult conversations. Articulation is not just about naming traits—it's about *structuring identity through aligned action.*

Integration is where the design meets reality. It involves embedding the new draft into lived experience. This requires consistency, but not rigidity. Integration is the difference between someone who *says* they are becoming more patient, and someone who *designs their daily environments*—their calendar, their commitments, their relational expectations—to practise patience under friction. The built self, like any good structure, must be stress-tested. Integration is how you know whether your new draft holds up.

At this stage, it's vital to acknowledge: no draft is final. Life will introduce new forces—births, endings, revelations, crises—that demand redesign. But this is not failure. It is fidelity to reality. The most resilient identities are not the most fixed, but the most *adaptive.* Like well-designed buildings, they account for load, weather, time, and movement.

There's a quiet power in seeing your identity not as a noun, but as a verb. *Not a label, but a design process.* This shift is liberating. It means you are never stuck. It means that even after disillusionment, after burnout, after public or private collapse—you are not at the mercy of circumstance. You are still the drafter. You can return to the page. You can revise the blueprint. You can, with enough honesty and discipline, build a self that feels inhabited—not performed.

So ask yourself—not what you should be, or what you've always been told you are—but what kind of human *you want to design towards.* Not to impress. Not to conform. But to inhabit the life you now understand you want to live.

This is identity as conscious construction. This is what it means to draft the new self.

From Storytelling to Storybuilding – Shifting Focus from Past to Designed Future Narratives

At some point in adulthood—often after a major disruption, transition, or quiet existential reckoning—we become aware that the story we've been telling about ourselves no longer fits. The events are still true. The characters remain familiar. But the narrative frame begins to feel tired, even constrictive. The past has had too much say, and the future too little design. The issue is not with memory. It is with the architecture of meaning.

Storytelling, in psychological terms, is how we make sense of what has happened. It is retrospective. It gathers, organises, and assigns emotional tone. It tells us who we think we are, based on where we've been. But identity confined to storytelling becomes inert. The individual becomes a curator of their own archive, endlessly replaying a loop of explanation. Storybuilding, by contrast, is prospective. It uses narrative as *design material*—constructing forward-facing structures of becoming, not just backward-looking accounts of experience.

This distinction is not semantic. It's strategic. Storytelling can heal, but storybuilding can *transform*.

The concept of narrative identity—the internalised and evolving story of the self—was first articulated in scholarly form by psychologist Dan McAdams. He argued that people make sense of their lives by weaving experiences into narrative coherence. That coherence can provide meaning, but it can also ossify. When life scripts become overly defined by trauma, by old roles, or by inherited expectation, they become psychological scaffolding that limits movement.

Consider a person whose narrative identity is deeply anchored in being a "survivor." This framing may initially be empowering, a signal of resilience. But over time, it can become a kind of trap. Every event is interpreted through the lens of what one had to *overcome*. Every decision is weighed against a story of damage, not design. This is where storytelling reaches its limitation. It can preserve meaning, but it rarely *expands possibility*.

Storybuilding, on the other hand, asks not, "What happened to me?" but "What am I building from here—and who must I become to inhabit it?"

This shift is not merely motivational—it is *architectural.* When one moves from storytelling to storybuilding, the past is no longer the blueprint. It is the foundation material. And like all building materials, it can be repurposed, restructured, even discarded. What matters most is what you choose to construct *on top* of it.

Psychologically, this aligns with the concept of narrative future orientation. In contrast to ruminative self-reference, future-oriented narratives activate goal-directed cognition, positive affect, and broader behavioural flexibility. Neuroscience supports this: studies of the brain's default mode network—active during introspection and future simulation—suggest that imagining meaningful futures activates similar brain regions as autobiographical recall, but with greater potential for novel connection-making. In other words, *how you imagine the future can rewire your relationship to the past.*

This is not a call to disown your history. Rather, it is a call to *reposition* it. Instead of holding your past as your compass, hold it as your context. It explains how you arrived here—not where you are going.

So how does one begin to build a new story? The process demands several intellectual and emotional moves: reframing memory, de-authorising old narrators, introducing new plotlines, and designing for narrative tension with clarity—not avoidance.

The first move is *decoupling identity from trauma or default roles.* Trauma-informed psychology has rightly emphasised the need to honour lived experiences of suffering. But that honouring must not harden into identity. To say, "This is what happened to me," is not the same as saying, "This is who I am." You are not your interruption. You are your *intention.*

The second move is *reclaiming authorship*. This means naming where the existing story was inherited or imposed. Who defined the values you've been performing? Who cast you as the peacemaker, the overachiever, the rebel, the martyr? Were these roles chosen, or merely accepted? Many people mistake their biography for their identity. But biography is not destiny. The moment you begin editing the story instead of merely narrating it, you re-enter the creative domain of becoming.

Crucially, storybuilding is *not fantasy*. It is structured imagination. The architect does not dream of a building and walk away. They draft. They test. They adjust for constraints. Storybuilding works similarly. It demands *deliberate vision*. Not just hopes, but frameworks. What kind of relationships will your new narrative prioritise? What internal values must it reinforce? What risks will it allow? What regrets will it forgive?

Therapeutic modalities like Acceptance and Commitment Therapy (ACT) and Narrative Therapy already incorporate this kind of future-forward scaffolding. ACT, for instance, helps clients clarify values and build actions that move them toward those values, even in the presence of discomfort. Narrative Therapy invites clients to "externalise" problems and re-author their stories with agency. But outside the therapy room, these tools are rarely translated into proactive life design.

To storybuild well, one must think like a designer: experimenting, iterating, returning to core intentions. It involves editing out inherited scripts that no longer align, revising self-narratives that restrict growth, and prototyping new self-concepts *through lived behaviours*, not just internal shifts.

Let's consider a practical example. Imagine a professional who has spent two decades telling themselves the story of being "the reliable one"—the steady executor, the silent backbone of their company. It is a story that has brought them recognition and security. But privately, they feel dislocated from their creativity, their inner eccentricities, their philosophical curiosities. They sense a new story forming—perhaps one of becoming a thought leader, or an entrepreneur, or a mentor. If they remain locked in storytelling mode, they will keep revisiting the reasons why their current identity "makes sense." But if they move into storybuilding, they will begin drafting a new narrative arc. One that is *designed*, not merely deduced.

They might reframe past moments of constraint as preparation, not punishment. They might explore small narrative experiments: writing publicly, mentoring selectively, changing how they show up in meetings. These aren't declarations. They're *narrative actions*. Small architectural moves that shift the story from memory to design.

Another powerful dimension of storybuilding is embracing *narrative multiplicity*. That is, allowing yourself to build more than one future self. Psychologist Robert Kegan's work on adult development highlights the complexity of meaning-making in later life stages. Mature identity is not singular. It is complex, nuanced, often paradoxical. Storybuilding does not require simplification. It requires *coherence across layers*. One can be both the pragmatic parent and the late-blooming artist. Both the cautious planner and the occasional disruptor. Storybuilding allows these tensions to coexist *by design*—not as accidents, but as architecture.

Yet perhaps the most under-acknowledged skill in storybuilding is the management of narrative gaps. Any meaningful future-oriented narrative will contain moments of doubt, delay, ambiguity. You won't always know if it's working. You'll be between selves—no longer who you were, not yet who you're becoming. This is not a flaw in your process. It is a feature. Architects call this the "in-between phase"—when the skeleton of the building stands but the interior is unfinished. Identity works the same way. The key is to stay in the draft. Stay with the tension. Keep building.

So much of modern discourse around identity overemphasises authenticity and underemphasises authorship. We ask if something "feels true" instead of asking if it *moves us forward with integrity*. But not everything that feels true is useful. And not every identity that feels real is relevant to the life we now need to live.

The practice of storybuilding does not deny authenticity—it *upgrades it*. It moves from reactive storytelling to intentional authorship. It transforms you from narrator to *designer*. It allows you to honour your past without being hostage to it.

To shift from storytelling to storybuilding is to say: the story I've been told is not the story I have to live. And the self I've been reciting is not the limit of the self I can now design.

This is not about changing your life overnight. It is about rewriting the story that makes change *thinkable*.

Becoming Architect and Resident – Empowering the Self to Build and Dwell Within

At some point, every serious reflection on personal growth reaches an unspoken threshold: it is no longer enough to analyse the self; the self must now be *built*. This is where most self-help models quietly falter. They remain committed to incremental change within a pre-existing identity—refining habits, reframing thoughts, managing emotions—but rarely do they challenge the foundational premise: that identity is fixed and the self is simply a tenant in its rooms. This chapter challenges that premise at its root.

To live well—psychologically, emotionally, ethically—one must learn to become both the *architect* and the *resident* of their inner world. This is not a metaphor. It is a functional dual role. You are responsible not just for occupying your mind, but for constructing its contours, designing its flow, maintaining its structural integrity, and—just as crucially—inhabiting it with awareness and care.

The self is not found. It is *formed*. And like any meaningful construction, it is shaped by plans, materials, and maintenance—not sentiment or spontaneity alone.

Let's begin with the concept of *inner architecture*. In physical terms, architecture is the discipline of translating intention into structure. It deals with weight distribution, spatial purpose, aesthetics, constraints, and function. It accounts for the needs of both the builder and the user. When we apply this rigor to the inner life, a remarkable shift occurs. Emotional resilience is no longer seen as an abstract trait; it becomes the result of mental engineering. Identity is not inherited—it is *constructed.* Thoughts are not passive phenomena—they are internal design elements. The self stops being a vague psychological space and starts becoming *a deliberate psychological environment.*

Cognitive science has begun to echo this sensibility. Research in neuroplasticity confirms that our neural architecture is malleable—not only in childhood but throughout adulthood. The thoughts we rehearse, the values we prioritise, the environments we expose ourselves to—these shape the structure and efficiency of our cognitive systems. In essence, our minds are not containers of experience; they are sites under continuous construction. And crucially, the builder is not external. It is us.

But here lies the challenge: the builder of the mind must also *live* inside it. This dual role can create tension. The architect is concerned with vision, coherence, long-term alignment. The resident seeks comfort, immediate relief, familiarity. Growth requires designing uncomfortable rooms before we're ready to live in them. Stability demands inhabiting what we've built—even when it feels unfamiliar or incomplete. The tension is productive *if we learn how to manage it.*

One of the most persistent errors in modern personal development is mistaking design for decoration. People attempt to patch cracks in their identity with affirmations, retreats, or personality quizzes—when what they need is a new structural blueprint. Architecture, internal or external, requires depth of planning. You do not build a house by repainting the walls. You examine the foundation, test the load-bearing walls, account for climate, and then draft with precision. The same is true of mental infrastructure.

Consider the example of someone reconstructing their sense of self after a major relational rupture—divorce, estrangement, or betrayal. The old identity was often built around roles: spouse, confidant, provider, protector. When that scaffolding collapses, what remains? If the individual sees themselves only as a *resident* of the emotional aftermath, they may descend into chaos, attempting to feel better without changing anything fundamental. But if they take up the role of *architect*, they can begin to ask generative questions: What values will define my new identity? What must be demolished, and what can be repurposed? What rituals or structures will support the kind of life I now want to live? And then, most critically, they must *enter* the new identity—not as a tourist, but as a resident. They must live in the discomfort of their new self until it becomes habitable.

This interplay between building and dwelling finds echo in phenomenology, particularly in the work of philosopher Martin Heidegger, who wrote extensively on the notion of *dwelling*—not simply as occupying space, but as *being at home in the world.* His insight applies inwardly as well: one must not merely construct mental edifices, but learn to live *well* within them. A well-structured identity without presence is just as hollow as a chaotic one. Inner architecture is not only about clarity of design—it is about *intimacy with the design you've created.*

Let us be practical. To become both architect and resident of the self, three key principles must be internalised.

First: Self-design requires intentional constraint. Just as architects must honour constraints of gravity, material, and cost, so too must inner designers work within psychological limits. Not every potential identity is available to us. Some values are incompatible. Some dreams must be adapted. We cannot live a hundred lives at once. The work is not to maximise options, but to clarify fit. Inner peace is not found in boundless choice, but in *disciplined design.*

Second: Habitation requires repetition. The mind acclimates through familiarity. A newly constructed mindset will feel foreign at first. That does not mean it's wrong. It means it's unpractised. To dwell in a new self requires returning—again and again—to behaviours, reflections, conversations, and environments that *support the structure you've built.* The shift from impostor syndrome to integration comes not from a sudden insight, but from sustained *dwelling* in the truth of your own construction.

Third: Maintenance is non-negotiable. No architecture is immune to erosion. Thoughts decay. Habits slip. Beliefs become brittle. This is not failure. It is entropy. The architect must return to the design with vigilance. The resident must notice when the home no longer fits and participate in renovation. The self is not a project you finish. It is a *practice* you maintain.

This dual role also invites a different kind of ethical reflection. Many people outsource their mental architecture to institutions—families, faiths, careers. Others abdicate it to internalised narratives they never authored. But authentic identity requires authorship. To be the builder of your mind is to take responsibility for its contents. To be the dweller is to honour your built environment with congruent action.

The stakes are not abstract. A person who has not consciously constructed their mental environment is vulnerable to ideological capture, emotional disarray, and chronic misalignment. They will build according to others' blueprints. They will live in rooms they never chose. Over time, they will call this "fate" or "personality." But in reality, it was *neglect*. To build is to reclaim that which default living has surrendered.

Psychological well-being, therefore, is not just emotional regulation or behavioural functionality. It is architectural fluency. It is the capacity to imagine and inhabit the self you have reason to value—without waiting for permission or certainty.

This is not easy work. Becoming the architect and resident of your inner world requires discomfort. It asks you to tear down what once felt safe. It asks you to design values into behaviour—not just name them abstractly. It asks you to tolerate dissonance while new frameworks are being constructed. But the alternative is a life lived in borrowed structures, among inherited beliefs, under someone else's roof.

And so the call is this: stop waiting to feel at home in a mind that was never designed for who you are becoming. Begin building. Begin dwelling. Become both the blueprint and the inhabitant. There is no one coming to construct you.

That is your work.

Chapter 11
The Structural Audit – Testing Your Inner Architecture

We tend to admire resilient minds much in the way we revere enduring architecture: by their capacity to hold steady under duress. But, as even the most celebrated structures require periodic inspection to ensure their integrity remains intact, so too do the internal frameworks that support us. Stability is not merely the absence of collapse—it is the sustained presence of coherence under prolonged stress, contradiction, and the relentless press of time.

And yet, how often do we pause to examine the architecture within? Belief systems, coping strategies, identity scaffolds, the grooves of thought we travel so reflexively—are these mental structures still serving their purpose? Or are they, quietly, becoming liabilities? Too often, we conflate resilience with personality, and endurance with health. We wear survival as a badge, mistaking its presence for soundness. But buildings don't fall all at once. They fracture slowly—hairline fissures, creeping stress fractures—until the damage is too evident to ignore.

The same holds true for the psyche. This chapter doesn't advocate tearing everything down. Rather, it makes a gentler, though no less urgent, proposal: that we audit what we've built. With precision. With honesty. With respect for the complexity of what holds us up.

To forge a resilient self, one must evolve from mere construction into the ongoing discipline of inspection. A well-built bridge isn't assumed safe indefinitely; it's tested, stressed, monitored. The same diligence is required internally—not to cause breakage, but to assess capacity. Can this structure flex? Will it hold? Does it still function under the weight of real life?

Here we introduce a new concept: the psychological structural audit. A methodical, reflective inquiry into the state of your internal systems. It involves probing the stability of your mindset under pressure, checking whether your identity still aligns under friction, and examining how your emotional mechanisms respond to the weight of repeated stress. This isn't an exercise in achieving flawlessness. It's about building in reinforcement where it counts. Weakness, in this context, is not shameful—it's instructive.

We begin with a practical metaphor: load points. These are the internal anchors that bear the heaviest psychological strain, though often we're unaware of them until they start to fail. Perhaps for you, it's the need to be indispensable. For someone else, it might be the compulsion to appear invulnerable, or a belief—quiet but constant—that love must be earned, not received freely. These convictions, often mistaken for personality traits, can quietly bear the weight of an entire identity. But were they ever truly designed to do so?

The audit starts with a deceptively simple question: *Where does it hurt when life gets heavy?* More often than not, our answer points us in the wrong direction. We tend to blame the obvious disruption—a lost job, a betrayal, a moment of rejection. But what actually cracks is not the circumstance itself—it's the hidden dependency we had on it for meaning, validation, or stability. The pain isn't just situational; it's structural. And because it has woven itself into the very fabric of the self, it rarely gets named.

We must also challenge a culturally pervasive and misguided belief: that the need for internal maintenance signals failure. This is nonsense. Architects don't wait for buildings to collapse before inspecting the foundation. Nor should we. Psychological maintenance is not indulgent—it is the quiet, mature discipline of those who understand that strength requires stewardship. It's not about being fragile. It's about being responsible for one's internal design.

Maintenance, then, must be redefined—as an act of integrity, not insecurity. The most robust among us are not those who posture invincibility, but those who routinely ask themselves: *Does this still support me? Is this still aligned with who I am becoming? Is this structure still worthy of the weight it bears?* And when the answer is no, they adjust—not in panic, but with intention.

Here, the conversation shifts towards an evolved model of selfhood: a movement away from rigid strength toward regenerative resilience. A building may endure a storm, but a tree responds. It adapts. It reallocates. It heals around the break. The same principle must apply within us. Our mental systems must learn not only to withstand strain, but to grow because of it.

To that end, this chapter offers tools—not prescriptions, but instruments for adaptive design. Reflective rituals, recalibration of values, narrative testing, and practices drawn from psychology and architecture alike. We draw from systems thinking, the stoics, contemporary resilience theory, and clinical interventions like acceptance and commitment therapy (ACT).

One such tool is *value cycling*, a practice adapted from ACT that helps you distinguish between values that are truly animating your decisions versus those that have become decorative or outdated. We'll also explore how to embed psychological flexibility into daily living—not merely as a crisis response mechanism, but as a default mode of navigation.

At every turn, we return to the metaphor of the self as structure. Under pressure, the test isn't whether you can avoid stress—that's fantasy. The real test is how your inner systems respond. Do they crack? Absorb? Redirect? Or adapt and renew?

Harder questions inevitably arise: Which internal structures no longer serve? What identities, beliefs, or patterns were once crucial for survival, but have since ossified into dead weight? Sometimes, soundness isn't about reinforcing what's weak. It's about letting go of what's obsolete. Some rooms of the self are elegantly decorated but structurally precarious. We must be willing—courageously—to demolish them.

And yes, that process can look like loss. But viewed correctly, it is refinement. Just as a skilled architect will eventually discard a beloved but unsound design in service of coherence, safety, and beauty, so too must we learn to part with outdated internal architecture.

This chapter does not offer a tidy sequence of steps. There is no formula. Only tools, and questions, and space to think. The audit is yours alone to conduct—but it must be intentional. Because even the most elegant structures decay if left unaudited. Decay is silent, insidious, and, over time, inevitable.

If earlier chapters were concerned with the building of the self, this one is about its testing. Not to confirm your strength for its own sake, but to expose the gaps. Not to shame what breaks, but to rebuild with greater honesty, and sharper clarity. Here, you will learn to apply pressure—diagnostically, not destructively—to your values, your routines, your most trusted assumptions.

The goal is not perfection. The goal is coherence. Responsiveness. Structural trust.

Because, in the end, what proves the worth of any structure—mental or material—is not how cleanly it appears in design. It is how faithfully it performs when put to the test.

And if you're willing to inspect the architecture you live within, you're already proving that you deserve to dwell in it securely.

Simulate the Storm – Helps Readers Test Their New Mindset Safely

Most people only discover the strength of their mindset when it's too late to improve it. A crisis arrives. A loss occurs. An expectation collapses. In that moment, they either withstand the pressure or fracture beneath it. Yet if we accept that mindset is not a fixed trait but a designed structure—an architecture of belief, attention, interpretation, and response—then it stands to reason that it should be tested *before* the storm, not during it. This subchapter makes a case for proactive psychological simulation: a disciplined, reflective practice where individuals safely expose their minds to hypothetical strain in order to test their cognitive integrity and resilience design.

This is not simply a philosophical argument. In fields like aviation, medicine, and elite sports, simulation is a cornerstone of preparation.

Pilots train for engine failure in controlled environments so that panic doesn't impair performance at 30,000 feet. Surgeons rehearse rare procedures in high-fidelity simulations before ever making the first incision. Olympians visualise not only their best performance, but also the moments their muscles might cramp or their confidence might falter. These practices don't just enhance performance—they *reveal weaknesses before reality does*. The same principle applies to mental architecture. A resilient mindset is not one that denies adversity, but one that is *built to anticipate it*. Designing for mental adversity means simulating the very conditions that could challenge, distort, or dismantle our core operating beliefs—deliberately, intelligently, and within psychologically safe bounds.

Consider an example: a professional who believes they've outgrown their fear of failure. They've done the reading, revised their self-talk, and reframed their relationship to risk. But what happens when they imagine pitching a bold idea and being met with public rejection? Or discovering that a peer received praise for the very thing they hesitated to attempt? Or worse, being told their value to the organisation is in question? These are not morbid scenarios—they are likely, even inevitable, in dynamic environments. The strength of their mindset cannot be proven in calm. It must be tested in simulation, where the emotional circuitry is safely triggered and then studied. *Can I remain composed? Do I default to defensiveness, withdrawal, or overcompensation? Do I return to old scripts—"I'm not good enough", "I knew I'd mess this up"—or stay anchored in the updated narrative I've worked so hard to construct?*

Psychological simulation, when done well, invites this kind of inquiry. But it must be distinguished from catastrophising or rumination. The goal is not to spiral into worst-case fantasies or relive past traumas. Rather, it's to create structured, guided stress tests that reveal whether your mindset is flexible, coherent, and scalable under pressure. In cognitive behavioural therapy (CBT), a related concept is "behavioural experiments"—a technique where clients test the validity of their beliefs through intentional exposure. In elite performance coaching, mental contrast and pre-mortem analysis serve a similar function: envision the challenge, examine your default reactions, and install proactive adaptations. The practice becomes less about proving yourself right, and more about building yourself ready.

There are several design principles that govern effective storm simulation. The first is emotional authenticity. The scenarios must elicit real internal tension, otherwise the test is irrelevant. This doesn't mean plunging into anxiety, but it does mean resisting the temptation to sanitise hypothetical adversity. A simulated storm should mirror the types of psychological turbulence that threaten your mental equilibrium—rejection, ambiguity, loss of control, diminished status, or identity threats. These are the real earthquakes of modern life, and they often hit without warning. If your imagined stressor is too mild, you'll learn nothing. If it's too overwhelming, you'll regress. The balance is key: high-fidelity emotional realism within a safe cognitive frame.

Second is *response rehearsal*. Simulation without analysis is mere drama. The objective is not just to feel something, but to *observe how you respond to what you feel*. Do you rationalise? Deny? Blame? Or do you recalibrate with flexibility and agency? Journaling the simulated experience in real time—What did I feel? What meaning did I assign to this discomfort? What pattern did I default to?—can uncover beliefs and blind spots invisible during ordinary self-reflection. This is not abstract work. A professional preparing for redundancy, a parent anticipating an empty nest, or an athlete nearing retirement must engage their internal systems with enough clarity to prepare *before* reality imposes itself.

The third principle is *iteration*. A single simulation offers insight, but consistent simulation cultivates robustness. Much like progressive overload in physical training, psychological resilience is forged through cumulative exposure to increasingly complex stressors. Start with manageable discomfort: imagine receiving sharp feedback on your performance. Then increase the stakes: imagine being passed over for an opportunity you felt entitled to. Then increase the abstraction: imagine confronting the reality that a long-held identity—"the high-achiever", "the dependable one", "the fixer"—no longer fits. With each simulation, your mindset architecture is tested not only for strength but for elasticity.

It's worth noting that storm simulation is especially valuable in times of *relative calm.* When life feels stable, most people assume their mindset is sound. Yet this period of calm is when the scaffolding of cognitive resilience should be inspected most carefully. Mental strength is not the absence of emotion under stress—it is the ability to remain psychologically cohesive while in emotional motion. That cohesion must be engineered *before* it is demanded.

One of the most underappreciated benefits of mental simulation is the cultivation of *meta-cognition*—the capacity to think about your own thinking. This is what separates reaction from response. A simulated storm reveals where your cognitive automation serves you, and where it betrays you. Perhaps you discover that your instinct is to problem-solve prematurely, bypassing emotional processing. Or that you intellectualise pain instead of honouring it. Or that you overcorrect into self-blame in the name of accountability. These tendencies are not flaws. They are unexamined defaults, and simulation allows you to make them conscious—where real change begins.

This subchapter is not about encouraging paranoia or anxiety. It's about empowering individuals to take agency over their mental infrastructure by stress-testing its integrity. In organisations, this is called scenario planning. In engineering, it's known as load testing. In medicine, it's clinical rehearsal. In personal development, it should be seen as a moral obligation: *to be honest enough to test what we believe we've built.*

Storm simulation doesn't require a therapist or a coach, though both can enhance the process. It requires structured imagination, radical honesty, and a willingness to witness one's mental responses with precision rather than judgement. It requires, in short, the humility to ask: *Have I built a mindset that can weather disruption—or only one that performs in calm?*

Ultimately, mindset is not a product of information. It is the architecture of applied interpretation. We don't rise to the level of our affirmations—we default to the level of our design. And as with any structure, design is only as good as its ability to endure stress without collapse.

You are not just the resident of your mindset—you are its architect. But every architect tests their design before the flood arrives.

Check Your Load Points – Provides Tools to Identify Mental Weak Spots

Most buildings are overengineered for the expected. It's not the normal weight of daily use that causes failure; it's the subtle, cumulative stress in places no one thought to reinforce. The same is true of people. Most of us don't break because of the major pressures we expect—illness, deadlines, public speaking. We break because of hidden mental weak spots that collapse under the compounded load of ambiguity, micro-failure, and internal contradiction. These aren't visible to the outside world, and often not even to us—until they fail. The purpose of this subchapter is to challenge the reader to engage in a structured audit of their cognitive framework. *Where does your mind consistently falter under pressure—and what does that reveal about your psychological architecture?*

Understanding mindset as architecture demands a diagnostic lens. Engineers don't wait for a bridge to fall to identify structural failure—they apply load testing, stress mapping, and fatigue analysis. Similarly, a healthy mindset is not one that simply functions in the absence of stress. It is one that has been evaluated for structural integrity under pressure. But identifying mental weak points isn't merely about noticing when you feel "off." It requires forensic attention to *patterned collapse.* Repeated anxiety in specific interpersonal dynamics. Disproportionate reactivity to feedback. Sudden paralysis in decision-making despite prior confidence. These are not anomalies. They are *load points*—places where your beliefs, habits, and self-concept come under unsustainable strain.

To locate your psychological load points, begin with this core principle: *stress is not random; it is directional.* Every mind has zones of greater and lesser reinforcement, typically shaped by early experience, belief conditioning, social scripts, and adaptive overuse. For instance, consider the person who thrives in high-pressure deadlines but unravels when asked to set boundaries in personal relationships. Or the leader who handles organisational chaos with grace but panics at the prospect of appearing emotionally vulnerable.

These aren't personality quirks. They're stress concentrations—areas where the mental scaffolding hasn't caught up with the demands of real life.

Neuroscience and behavioural psychology offer useful frameworks here. The concept of *predictive coding* suggests that our brains are constantly constructing mental models of the world and updating them based on feedback. When the incoming data severely violates the model—when an assumption about control, worth, or competence is shattered—stress amplifies. The mind tries to reconcile the gap, and where the internal model is rigid or outdated, breakdown occurs. Identifying load points, then, is not about avoiding discomfort but recognising where your mental models are too brittle to flex.

One tool that facilitates this recognition is reflective counter-patterning. This involves systematically tracking the moments when your mindset destabilises and working backward to identify the narrative architecture underneath. Not just *what* triggered you, but *why* that specific type of trigger is repeatedly disorienting. If, for example, being overlooked for credit causes disproportionate distress, what belief does that threaten? Perhaps it's not simply about validation, but about your internalised sense of fairness, or your core narrative of "I must prove my worth to be safe." In this sense, your response is not irrational—it's overdetermined. It points to a concentrated load bearing more psychological weight than it was built to handle.

Another effective method is stress rehearsal via guided journaling. Instead of reflecting solely on past events, simulate anticipated stress scenarios and observe your mental posture. Imagine your team failing publicly. A personal relationship ending. A goal becoming unachievable. How does your mind narrate those scenarios? What inner monologue arises? Are you prone to control, denial, blame, or despair? These responses are not arbitrary—they follow the path of least structural resistance. *Mental weak spots are not just where you feel bad; they are where your mental operating system runs out of bandwidth to make meaning constructively.*

Importantly, not all load points are created equal. Some are *chronic*—long-standing vulnerabilities that trace back to early conditioning or identity. Others are *contextual*—arising from current environmental mismatch, like a role you've outgrown or an ethos you no longer believe in. A healthy audit distinguishes between the two. Chronic load points require re-architecting belief systems. Contextual ones may require environmental redesign—changing the structure around you rather than just within you.

Let's take a practical case. A high-achieving executive begins to exhibit burnout symptoms: difficulty sleeping, irritability, loss of meaning. At first glance, this seems like a capacity problem—too much work. But closer inspection reveals that her psychological load point isn't the hours; it's the *meaning fragility* underneath the performance. Her internal schema equates achievement with identity: "If I'm not excelling, I'm irrelevant." The work, once fulfilling, now feels like endless validation theatre. Her collapse is not from external load but from an unsustainable belief load—a cognitive construction that cannot withstand the long arc of reality. Without identifying this, any solution would treat symptoms, not structure.

A sophisticated mindset doesn't aim to eliminate all weak points. That's neither possible nor human. Rather, it commits to continual structural auditing. In high-integrity systems, maintenance is not a sign of failure—it's a feature of design. Just as skyscrapers are inspected post-earthquake, even if they appear intact, our mental structures should be assessed after major decisions, emotional disruptions, or identity shifts. *What load did this experience place on my inner framework—and where did I bend or break?*

There is also a cultural tension worth exploring. In many professional and personal environments, admitting to weak points is still perceived as weakness. People mask vulnerability under performance, polish over doubt with bravado. But a mindset that cannot admit its own fracture points is one already at risk of collapse. Adaptive mental architecture is honest by design. It doesn't romanticise its resilience. It investigates its limitations with intellectual courage and emotional precision.

Philosophically, this process invites us to rethink what constitutes strength. True resilience is not the absence of fracture—it's the capacity to detect, interpret, and reinforce where fracture is likely. If you do not know your cognitive fault lines, then your growth is built on luck, not design. But when you do know them—when you name them without shame—you gain a diagnostic clarity that separates noise from signal. Not every emotional spike is a warning sign, but repeated patterns are data. And data, honestly interpreted, is design gold.

To close, checking your psychological load points isn't a task to be rushed, outsourced, or glossed over. It's foundational work. Not because we must be perfect, but because we are already under load—daily, hourly, incrementally. What we do not assess, we cannot reinforce. And what we cannot reinforce will fail, not because we are broken, but because we have not built consciously.

Your mind is not just a mirror of the world. It is a structure you inhabit. Know where the beams creak. Know where the frame bends. Not to be afraid—but to be ready.

Maintenance Is Not Failure – Reframes Ongoing Inner Work as Integrity, Not Imperfection

There is a pervasive cultural illusion—quiet, corrosive, and persistent—that personal maintenance signals defect. The idea runs beneath productivity mantras and self-help slogans: that the highest form of success is self-sufficiency, that inner work is a remedial task for the broken, and that those who "have it together" don't need routine recalibration. This narrative is not only intellectually dishonest—it is architecturally dangerous. No well-designed structure, from a bridge to a brain, maintains integrity without maintenance. *The mature mind does not conflate tune-ups with failure. It recognises them as markers of structural wisdom.*

When we speak of personal growth, the conversation is often hijacked by climactic metaphors: transformation, breakthroughs, reinvention. These moments are celebrated, dramatised, and commodified. What receives far less attention—but is arguably more important—is the quiet discipline of maintenance. The intentional, often invisible, effort to preserve the internal coherence of one's values, beliefs, and behaviours under real-world strain. Not because you are falling apart, but because you are still in motion.

Modern psychology offers helpful insights here. Cognitive Behavioural Therapy (CBT), for instance, is not designed merely for intervention during crises; it is equally powerful when applied as a *preventative hygiene system*—a method of inspecting the foundational assumptions we live by, especially as life conditions change. But even among those who study or practise these tools, the expectation often lingers that if you've done the work "right," you shouldn't need to do it again. This is a misreading not just of the therapy, but of human nature itself.

No human being is a static structure. Our environments shift, roles evolve, relationships fray and reform, and the scaffolding of meaning we once relied upon must be reexamined. *Maintenance, in this context, is not regression. It is reverence for the fact that you live inside a dynamic system.* To deny yourself that upkeep is not strength—it is neglect, cloaked in stoicism.

A useful analogy can be drawn from systems engineering. In resilient design frameworks, routine maintenance is not just accommodated—it is scheduled, funded, and built into the lifecycle of the system. An aeroplane engine, for instance, is considered flightworthy not because it never requires inspection, but because it is inspected so regularly that risks are caught before failure. To transpose this thinking to inner architecture: a resilient mindset is not one that never falters. It is one that is *regularly audited, restored, and recalibrated with dignity.*

Yet, in personal development discourse—especially the commercialised strains—maintenance is still framed as a subtle confession of inadequacy. The self-help aisle is saturated with titles that promise finality: "fix your mindset," "master your emotions," "unlock your potential." But humans are not puzzles to be completed. We are living frameworks, always under some form of psychological load, always subject to weathering. *To maintain is to respect complexity, not confess defeat.*

Moreover, the resistance to maintenance is often rooted in ego. People who value competence—especially high-functioning individuals—can feel threatened by the idea that their inner world needs upkeep. They have internalised the dangerous idea that consistency is proof of character. In reality, *adaptation is a more mature measure of integrity than unyielding stability*. What looks like inconsistency to the untrained eye is often a deeper form of loyalty—to context, to truth, to the evolving nature of life.

There's also a deeper, often unspoken ethical component. Ongoing inner work is not just a favour you do for yourself—it is an act of responsibility toward others. Emotional self-regulation, unlearning harmful scripts, repairing faulty assumptions: these are not solo projects. They are forms of social maintenance. If you refuse to inspect your beliefs, your biases, your blind spots, the burden of their impact will be borne by those around you. *Maintenance, then, is not just personal hygiene—it is moral architecture.*

Consider the concept of *planned recalibration*. Instead of waiting for burnout, breakdown, or interpersonal rupture, individuals and organisations alike can establish maintenance rituals. These might include quarterly value audits: Are my current behaviours still aligned with my stated beliefs? Or cognitive tension scans: Where in my life do I feel persistently drained, and what does that reveal about unmet psychological needs? These are not indulgent exercises. They are precision diagnostics. Not unlike running a diagnostic on a server that never crashed—not because it won't, but because *it shouldn't have to before attention is paid.*

Another critical dimension is narrative maintenance. Our identities are shaped by stories we tell about who we are and why we matter. But these narratives age. They accrue distortion, irrelevance, and rigidity. What once felt like a noble truth—"I must be strong for everyone," "success means never needing help"—may no longer serve your evolving self. And yet, without maintenance, these internalised scripts harden into dogma. Regular narrative inspection—asking, "Is this still true? Is it still helpful?"—is not naval-gazing. *It is the architecture of coherence.*

Philosophy, too, offers corroboration. The Stoics, often misread as paragons of emotional suppression, actually emphasised a disciplined, ongoing introspection. Marcus Aurelius' "Meditations" is not a victory lap; it is a maintenance log—a private ledger of adjustments, reinforcements, and recalibrations. He was not seeking to reach a point where reflection became unnecessary. He was maintaining the inner fortress of reason, knowing full well it was never complete.

Even in spiritual traditions, the concept of *ongoing refinement* is a recurring theme. In Zen Buddhism, for example, the practice of "zazen" (seated meditation) is not a path to enlightenment so much as a form of maintenance—daily alignment with impermanence, humility, and presence. *The work is never done, and that is not the problem. That is the point.*

So why does resistance to maintenance persist? Because maintenance is invisible. It doesn't produce dramatic before-and-after stories. It cannot be packaged as a single event or achievement. Maintenance is work without spectacle. But *it is the work that makes everything else sustainable.*

In practice, embracing maintenance as integrity means rethinking what counts as progress. It's not only new insight, radical change, or measurable gains. It's also *repetition done with intention.* Reviewing your values not because they've changed, but because you've changed. Relearning emotional regulation not because you've forgotten, but because your stressors have evolved. Restating your boundaries not because they're invalid, but because context demands reinforcement.

To be clear, this reframing is not about lowering standards—it's about refining definitions. Progress is not linear, and it is not binary. Sometimes the most advanced form of inner work is *looping back to foundational practices with deeper awareness.* It's the person who re-reads the basics with new eyes. Who doesn't just meditate once, but maintains the practice. Who doesn't just set boundaries when it becomes unbearable, but routinely checks them for structural soundness.

Finally, there is power in making this reframing explicit. Speak it aloud. Model it in leadership. Build it into systems. Whether you're managing a team, raising a child, or stewarding your own life, make it clear that *maintenance is a form of care, not correction.* It is an act of design fidelity—a commitment to the idea that what you build, internally or externally, deserves sustained stewardship.

No architect feels ashamed when a building requires inspection. No pilot questions their competence when an engine gets routine servicing. Why should the mind be different?

Designing for Regeneration – Building Frameworks That Replenish Rather Than Deplete

There is a dangerous misconception—quietly embedded in cultural norms, professional environments, and even personal development literature—that strength is the capacity to endure indefinitely. The idea that once we've "healed," "built," or "grown," we should remain unshakeable thereafter is not only psychologically naive, it is structurally unsound. Any system—biological, architectural, or psychological—that cannot regenerate eventually fractures. *The human mind, no matter how refined or disciplined, is not exempt.* To design a truly sustainable and adaptive mindset, one must not merely build for function or endurance, but for regeneration. That is: *the ability to self-replenish, self-correct, and evolve while in use.*

This subchapter explores regeneration not as a poetic metaphor, but as a deliberate design principle for inner architecture. What does it mean to engineer a mindset that doesn't simply recover from stress, but integrates fatigue as a design signal? How do we create cognitive and emotional scaffolding that becomes stronger through restoration—not merely despite it? And what frameworks allow individuals to respond to psychological demands not with depletion, but with durability?

These are not philosophical indulgences. They are *urgent psychological realities* for modern professionals, leaders, and individuals attempting to remain coherent under increasing cognitive load.

Regeneration Is Not Rest: It Is Adaptive Integration

Before proceeding further, let's clarify terms. Regeneration is not synonymous with recovery or relaxation. It is not "taking a break" or "bouncing back." Those ideas imply interruption—something external to the main system. *Regeneration is intrinsic.* It's what the body does while sleeping, what forests do through seasonal change, and what a psychologically healthy mind does in response to complex life demands.

In the psychological realm, regeneration involves the ongoing integration of new experience, the capacity to process failure without permanent identity damage, and the ability to recalibrate purpose without existential collapse. It is the anti-fragile element of the human psyche: the part that improves through intelligent stress.

To cultivate this, we must move beyond models that view mental wellbeing as either high-functioning or dysfunctional. Instead, we must ask: *What is the daily regenerative capacity of your inner system? And is it being designed for or accidentally neglected?*

Case Study: Burnout in High-Performing Individuals

Consider the example of a senior healthcare executive—let's call her Dr. Meera—who had spent over two decades navigating hospital leadership during systemic upheaval. Her career was steeped in resilience language: "grit," "holding the line," "staying strong for the team." But when her father passed unexpectedly and her organisation merged in the same quarter, Meera—by all outward measures still competent—lost her internal elasticity. Decision-making dulled. Motivation hollowed. What she thought was strength had actually been strain accumulated without release.

Psychological debriefing revealed a critical flaw: her identity structure had no designed mechanism for emotional integration. Everything went into performance storage. Nothing was metabolised. She had systems for workflow and patient triage, but *no regenerative framework for herself.*

What eventually helped was not time off, but structured emotional processing, values re-alignment, and, most crucially, the building of a regenerative internal framework. One that included recurring check-ins not for efficiency metrics, but for internal coherence.

The lesson: regeneration is not automatic, even for the competent. It is architectural.

Three Foundational Elements of Regenerative Mindset Design

Just as physical structures require materials, reinforcement, and drainage, psychological frameworks for regeneration require internal design strategies that support *both durability and flexibility*. Let's examine three critical elements.

1. Meta-Cognition as Scaffolding

A regenerative mind is one that is aware of its own operations. Meta-cognition—thinking about how we think—is often under-leveraged. In regenerative terms, it functions as internal scaffolding: it allows the thinker to recognise strain *before* collapse, to adjust approaches before they fossilise.

Rather than asking, "How do I fix this thought?" the regenerative question is: *'What process generated this thought—and does that process serve me long-term?"*

By routinely engaging in this form of reflection (e.g., post-conflict self-assessment, or end-of-week narrative reviews), individuals install a kind of architectural intelligence. Weak points are not hidden. They're mapped.

This self-awareness is not indulgence; it's infrastructure.

2. **Scheduled Integration Points**

Much like engineered joints in a bridge allow movement without structural failure, integration rituals allow psychological flexibility without breakdown. These are not vague habits, but scheduled points of regenerative alignment.

Consider the psychological utility of a monthly narrative journal. Not a diary, but a deliberate re-narration of events through your current values and future lens. Or weekly pattern-tracking: noting what thoughts or behaviours repeat under stress, and adjusting course not reactively but strategically.

These rituals *do not simply manage emotions—they metabolise them* into insight and adjustment. That is the essence of regenerative design: building self-reflective rituals into the daily structure, not bolting them on during a crisis.

3. **Values-Based Stress Filters**

A regenerative system must be selective about which forms of stress it allows through. Not all stress is toxic. Some is necessary. The key distinction is whether the stress encountered is *aligned* with personal values and long-term identity architecture.

Research in motivational psychology has long distinguished between *eustress* (positive, growth-inducing stress) and *distress* (negative, identity-eroding stress). Regenerative minds are designed to filter incoming pressures through the lens of chosen values. When a person encounters a difficult challenge that *aligns* with their purpose, the stress becomes constructive.

For example, a parent staying up late to help a child study may feel physically drained but emotionally congruent. Compare that to staying late for a third corporate rebranding initiative that contradicts personal ethics. One is costly but coherent. The other is corrosive.

A regenerative architecture must include valves of discernment: a filtration system that distinguishes meaningful demands from unsustainable ones.

Regeneration Is a Metric of Integrity, Not Indulgence

One of the greatest cultural distortions around inner work is the belief that "maintenance" signals deficiency. That needing reflection, therapy, or rest is evidence of inadequacy rather than precision. The regenerative model dismantles this thinking.

In architecture, scheduled maintenance is not weakness—it is *safeguarding against collapse.* Likewise, checking internal frameworks for psychological stability, updating thought patterns, and re-aligning behavioural responses is not a deviation from strength. It *is* strength.

This is particularly vital in fields that romanticise self-sacrifice: healthcare, education, entrepreneurship. In such cultures, the absence of breakdown is mistakenly taken as proof of robustness. But just as the silent corrosion of a beam eventually leads to structural failure, so too does unaddressed psychological strain—no matter how competent the surface.

To regenerate is to respect complexity. It is to *design for continuity.*

Adaptive Design: Regeneration in Dynamic Systems

Lastly, it is worth noting that regenerative mindsets are inherently *adaptive.* They are not static structures, but dynamic ecosystems that adjust according to context.

This means that what regenerates you at age 25 may not at 45. What fortifies you during career growth may not during loss. And what stabilises your thinking under pressure in one season may no longer serve in another.

Therefore, *regeneration must be audited.* Not through sentiment, but through practical observation. Ask:

What thoughts do I return to when strained?

Which actions restore coherence?

Which inputs consistently deplete me, and why are they still permitted?

To design for regeneration is to make room for self-adjustment without shame. It is to accept evolution not as optional, but as fundamental to sustainable inner architecture.

Final Thought

Resilience, by itself, is no longer a sufficient model. The ability to "bounce back" assumes the same shape can hold. But minds—like structures—change form under pressure. A regenerative framework doesn't aim to restore the old shape. It *builds capacity to become a stronger one.*

Regeneration is not recovery. It is design intelligence in action. It is the strategic insertion of flexibility, integration, and self-awareness into the fabric of one's mindset—not for comfort, but for longevity.

And in that, it is not merely a psychological luxury. It is *existential engineering.*

Conclusion
The Builder's Mindset

We were never meant to remain fixed. No insight, no transformation, no psychological turning point can sustain itself unless it is treated as a structure—something erected, not stumbled upon. At the heart of any mindset built to last lies a largely neglected but vital principle: constructive agency. You don't wait around for your perspective to settle. You build it—layer upon layer. Meaning isn't simply discovered; it's deliberately crafted, especially under strain. This isn't some poetic analogy. It's a principle borrowed straight from architecture.

This chapter doesn't serve as a tidy wrap-up. Rather, it offers a shift in position. You are no longer merely the subject inside your own psyche—you become the designer of it. Everything you've encountered so far hasn't just been insight; it has been scaffolding. And now, at the close, we uncover the blueprint that supports it all: the builder's mindset. This is not a mindset that simply survives hardship or repeats mantras. It's one that regards the self as an evolving construction—an entity to be maintained, refined, and reshaped with intentional care.

To adopt the builder's mindset is to alter your relationship with inner work from the ground up. Many pursue personal growth as a kind of excavation—as if somewhere beneath the layers of pain, confusion, or distraction, the "real" self lies waiting to be uncovered. But this view rests on a false premise: that the self is static. The builder rejects this. The self, in their view, is an ongoing project—not retrieved from childhood memories or personality inventories, but drafted, torn down, and revised, again and again. And no, the work is never really done.

This shift carries significant psychological implications. If the self is built, then so too are your notions of stability, resilience, identity. Each shift in awareness isn't a magical epiphany—it's a deliberate renovation. That doesn't mean gut instincts or raw emotions are without value. It means that feeling alone isn't enough. Even the most powerful instinct needs a structure—something to hold it, make sense of it, guide it. Just as architectural flair without sound engineering results in collapse, passion without inner scaffolding leads nowhere stable.

Three qualities form the backbone of the builder's mindset: deliberate design, continuous calibration, and regenerative discipline. Let's break those apart, one by one.

Deliberate Design begins with ownership. You're not simply at the mercy of your emotional storms, habitual patterns, or knee-jerk responses. You are the one laying the bricks. That doesn't mean pretending you can control everything—far from it. But it does mean that how you frame events, how you draw meaning from experience, is your domain. Builders don't wait for clarity to arrive neatly packaged. They begin drafting it, knowing the first version might be flawed. No matter. Drafting is the first sign of agency.

This mindset finds its echo in various therapeutic models—cognitive behavioural therapy, dialectical frameworks, narrative therapy—all built on one idea: thoughts and beliefs are constructions, not certainties. And anything constructed can be redesigned. When upheaval strikes, what haunts people isn't usually the event itself—it's the interpretive scaffolding hastily thrown up around it. The builder learns to slow this reflex, inspect the integrity of that narrative, and redesign one that better supports life going forward.

Next comes Continuous Calibration. This is the trait that distinguishes builders from perfectionists. To build doesn't mean you're chasing a polished endpoint. It means you're willing to stay in conversation with the structure—adjusting, realigning, upgrading. Growth is not a finish line. The "final" self doesn't exist. What does exist is a relationship—between your current internal architecture and the demands of the present moment. When either shifts, recalibration isn't failure; it's function.

Too much of contemporary self-help worships the breakthrough while neglecting the follow-up. But in architecture, a design that can't be maintained is useless. Builders understand that maintenance is not a chore; it's the heartbeat of sustainability. They welcome updates. They expect the need for reconfiguration. This is why they bend under pressure but don't break. It's what allows the overcommitted executive, the stretched parent, the resilient leader, to adapt their inner systems without guilt. Because recalibration is not fragility. It is wisdom made operational.

Finally, there is Regenerative Discipline—the engine room, if you like. Resilience often gets discussed as the capacity to bounce back. But regeneration? That goes deeper. It's about designing your inputs—what you consume, whom you spend time with, how you recharge—so that your capacity isn't just preserved but renewed. A regenerative system isn't marked by its ability to endure one crisis. It's marked by its ability to remain useful, responsive, even creative in the aftermath.

Here's the difference, in plain terms: a mindset reliant on inspiration flares up when conditions are perfect. A regenerative mindset ticks along regardless. Builders don't depend on ideal moments or external affirmation. They build emotional environments that can run reliably across seasons—joyful, stressful, or mundane.

What this chapter urges is a move away from abstract self-identifiers—being "resilient" or "disciplined" or "confident"—toward a more grounded question: what have you built to sustain yourself when those traits falter? Not how you feel today, but what scaffolds you've put in place to keep functioning when tomorrow feels different. Not what you believe in theory, but how those beliefs translate into systems, habits, and decisions that hold over time.

Let's be clear: this is not another sermon on endless optimisation. The builder's mindset is not about being hyper-productive or aesthetically polished. It's about stewardship—an ethical responsibility to maintain what you've built. A recognition that strength isn't found in the absence of weakness, but in the habit of returning to coherence again and again. That even the best structures need regular checks. And that mental soundness is not a passive gift, but a craft.

A builder doesn't obsess over flawlessness. What they care about is structural integrity. Will it hold? Will it flex when needed? Will it evolve with purpose rather than disintegrate under stress? These questions don't just apply to the psyche. They echo through relationships, professional lives, community roles. Eventually, the inner dialogue shifts: from "Am I good enough?" to "Is this framework supporting me well enough?" From "What's broken?" to "What needs reworking?" From "Who am I?" to "What am I choosing to construct now?"

Over the course of this book, you've been offered tools—emotional containment, narrative engineering, values recalibration, and more. But this final chapter takes a step back. Not to admire the build. To remind you: you are the builder. Mindset isn't luck. It isn't fixed. It isn't a trait. It is a designed space. And it is yours.

And unlike most buildings, this one never truly finishes. That's not a design flaw. That's the brilliance.

Your Mind Is Not a Garden to Grow. It's a Structure to Build, Reinforce, and Revisit

The final message reframes personal development as architectural integrity, not emotional patchwork.

The language we use to describe the mind shapes how we relate to it. For decades, popular psychology and wellness culture have leaned heavily on the metaphor of the mind as a garden: a delicate terrain in need of nurturing, free from weeds, in search of constant bloom. This framing, while poetic, has become misleading. It encourages a passive, reactive model of personal growth—where success means being "in bloom" and struggle implies something diseased, dry, or dead. But the human mind is not seasonal. It does not flourish according to sunlight and water. It is not something we merely tend. *It is something we construct.*

To understand personal development not as cultivation but as *construction* is to radically change the nature of your engagement with it. Instead of waiting for clarity or healing to arrive like spring after winter, the architect of the self gets to work. They do not sit with their pain hoping it transforms. They study its angles, map its load-bearing walls, test its pressure points, and reinforce its foundation.

This is not an abandonment of emotional care. It is an evolution of it.

To suggest that the mind is a structure—and not a garden—is not to devalue emotion or inner richness. It is to assert that true resilience is engineered. Just as a building is designed to withstand stress, expansion, contraction, and age, *a well-built mindset is not something that feels good—it is something that holds.*

Most traditional models of personal development follow a "fix and grow" logic. The assumption is that something inside us is broken, or stunted, and with enough mindfulness, love, or affirmation, it will eventually become whole. While well-intentioned, this frame implies a linear path with a final state of psychological flowering. That belief is responsible for much of the despair people feel when, after years of inner work, they still encounter anxiety, grief, doubt, or anger. They believe they must have done something wrong. That they are somehow failing at self-development.

But if we discard the garden metaphor, a more robust and honest alternative emerges. The architect does not ask whether a wall feels whole. They ask whether it holds under pressure. The builder does not expect a room to remain untouched by time or use. They plan for maintenance, reinforce supports, and design for flexibility. *This is the mindset that must replace the fragility of emotional idealism.* Personal development is not about blossoming—it is about *structural coherence.*

In cognitive science, this architectural metaphor finds clear resonance. The brain is not a passive vessel for feelings—it is a dynamic, plastic organ constantly shaping, pruning, and reinforcing neural pathways in response to behaviour, not desire. We do not "grow" happiness. We *construct cognitive frameworks* that generate conditions under which sustainable emotional stability can emerge. Practices like cognitive behavioural therapy (CBT), acceptance and commitment therapy (ACT), and schema therapy all rest on this truth: beliefs, reactions, and habits are not inherent. They are *designed—sometimes by default, sometimes with intention.* The difference lies in whether the mind's owner chooses to act as architect or tenant.

Architects work with *form and function.* That means not every part of your mindset has to be beautiful—it has to be *sound.* One of the most damaging myths in self-development is the obsession with coherence as a feeling rather than as a structure. People are told that alignment is when they "feel in flow," or when "everything makes sense." But in practice, internal coherence often feels like friction. Because to reinforce a structure, you must test it. You must expose weak points. You must examine corners you've previously avoided.

This testing is not failure—it is proof of integrity. Well-built identities, like well-built buildings, are not immune to stress. They *are defined by their ability to carry it.* And that ability is not innate. It's constructed through conscious internal design: clarifying one's values, mapping one's narratives, stress-testing one's coping strategies, and embedding redundancies for times of overload.

There is a secondary cost to the garden metaphor that goes largely unnoticed: it primes people to avoid "ugliness." In gardens, decay is undesirable. Withered leaves are shameful. In structural thinking, *decay is data.* A crack is an invitation to examine foundations. A leak means something has shifted—and gives you a chance to correct the load before collapse. This approach eliminates guilt from the process of struggle. Instead of asking "Why am I still not healed?" the builder asks "What part of this design needs strengthening?"

We also move away from the seduction of perfection. A perfectly constructed mindset is neither possible nor desirable. Rigidity is the enemy of adaptability. The builder's goal is not an invulnerable structure—it's a *regenerative one.* In architecture, the most advanced buildings are designed not to resist change, but to *integrate it.* They include expansion joints, flexible materials, and adaptive frameworks. So too must our inner architecture.

Let's bring this down to the everyday: when someone faces burnout, the garden model tells them to retreat, rest, and regrow. The architectural model asks: *What was overloaded? What part of this system lacked support? What internal assumptions or values allowed the stress to accumulate unchecked? What needs redesigning—your calendar, your boundary scripts, your perfectionism algorithm?* The questions change. The power shifts. And with that shift comes sustainable agency.

Consider identity. Most people inherit their psychological identity much like a tenant inherits the layout of a rented space. They adapt to it, decorate it, maybe even complain about it—but rarely do they think to *redesign the floorplan.* Identity is not discovered. It is *drafted, tested, reinforced, and revised.* To own this process is to stop waiting for yourself to emerge and to begin constructing the self that is aligned with your chosen principles—not your past defaults.

None of this makes the work easier. But it *makes it real.* Emotional bypassing, excessive reliance on affirmation, or spiritualised avoidance of hard psychological labour are all consequences of seeing the self as a thing to be grown. When we reframe mindset as structure, we drop the illusion that clarity, confidence, or contentment are destinations. We stop asking when we will *feel better*, and start building lives that can *carry complexity* without breaking.

This reframing also changes how we relate to setbacks. Gardens can be ravaged by weather, insects, drought. There is a helplessness to that metaphor. A sense that we are at the mercy of forces beyond our control. But the builder does not ask for better weather. They reinforce the roof. They design for wind shear. They install drainage. Setbacks are no longer proof of failure—they are part of the audit. *The measure of a mindset is not how it functions on a good day. It's how it holds when pressure mounts.*

And when it does break—because sometimes it will—that too is within the paradigm. Structural failure is feedback. And architects revisit blueprints. They adapt. They strengthen the next iteration. That's the difference between emotional patchwork and architectural integrity. The former is reactive. The latter is intentional.

Ultimately, to build a mind is to stop outsourcing your internal life to weather, mood, or other people's approval. It is to stand with responsibility, not over your emotions—but over the systems that hold them. It is to ask not "What do I feel right now?" but "What system have I built to contain this? To make sense of it? To transmute it into aligned action?"

You are not a gardener tending to a fragile terrain. You are a structural designer of your own interior landscape. The work is not seasonal. It is foundational. And it never ends—not because something is wrong, but because something is right.

So keep your tools close. Revisit the blueprint. Audit the load. Reframe the crack. Strengthen the beam. Not because you are broken. But because you are building.

And builders build.

About the Author

Kiran Saito is a behavioural design thinker and resilience strategist who explores the intersection of habit formation, minimalism, and psychological recovery. With a background in cognitive science and an enduring passion for Eastern and Western philosophies of the mind, Kiran writes for readers navigating major life transitions—burnout, identity loss, or reinvention. Drawing from over a decade of research and personal exploration, Saito offers frameworks that help people not just bounce back, but rebuild themselves from the ground up. Kiran's work combines the precision of science with the soul of introspection, guiding readers to create mental infrastructure that endures life's inevitable tremors. The Inner Architect is his most defining work to date—a blueprint for becoming structurally resilient in a world that rarely pauses.

www.ingramcontent.com/pod-product-compliance
Lightning Source LLC
Chambersburg PA
CBHW031340230926
51848CB00002B/323
* 9 7 8 9 3 7 1 3 4 0 9 4 6 *